TRAUMA AND THE FAILURE OF HISTORY

SEMEIA STUDIES

Steed V. Davidson, General Editor

Number 94

TRAUMA AND THE FAILURE OF HISTORY

Kings, Lamentations, and the Destruction of Jerusalem

David Janzen

SBL PRESS

 **PRESS**

Atlanta

Copyright © 2019 by David Janzen

Library of Congress Cataloging-in-Publication Data

Names: Janzen, David, 1968– author.
Title: Trauma and the failure of history : Kings, Lamentations, and the destruction of Jerusalem / by David Janzen.
Description: Atlanta : SBL Press, 2019. | Series: Semeia studies ; Number 94 | Includes bibliographical references and index.
Identifiers: LCCN 2019014656 (print) | LCCN 2019018717 (ebook) | ISBN 9780884143390 (ebk.) | ISBN 9781628372274 (pbk. : alk. paper) | ISBN 9780884143383 (hbk. : alk. paper)
Subjects: LCSH: Bible. Kings—Criticism, interpretation, etc. | Jerusalem—History—Siege, 586 B.C. | Bible. Lamentations—Criticism, interpretation, etc. | Psychic trauma—Biblical teaching.
Classification: LCC BS1335.52 (ebook) | LCC BS1335.52 .J36 2019 (print) | DDC 222/.506—dc23
LC record available at https://lccn.loc.gov/2019014656

Printed on acid-free paper.

For Patricia

and for my parents

Contents

Abbreviations

1QIsaᵃ	Isaiahᵃ (Great Isaiah Scroll)
4QLam	4Q111
ABC	*Assyrian and Babylonian Chronicles*. Albert K. Grayson. TCS 5. Locust Valley, NY: Augustin, 1975.
ABD	*Anchor Bible Dictionary*. Edited by David Noel Freedman. New York: Doubleday, 1992.
ABR	*Australian Biblical Review*
ABRL	Anchor Bible Reference Library
ABS	Archaeology and Biblical Studies
AIL	Ancient Israel and its Literature
ANEM	Society of Biblical Literature Ancient Near Eastern Monographs
ANET	*Ancient Near Eastern Texts Relating to the Old Testament*. Edited by James B. Pritchard. 3rd ed. Princeton: Princeton University Press, 1969.
AOAT	Alter Orient und Altes Testament
AOTC	Abingdon Old Testament Commentaries
ASB	*Austin Seminary Bulletin*
ATANT	Abhandlungen zur Theologie des Alten und Neuen Testaments
BASOR	*Bulletin of the American Schools of Oriental Research*
BCP	Blackwell Companions to Philosophy
BEATAJ	Beiträge zur Erforschung des Alten Testament und des antiken Judentum
BETL	Bibliotheca Ephemeridum theologicarum Lovaniensium
Bib	*Biblica*
BibInt	*Biblical Interpretation*
BibInt	Biblical Interpretation Series
BibOr	Biblica et orientalia
BibSem	The Biblical Seminar

BR	*Biblical Research*
BT	*The Bible Translator*
BZ	*Biblische Zeitschrift*
BZAW	Beihefte zur Zeitschrift für die alttestamentliche Wissenschaft
CBQ	*Catholic Biblical Quarterly*
CHANE	Culture and History of the Ancient Near East
CIS	Copenhagen International Seminar
Clio	*Clio: A Journal of Literature, History, and the Philosophy of History*
CMP	Cultural Memory in the Present
ComCrit	*Comparative Criticism*
CovQ	*The Covenant Quarterly*
CriInq	*Critical Inquiry*
CSALC	Cambridge Studies in American Literature and Culture
CSS	Cambridge Social Studies
DJD	Discoveries in the Judaean Desert
DSM-5	American Psychiatric Association. *Diagnostic and Statistical Manual of Mental Disorders*. 5th ed. Washington: American Psychiatric Publishing, 2013
Dtr	The Deuteronomistic History
Enc	*Encounter*
ESHM	European Seminar in Historical Methodology
FAT	Forschungen zum Alten Testament
FCI	Foundations of Contemporary Interpretation
FRLANT	Forschungen zur Religion und Literatur des Alten und Neuen Testaments
GN	Geographical name
HBM	Hebrew Bible Monographs
HBS	Herders biblische Studien
HCOT	Historical Commentary on the Old Testament
HS	*Hebrew Studies*
HThKAT	Herders theologischer Kommentar zum Alten Testament
HUCA	*Hebrew Union College Annual*
HvTSt	Hervormde Teologiese Studies
IBHS	Waltke, Bruce K., and M. O'Connor. *An Introduction to Biblical Hebrew Syntax*. Winona Lake, IN: Eisenbrauns, 1990
IJPA	*International Journal of Psychoanalysis*

Int	*Interpretation*
ISBL	Indiana Studies in Biblical Literature
JANES	*Journal of the Ancient Near Eastern Society*
JAOS	*Journal of the American Oriental Society*
JBL	*Journal of Biblical Literature*
JHebS	*Journal of Hebrew Scriptures*
JSOT	*Journal for the Study of the Old Testament*
JSOTSup	Journal for the Study of the Old Testament Supplement Series
LCBI	Literary Currents in Biblical Interpretation
LHBOTS	The Library of Hebrew Bible/Old Testament Studies
LSTS	The Library of Second Temple Studies
LXX	Septuagint
MT	Masoretic Text
NCBC	New Century Bible Commentary
NEAEHL	*The New Encyclopedia of Archaeological Excavations in the Holy Land.* Edited by Ephraim Stern. 4 vols. Jerusalem: Israel Exploration Society & Carta; New York: Simon & Schuster, 1993
NLH	*New Literary History*
OBO	Orbis Biblicus et Orientalis
OG	Old Greek
OTL	Old Testament Library
OTM	Oxford Theological Monographs
OtSt	Oudtestamentische studiën
PCI	Post-Contemporary Interventions
PEQ	*Palestine Exploration Quarterly*
PRCS	Parallax: Re-visions of Culture and Society
Proof	*Prooftexts: A Journal of Jewish Literary History*
PSB	*Princeton Seminary Bulletin*
RB	*Revue biblique*
RBS	Society of Biblical Literature Resources for Biblical Study
SAA	State Archives of Assyria
SAAB	*State Archives of Assyria Bulletin*
SANt	Studia Aarhusiana Neotestamentica
SBLDS	Society of Biblical Literature Dissertation Series
SBLMS	Society of Biblical Literature Monograph Series
SBLStBL	Society of Biblical Literature Studies in Biblical Literature
SBT	Studies in Biblical Theology

SBTS	Sources for Biblical and Theological Study
SEÅ	*Svensk exegetisk årsbok*
SemeiaSt	Society of Biblical Literature Semeia Studies
SJOT	*Scandinavian Journal of the Old Testament*
SPEP	Studies in Phenomenology and Existential Philosophy
SPOT	Studies on Personalities of the Old Testament
SSN	Studia Semitica Neerlandica
STL	Studia theologica Lundensia
SymS	Society of Biblical Literature Symposium Series
TBAT	Theologische Bücherei. Altes Testament
TCS	Texts from Cuneiform Sources
THL	Theory and History of Literature
THOTC	Two Horizons Old Testament Commentary
Transeu	*Transeuphratène*
TSS	Themes in the Social Sciences
TThSt	Trierer theologische Studien
TynBul	*Tyndale Bulletin*
UF	*Ugarit-Forschungen*
VT	*Vetus Testamentum*
VTSup	Vetus Testamentum Supplement
YCSS	Yale Cultural Sociology Series
ZABR	*Zeitschrift für altorientalische und biblische Rechtsgeschichte*
ZAW	*Zeitschrift für die Alttestamentliche Wissenschaft*
ZDPV	*Zeitschrift des deutschen Palästina-Vereins*

1

Introduction:
The Nature of History and the
Nature of Trauma

"When I got home from the Second World War twenty-three years ago," writes Kurt Vonnegut near the beginning of *Slaughterhouse-Five*, "I thought it would be easy for me to write about the destruction of Dresden, since all I would have to do would be to report what I had seen." What he had seen and survived as a prisoner of war was the Allied bombing of the city in 1945, which may have killed as many as twenty-five thousand people, but, he continues, "not many words about Dresden came from my mind then—not enough to make a book, anyway. And not many words come now, either" (Vonnegut 1969, 2). This novelist, whose career was built on finding words for stories, could, despite his best efforts, find none for his own, as he tells us in the opening pages of the book, and so he writes a different story instead, one that begins,

> Listen:
> Billy Pilgrim has come unstuck in time. (23)

Billy Pilgrim is an American soldier captured by the Germans who survives the bombing of Dresden as a POW, just as Vonnegut did. Billy, however, lives an achronological life, constantly and uncontrollably moving back and forth in time, to and from the story that makes its way through the novel and culminates in the destruction of Dresden. The joint not-story of Vonnegut and story of Billy Pilgrim in *Slaughterhouse-Five* tells us something about trauma, for there are no words for it, not even from skilled novelists. It is not simply a matter of reporting what one has seen, as Vonnegut discovered. But trauma is a powerful force, returning victims to events for which they can find no words, events that they cannot in fact remember but that they are forced to relive, just as Billy Pilgrim, come unstuck in time, is continually returned to the events of his capture on the battlefield, his time in a POW camp, and the destruction of Dresden.

In this monograph we explore the nature of trauma that cannot be remembered or articulated but only relived, and we contrast it with history, the study of which has been so central to the modern field of biblical studies. The following chapters argue that trauma is antihistory, not merely what history is not but something that rejects historical explanations and that cannot be comprehended by historical narrative. The nature or essence of history is explanatory narrative that conveys meaning; it is the production of a true past that reflects a writer's and culture's worldviews and concerns. But unlike history, trauma cannot be formed or understood in narrative created by the belief systems of worldviews, in part because trauma is not something victims can believe. If one could speak of a nature or essence of trauma, then it would be an absence of meaning and knowledge that stems from victims' failure to fully experience the events that traumatized them, a failure that has prevented the trauma from becoming part of the past at all. In this part of the book we juxtapose the natures of history and trauma not only to clarify and explain the differences between them, but to demonstrate how they are manifested differently in response to great traumatic events. Histories create and explain those events in particular ways, and function to reinforce or reform the worldviews that bind communities together in shared belief systems, since the explanations are rooted in ways of making sense of things defined by those worldviews. For a community to agree that a history has presented the past as it really happened is for it to tacitly assent to the validity of the worldview that has shaped it. But for trauma victims who have failed to fully experience and know those events, there is no explanation, and so history fails in the face of trauma.

One of the ways that we examine how history and trauma react differently to massive traumatic events is to read both Kings and Lamentations, two works composed in the wake of the same basic catastrophe, the geopolitical disaster that annihilated Judah in the sixth century BCE. In 587/6 BCE, the Babylonians besieged and destroyed Jerusalem, and the slaughter and destruction throughout Judah in the early sixth century was horrific. The population of Judah at the beginning of that century was about 110,000 (so Lipschits 2005, 59),[1] but by the end it had fallen by 70 or 80

---

1. By Oded Lipschits's (2003, 267–71) calculations, at the beginning of the sixth

percent.[2] Concerned with Egyptian influence in the Levant, Nebuchad-nezzar largely wiped out fortified settlements in Judah and the Philistine coast, as well as in Ammon and Moab; after this point, the Philistines seem to have disappeared entirely, and by the Persian period their territory was controlled by the Phoenicians (Lipschits 1998; Stern 2004, 274–75; Faust 2012a, 23–32). Benjamin, the northern part of early sixth-century Judah, largely seems to have escaped this massive destruction (see, e.g., Stern 2001, 321–22; Carter 2003, 310; Lipschits 2003, 346–55),[3] and Oded Lip-schits (e.g., 2004b; 2011a, 191–94; 2011b) argues that many rural areas in Judah managed to survive,[4] yet archaeologists rightly link the widespread depopulation of Judah and surrounding regions to the Babylonian incur-sion and its concomitant aspects: the famine and disease that accompa-nied it, as well as the removal of some of the inhabitants to Mesopotamia.[5]

If the Judean communities in Palestine and Babylonia were to survive, then they had to demonstrate to their members that their worldviews were able to make sense of the horrific suffering they had witnessed and under-gone in this sixth-century disaster. One can see, for example, that a belief system that maintained that YHWH controlled historical events might be badly shaken by an invasion and occupation that killed off a significant part of the population and forced others to migrate to Mesopotamia, but a failure to make sense of those events through the community's worldview

---

century about ninety-five thousand lived in the area that would make up the Persian-period province of Judah.

2. Lipschits (2003, 355–64; 2005, 267–71) puts the population of the area covered by early sixth-century Judah at about thirty thousand by the end of that century, a 70 percent drop in the population of the region, while Avraham Faust (2012a, 119–47; 2012b, 118–21) puts the population decline in the wake of the Babylonian invasion at 80 percent.

3. Faust (2012a, 209–31), however, argues that Benjamin suffered a massive decline in settlements in the wake of the Babylonian invasion as well.

4. Lipschits points to Ramat Rahel as an administrative center in Neo-Babylonian Judah, where taxes in kind were gathered from the province, and argues that some rural sites continued to exist to supply the products collected there as tax. Faust (e.g., 2003; 2012a, 45–48, 56–57), on the other hand, argues that most rural sites in Judah were destroyed by the Babylonians. See also Valkama, 2010, 43–44.

5. For the factors that led to the massive population drop in Judah, see Middlemas 2009, 174–75; Faust 2011. The region was so deeply shaken that the archaeological record provides evidence for important societal changes, such as, for example, the four-room house disappearing entirely at the end of the Iron Age (see Faust 2004; 2012a; 2012b).

might well cause group members to doubt its validity, leading them to demand important changes in the society or perhaps to abandon it altogether. The book of Kings provides one explanation of the disaster, an account that, for those who assent to the author's worldview, explains what really happened, but to read Lamentations is to come across successive rejections of explanations for the victims' suffering, which repeats over and over in the book's poems as they relive their trauma. An examination of Kings and of the Deuteronomistic History as a whole shows a work that supplies and explains a past, whereas Lamentations provides only an ever-present trauma of suffering in which attempts to explain it fail and are drowned out by the survivors' repeated articulations of their pain. For Lamentations as a whole, we could say, there is no past disaster to explain, only the continual repetitions of a present and unexplainable trauma. The reactions of Kings and Lamentations to the same basic set of events could not be more different, and this is because Kings can be seen as part of a history, something that confirms the ability of the group's worldview to make sense even of the disaster that struck Judah, while Lamentations is largely a series of testimonies to trauma that reject history.

We begin our study of the antithetical natures of history and trauma in chapter 2, where we explore the nature of history and see that histories are narrative creations of the past that readers recognize as meaningful insofar as they understand them to provide true representations of what really happened, not just in regard to the events they discuss but also in the explanations and causal relationships the narratives claim existed among them. Not all readers can acknowledge the same writing to be a history, for not all readers can believe that it is true; the pasts created by historians are formed by their worldviews, which limit the ways they can understand and explain things, and only readers whose belief system overlaps significantly with the author's are able to understand a given writing to be a history rather than a work of fiction. If, for example, one encounters a work that explains past events with descriptions of divine intervention, one is only in a position to accept it as an account of what really happened if one shares the author's beliefs concerning the work of the divine in history. For an atheist, it would be a work of fiction. The past can only exist for us in ways we find to be meaningful, and so it can only exist for us in stories that cohere with the worldviews we hold, although we can, of course, be convinced to change some of our important beliefs and alter our worldviews.

One's belief system is thus key in determining what one can understand to be a true account of the past, a point discussed not only in chapter

2 but also in chapter 3, when we examine how Dtr, and particularly the book of Kings, creates a past of traumatic events for its ancient Judean readers, some of whom would have been able to recognize it as a work of history that accurately explained the destruction of Judah and Jerusalem they and their community had survived. The Deuteronomist's worldview, which shaped the past he or she produced in the writing, seems to have been based on features of a belief system broadly shared by Judeans, at least as far as other biblical writings would lead us to conclude. There were particular aspects of the Deuteronomist's worldview, such as a belief in the eternal divine support for Davidic rule and the innate sinfulness of the people, that resulted in a creation of a past that perhaps not all sixth-century BCE Judeans could have accepted, but for those who saw a true past in Kings and Dtr as a whole, the work relates events that really happened and correctly explains the suffering the sixth-century exilic community in Babylonia had undergone.

The book of Lamentations responds to the same basic set of traumatic events that Dtr does, yet our reading of Lamentations through the lens of trauma theory finds not narrative, explanation, and history, but a failure and rejection of such things. We begin our contrast of trauma with history in chapter 4, with a discussion of why trauma results from victims' failure of experience of traumatic events, thus leading to an absence of knowledge and meaning of those events. So as we apply trauma theory to Lamentations in chapter 5, we embark on a sort of analysis different from our reading of Kings and Dtr, where we are interested in examining the narrative that creates and explains a preexilic past, as well as the Deuteronomist's worldview that resulted in the formation of this particular past. In Lamentations we do encounter attempts on the part of some of the speakers to create explanations for readers' suffering in the destruction of Jerusalem and its aftermath, only to see such explanations fail as they are contradicted or ignored or trail off into repetitions of the victims' pain. Applying what we know of trauma to Lamentations allows us to see not the explanation of history but history's failure to incorporate trauma into explanatory narrative. In Lamentations, trauma remains unknowable and so outside history, but repetitively present to the book's speakers, who, like Vonnegut's Billy Pilgrim, never seem to escape the time of their suffering, which cannot become past for them and so cannot be history.

As a note of clarification, I should mention at the outset that the book discusses both collective and psychological trauma and that these are two different things. I have already referred to psychological trauma as an absence of experience, knowledge, and meaning, but collective trauma is really a kind of history, one that focuses on traumatic events, and as such its essence is explanatory narrative. Collective trauma does not only create the events of a traumatic past; it explains them as it identifies perpetrators and victims of them. Collective trauma and psychological trauma are therefore not two species of the same genus but two incompatible things, and part of our analysis of Lamentations shows victims of psychological trauma repetitively rejecting the attempts of other speakers to impose the history of collective trauma that would mark them as the perpetrators of their own suffering. The root of psychological trauma is the missed experience of the traumatic event, and thus it is "unclaimed experience," as Cathy Caruth (1996) puts it, a powerful but unknowable force in the lives of survivors that exists outside meaning and narrative. But since collective trauma is a kind of history, it is the conscious creation of explanation and meaning in narrative, the claiming of a society's experience, to put it another way, and it should not be equated with the sum of the suffering of individual trauma victims within the group.[6]

One reason why it is important to make the distinction between history/collective trauma and psychological trauma in the context of the study of the Hebrew Bible is that biblical scholars using trauma theory have not always recognized how radically different they are. Works produced in the field sometimes assert that the explanatory narratives of collective traumas could have provided therapy and healing to victims of psychological trauma, claiming their experience on their behalf, as it were. As one example of this tendency, we can look to three rather recent collections of essays that include studies of Hebrew Bible texts through the lens of some sort of trauma theory: *Bible through the Lens of Trauma* (Frechette and Boase 2016) includes ten such essays, *Trauma and Traumatization in Individual and Collective Dimensions* (Becker, Dochhorn, and Holt 2014) has seven, and *Interpreting Exile* (Kelle, Ames, and Wright 2011) has four.[7] Of these twenty-one essays, about half make the argument or at least assume that

---

6. See, for example, the comments in Alexander and Breese (2011, xiv–xxii) that refer to the ways in which the essays in the collection they introduce have distinguished between social narratives about trauma and the collective suffering of group members.

7. Although the essay by Daniel Smith-Christopher in Kelle, Ames, and Wright 2011 does have the word *trauma* in its title, it focuses more on social and psychological approaches in general than on reading biblical texts through the lens of one kind of trauma theory, so I am not including it in the count of essays.

the unclaimed experience of psychological trauma can be claimed by the narrative of collective trauma in the sense that victims would have found narrative explanations of traumatic events therapeutic, either through accepting the meaning they found in such narratives[8] or by looking to some of the texts and their narratives as models to promote recovery.[9] Claims such as these rest on the assumption that psychological trauma can be healed as victims adopt the meaning of someone else's story, but, as chapter 4 discusses, psychological trauma is so different from the history of collective trauma that this is not possible. The use of social narratives to provide meaning for traumatic events tends only to repress the trauma; this is what Dtr appears to do, for it creates no space for psychological trauma at all, while the trauma victims who speak in Lamentations ultimately cannot accept the incipient narratives of collective trauma they are offered, narratives that could fit quite well in Dtr. Some victims of trauma certainly do publicly assent to social narratives that provide explanations of the events that traumatized them, but this is not equivalent to therapy.

Beyond the explanation of the distinction between history/collective trauma and psychological trauma, there are a number of other reasons why those who study the Hebrew Bible might find this sort of analysis of trauma in the context of reading biblical texts useful. That neither we nor

---

8. In *Bible through the Lens of Trauma*, see Boase 2016 (note particularly her discussion on p. 51, where she refers to Judith Herman's work on the recovery of victims from psychological trauma) and Odell 2016 (on pp. 113–14 she states that narrative helped individual traumatized Judeans in the process of "genuine healing"). In *Trauma and Traumatization*, see O'Connor 2014 (on pp. 213–17 she focuses on Jeremiah's prose and poetry as providing individual victims of trauma with explanations that promote "healthy functioning"). In *Interpreting Exile*, see Morrow 2011 (on pp. 281–83, 289 he claims that narratives in response to trauma can "help to rebuild a shattered sense of self"); Carr 2011 (on pp. 299–302 he focuses on prophetic literature as aiding the exiles as a community and as individuals to trust and to deal with shame); and Rumfelt 2011 (on pp. 325–29, she discusses the "narrative healing role" for individual victims of trauma as part of a discussion of biblical narratives).

9. In *Bible through the Lens of Trauma*, see Frechette 2016 (on p. 74 he points to the "healing function" of Isa 47 for individuals) and Strawn 2016 (pp. 154–55 are the conclusion of an argument that claims that "psalms can be seen, not simply as evidence of a therapeutic process but as that process itself" in regard to individuals). In *Trauma and Traumatization* see Nielsen 2014 (on pp. 68–69 she argues that Job provides a model for "how a traumatic experience can be worked through") and Frechette 2014 (pp. 71–72 form the introduction to a larger argument that some psalms "could have a healing function for people who have been traumatized").

the biblical writers nor the survivors of massive traumatic events such as the disaster that destroyed Judah and Jerusalem in the sixth century BCE could grasp the totality of those events, if only because the trauma that resulted from them cannot be grasped, is potentially of some importance. That both an ancient writer such as the Deuteronomist and modern historians and interpreters of the Bible might ignore the trauma of events such as the sixth-century disaster altogether, since trauma can enter neither narrative nor understanding, is also significant. The difficulty with ignoring or overwriting trauma is that this denies the existence of the trauma associated with the events, the events' key reality for trauma victims. The victims then become not victims but an "abstract element"[10] of the pasts that the worldviews of modern or ancient writers prompt them to create. The reality of their trauma then disappears entirely, replaced by the pasts that the writers, ancient and modern, prefer to see, pasts without trauma and so without trauma victims.

Lamentations, however, reflects the persistent articulation of an unknowable and unnarratable trauma in spite of attempts by some voices in the book to repress and overwrite it in collective trauma. Because this psychological trauma is not explainable and cannot be contained by narrative, historians could not integrate it into their stories of the past even if they wished to do so. But this does not mean, as we discuss in chapter 6, that they cannot make room for it beside their histories. Carving out space for trauma beside a history will not help to explain the trauma and, if anything, will result in a questioning of the conclusions in regard to the past that the histories present. Interpreters of the Bible interested in explaining Judean reactions to the sixth-century disaster can do more than include a discussion of Lamentations along with analyses of other writings that respond to it, such as Dtr, and can read Lamentations intertextually with such works, allowing the testimonies of trauma victims to jar and grind uncomfortably next to the explanations that would repress their trauma. This intertextual reading will not allow us to know the trauma, but it gives us some sense of how incompatible the trauma victims found totalizing explanations of the events with their own nonexperience of them. An intertextual reading gives us some sense as well of the difficulty they might have had accepting and believing the truth claims of a work such

---

10. See Saul Friedländer's (1997, 2) comment that Holocaust histories can turn victims "into a static and abstract element against a historical background."

as Dtr, and some sense as to how the suffering of their trauma repeated and potentially even drowned out such explanations. In such intertextual readings, at least, trauma victims are not reduced to an "abstract element" of factual data, and even if we cannot integrate trauma into the pasts that we create as historians and interpreters of the Bible, we can at least place it next to our histories and readings of texts to leave space for its unspeakable silence.

2

History, Narrative, and Collective Trauma

2.1. Historiography and Fiction

Given the project outlined in the introduction, this chapter needs to do a number of things. Since the basic point of the book as a whole is to contrast history with trauma and to explain why and demonstrate how histories and testimonies to trauma react so differently to the same traumatic events, we must discuss the nature of historiography and of history here. The chapter concludes that collective trauma is a kind of history, reflecting my earlier observation that psychological trauma and collective trauma are not two species of the same genus but two different things. Since we read Kings and the Deuteronomistic History as a whole as the manifestation of the worldview of one of the Judean exilic groups in its explanation of the past, we also need to show why and in what manner Kings and Dtr could be understood as a work of history. All of these goals demand that we be as clear as we can in this chapter as to what history is and does. History, as I argue in the first parts of the chapter, is a narrative creation of a true past, and in chapter 3 we see that ancient readers could have understood Dtr to be a work of history, although modern historians qua modern historians cannot; we then go on in that chapter to examine the specific ways in which Dtr uses narrative to create the past and collective trauma.

In the first section of this chapter we see that it can be difficult to distinguish historiographical narratives that explain what really happened in the past from narratives that create pasts that are not true; the chapter uses the catchall term *fiction* for this latter category.[1] Given this reality, we

---

1. Someone could, of course, analyze a text and conclude that, while it does not relate what really happened in the past, it is nonetheless true in some other way, perhaps in relating theological truth, for example. In my use of the term *fiction* here, I do

need to find some way to differentiate between them in order to clarify the nature of history. Since this discussion is taking place in dialogue with the field that studies the history of ancient Israel and Judah, we begin with the debate in that field as to the nature of history, a debate that is often bound up in a larger one concerning whether there is history writing in the Hebrew Bible. If the point of historiography is to discover "what really happened," the assertion of Leopold von Ranke, a parent of the modern field of historiography,[2] then, argue some historians of ancient Israel, we find none at all in the biblical literature. I maintain that history writings describe what really happened (even if that is not all that they do) and that it is possible to say, in a manner of speaking, that there are history writings within the biblical corpus, but to do this we have to engage with scholars who view the matter differently. From their point of view, histories must critically evaluate helpful materials about the past if they are to have any hope of describing what really happened, and writings in the Hebrew Bible do not do this. For Thomas Thompson, for example, a work such as Kings is interested in providing a theology of salvation history and creating a sense of Israelite identity, but not in referring to what he understands to be a real past.[3] The emphasis on salvation history in a writing such as Kings provides us with a "theory or philosophy of history" (Thompson 1992, 207); biblical authors focus not on what really happened but on what is eternal and unchanging that underlies experience, and critical evaluation of sources to establish what really happened and when is hardly their main point (Thompson 2000, 16–19). We thus encounter the same themes over and over in biblical writings that are (putatively) about the past, and the point at issue for their authors is to produce a sense of communal identity and connection to a transcendental power (23–33).

Lester Grabbe (1997, 32) has more confidence than Thompson that some biblical writings in some places can actually tell readers what really happened, but he does believe that biblical authors would not have under-

---

not mean to forestall such claims. The word is simply a reflection of my description of history as providing a true narrative of what really happened, and so I use it only to distinguish narrative creations of the past that are recognized as doing this from ones that are not.

2. For a brief discussion of von Ranke's understanding of historiography, see Gil 2011.

3. Thompson makes this point in a number of his works, but see, e.g., Thompson 1992.

stood the difference in genre that we moderns see between historical and theological writings, a position somewhat like that advanced by Thompson, who sees not historiography but theology in the Bible. Moreover, writes Grabbe, biblical writers such as those behind Kings and Chronicles did not critically weigh and evaluate evidence, unlike Greek historians such as Thucydides (2001, 161–71; see also Noll 2001, 58–59, 70–72), and this lack of a critical stance means that we cannot categorize them as historians. For Philip Davies (2008, 10–11), biblical writers did not produce histories in part because they lacked the sources to do so, such as access to archives, archaeological findings, and eyewitnesses, precisely the things that must be available so that historians can subject them to critical evaluation. This kind of data provides certain limits that a reliance on older textual and oral narratives does not; when it comes to archaeological data, for example, "there is no possibility of deliberate deception (forgery excluded!). Only texts, as a rule, can consciously lie" (Davies 2014, 15). Biblical authors would have relied on older narrative traditions, some of which were assumedly involved in "deliberate deception." A genre of historiography simply did not exist in the ancient Near East, writes Antti Laato (2005, 170–71), who argues that critical methods were not used to investigate the past and that royal courts produced "historical" documents to send ideological and political messages in which reconstructing what really happened was not the main goal.

This is hardly a full accounting of those who are dubious that we can describe any of the biblical writings as histories, but it gives us a sense as to why thoughtful scholars would make this kind of argument: the biblical writings were not critical investigations of the past because the authors lacked the sources for this sort of endeavor and because their goals were not those of real historians, since they aimed to make ideological, political, and theological points. A history, from this point of view, describes what really happened, but the biblical writers did not have the resources and critical mind-set to produce such a thing. Nonetheless, this position as to the absence of historiography in the Hebrew Bible is not shared by all historians of ancient Israel. Baruch Halpern, for example, argues that we can distinguish historiography from other genres through authorial intention (1996, 266–80); historians intend to write about what really happened, he argues, and the hands responsible for the composition of Kings and Dtr wrote with such intention. In this he disagrees with Thompson, who sees biblical writers as intending to do something else, and with Grabbe, who believes ancient Judean readers would not have distinguished between history and theology. Halpern (268) claims that ancient Judeans could and did distinguish between myth and history and would have known that Genesis 1 is not a history, while Dtr is.

Other scholars of the Hebrew Bible agree with Halpern's understanding of historiography as determined by authorial intention (e.g., Sternberg 1985, 25–35; Long 1994, 58–63; Amit 1999, 13–14; Kofoed 2005, 190–93, 235–47), but even if Thompson, for example, were to grant the point that the biblical writers were intending to produce the past as it really was, he would still conclude that they did not succeed in this since, he argues, works such as Kings were composed long after the events they purport to describe, and without proper sources about the past their narratives thus render a fictitious history of an Israel that never existed (2000, 31–34). Presumably, historiographies should tell us what really happened, or at least come close, if we are to understand them to be historiographies and not some other kind of writing; it would also seem that authorial intention does not matter at all if historians do not have access to sources that can tell them what really happened, or if they lack a critical worldview that would allow them to evaluate those sources properly, since then they would utterly fail to complete a central aspect of their job as historians.

Since I maintain that one of the most basic functions of historiographies is to tell readers what really happened, I am skeptical that referring to authorial intention alone helps us determine which writings are histories and which are not, and I am equally skeptical that other attempts within the field of the history of ancient Israel to define historiography have been entirely successful. John Van Seters (1983, 1), for example, borrows Johan Huizinga's definition of history as "the intellectual form in which a civilization renders an account to itself of its past." In this definition, says Van Seters, history writing is not primarily concerned with the accurate reporting of the past, but looks for significance in it in order to explain the present (4–5). In a somewhat similar manner, Rachelle Gilmour argues that a historiography must provide causation, meaning, and significance as it represents the past, arguing that a historiography explains the past and describes its significance (2011, 7–10). Marc Brettler describes a history as "a narrative that presents a past," a definition not at all dependent on whether the narrative in question describes what really happened (1995, 12).[4] The defi-

---

4. Brettler (1995, 152–53 n. 43) maintains that "historical facticity" is not a requirement for this definition.

nitions of Van Seters, Gilmour, and Brettler more or less seem to unchain historiography from the necessity to relate what really happened, and if that is the case then one wonders why we could not describe as a history any fictional writing that presents a past and makes it seem significant in some way. A writer might relate a whole series of events that did not happen while believing that they did, and describe their significance to and meaning for his or her society, but that begins to sound like a curious mix of history and fiction, if not fiction outright. After all, if we are going to define histories as things that present a past and describe its significance, then Shakespeare wrote them. For example, we refer to parts 1 and 2 of *Henry IV* and to *Henry V* as histories, and they do refer to events that really happened, such as the battles of Shrewsbury and Agincourt, and to figures involved in them, such as the eponymous kings and Henry Percy, but we somehow know that when we call these plays "histories" we mean something different from when we use the term for works produced by modern scholars, such as Israel Finkelstein and Neil Asher Silberman's (2001) *The Bible Unearthed* or Iain Provan, Philips Long, and Tremper Longman's (2003) *A Biblical History of Israel*. Both are works composed by modern scholars, experts with a great deal of experience in the study of the history of ancient Israel. Shakespeare's histories, we know, are largely fictional, but the other two works are histories in a way that Shakespeare's plays are not. Surely if we can make a clear distinction between history and fiction we have moved a step closer to deciding what a history is and whether Kings and Dtr as a whole match that definition.

One potentially obvious solution to this problem of distinguishing history and fiction is a formal one: histories have to do particular things if they are to discuss what really happened, and doing these things results in similar formal aspects, since what historians are trying to accomplish is not easy. The past is gone, and nothing about it is "directly accessible" (Grabbe 1997, 21), as only traces of it remain in things such as archaeological relics and texts and memories (Davies 2014, 21), and when dealing with events thousands of years ago, these relics and texts are few, and we have no guarantee that they are representative of the kinds of things people generally thought about and did (Knauf 1991, 26). Moreover, historians are driven by their own biases to form their histories in ways that reflect their interests and worldviews, a point widely acknowledged by historians of ancient Israel (e.g., Knauf 1991, 30–31, 50; Edelman 1996, 143; Whybray 1999, 183; Younger 1999, 314–15; Gilmour 2011, 13; Davies 2014, 17–19), and it would thus appear that an attempt to produce historiography can easily turn into theology or ideology or some other kind of nonhistory. If we continue to maintain that histories present to readers what really happened, then historians have to be able to deal with this paucity of evidence so that they can present what happened and ensure that their own biases do not turn history into fiction, and we might expect this to leave some sort of formal trace in real history writings. We sometimes refer to historians as pursuing a particular kind of method, and Philip Davies, for example, lists aspects of the method that historians must follow if they are to be historians: they must not privilege what is improbable, must not contradict the data that is at their disposal, must exclude "obvious bias" in the sources they use, must prioritize primary sources, and must engage competing interpretations of the past, among other things (2014, 22–23). If we see particular writings doing these kinds of things, then, it might seem, we should describe them as histories. Should Davies have this right, then we would have to conclude that Shakespeare did not write histories of the kind we are trying to define, since his history plays do not, for example, clearly address competing interpretations of what really happened, nor does he really seem to exclude obvious bias from works when, for example, he triumphantly portrays a glorious English victory at Agincourt in *Henry V*. Dtr also could not be a history, since at the least it would appear to privilege the improbable when using divine causation to explain events, and its author does not seem to be the least bit interested in addressing competing interpretations of the past.

If by *method* one means "a systematic and orderly series of steps a scholar follows" to produce historical analysis (George 2009, 459), then it is not clear to everyone that historians, ancient or modern, truly follow a method as they go about their work (e.g., Barr 2000, 47; Collins 2005, 4; Barton 2007, 62–67), but the kinds of things Davies discusses do intuitively seem like the sorts of things we expect historians to do, and we could perhaps see him as describing standards historians must adhere to and norms they must follow if they are to produce histories. However, there are aspects of his list for which we might want more explanation— What counts as improbable? What precisely is "obvious bias"?—and it would seem that a failure on the field's part to agree as to how to answer these questions has led it to disagree as to how to distinguish between history and fiction, regardless of whether works otherwise manifest the formal features that reflect a modern historiographic approach. Giovanni Garbini, for example, writes that a failure to recognize bias and improbable accounts in the biblical stories led a scholar such as John Bright to produce an "apologetic" rather than a history in a work titled *A History of Israel*; the same faults, he writes, mean that Georg Fohrer's "history" of Israel has a "lack of a real historical approach" (1988, 5–13). Niels Peter Lemche's survey of modern histories of ancient Israel (1998, 133–61) leads him to conclude that they often naively paraphrase the biblical writings created as ideological constructs and thus produce "an invented Israel" (165–66). Others argue, however, that the biblical texts provide us with our best source of knowledge about Israel's history and that it is "folly" to marginalize them in our historical work (Provan, Long, and Longman 2003, 73–74). Even as studies of ancient Israel seem quite similar on a formal basis, this has not helped the field distinguish between the scholarly works that are histories and those that are fictional. As a result, while Finkelstein and Silberman's book might seem to be a work of history, since they adhere to the kinds of standards Davies describes, one scholar of the Hebrew Bible calls it "very largely … a work of imaginative fiction, not a serious or reliable account of the subject" (Kitchen 2003, 464). The book by Provan, Long, and Longman is a "con," according to another historian of ancient Israel, and a confidence game involves the creation of a story that the author knows to be fiction (Grabbe 2011, 232). We can find many other charges such as this by scholars in the field describing the putatively historical works of their peers. Some are accused of writing "imagined narrative" and passing it off as history (Carroll 1997, 92–93), of creating material "belonging to the presently extremely popular genre of historical novels," material "that is closer to fiction than to historiography in the traditional sense of the word" (Lemche 2011, 149–50), of writing "nonhistories" (Dever 2001, 37), or of creating "mainly pure fiction from cover to cover" (Kitchen 2003, 462).

Seemingly, then, just because one scholar in the field writes a history that formally reflects the kind of standards and norms Davies discusses does not mean that others will not understand it to be fiction and refuse to recognize the scholar in question as a historian.[5] I have no reason to doubt that these writings labeled by some as "fiction" and "nonhistories" were intended by their authors to be taken as histories, since they are doing the sorts of thing Davies talks about as they prioritize primary sources, engage competing interpretations, and so on. But I also have no reason to doubt the sincerity of their critics, experts in the same field, who read

---

5. For an example of the latter point, see Knauf 2011, 40–50.

these works as fiction, and the most obvious conclusion to glean from this is that it is difficult to tell historiography and fiction apart and that readers do not always agree as to whether a particular work is one or the other. Fiction and historiography apparently have a lot in common, since historiography, like fiction, is a species of the genus narrative (see White 2010, 112), and formal aspects apparently do not always help us distinguish between the two, at least if there is ambiguity in regard to the exact sense of some of those aspects. As we discuss in the next sections of the chapter, at the heart of history is narrative that, first of all, creates a past, a definition of history close to Brettler's, and this part of the definition would appear to include Dtr, since it has a narrative that creates a past. This creation involves explanation that links past events together through causation and that indicates why they are significant, as Gilmour argues. The Deuteronomist was undoubtedly interested in explanation and significance, what we could call "meaning," yet since we expect histories not merely to create pasts but also to discuss what really happened, it is not enough only to say that Dtr creates a past in narrative; to be a history, it must also create a past that is true.

The difference between historiography and fiction, then, is that the past a historiography creates provides a true account of what really happened, whereas that created by a work of fiction does not. The difficulty in distinguishing between them, as we have seen, is that there is enough overlap that even people in the same intellectual culture do not always agree in which genre they should classify a specific work. What we choose to call a history is a narrative that creates a past that we largely believe to be true, whereas what we designate as fiction is a narrative that creates a past that we largely do not believe to be true. What we see as historiography coheres with our beliefs and worldview, because it contains events and explanations of them that we are predisposed to see as real. If, for example, we are not predisposed to believe that the divine world intervenes in history, then we cannot believe that a writing in which this is an important explanatory device truly explains what happened. This means, I am about to argue, that the difference between history and fiction is in the eye of the beholder, and if this seems ludicrous, recall that this is precisely the case among contemporary historians of ancient Israel as they discuss one another's works. In this definition it is not authorial intention that matters but readers' reception, and a particular writing, rather like Schrödinger's cat, is inherently neither one thing nor another until readers begin to observe it, and even then it can be both history and fiction at the same time if readers disagree as to how to classify it. I argue below that, from a modern scholarly point of view, Kings and Dtr as a whole cannot be considered to be a history, even though ancient Judeans could have understood it as one, as we discuss in chapter 3. Not all ancient readers of Dtr would have understood it to be a true account—one of the points we briefly discuss in the next section of this chapter is the Chronicler's revision of Kings, a revision that suggests the Chronicler did not always believe that Kings rightly represents what really happened—but some would have. Insofar as our interest lies in how some ancient Judeans thought about and responded to the events surrounding the destruction of Judah and the exile, then we can refer to Dtr as a history from the point of view of those who believed the Deuteronomist got things right.

But before we explain in chapter 3 the kind of past the Deuteronomist created, we need to describe more clearly the narrative nature of history. This helps us see why some ancient Judeans would have understood Dtr to be a true portrayal of the past, why collective trauma is a kind of history, and, as we discuss in later chapters, why psychological trauma is antithetical to historical narrative. Only then can we argue that the narrative of Kings and Dtr as a whole overwrites and represses psychological trauma while simultaneously creating collective trauma.

2.2. Historiography's Narrative Creation of the Past

If histories are concerned with what really happened, then it might seem that all they need to do is to provide facts about the past, but, as we see in this and the following section, the essence of history is an accurate explanatory narrative, and this is why no history is simply a list of facts in chronological order. Writings that only provide such a list are normally called annals or chronicles, and the *Annals of St. Gall* is one example of this latter genre, as are the Neo- and Late Babylonian chronicles, and both do no more than provide chronological lists of unrelated events. Here, for example, is a short excerpt from the *Annals of St. Gall* (trans. White 1987, 6–9):

709. Hard winter. Duke Gottfried died.
710. Hard year and deficient in crops.
711.

This is a chronological list of events, but the *Annals* does not explain why it is important to know that Duke Gottfried died in 709 or that the harvest was poor in 710, what the significance of these events is, what caused them, or what they caused. There is no explanation here, no sense as to why these events are significant or meaningful,[6] nor is any explanation provided for why no events at all are recorded for the year 711.

To take another excerpt from a different example of the genre, one of the Neo-Babylonian chronicles relates the events of Nebuchadnezzar's seventh regnal year as follows:

> Year seven. In the month of Kislev the king of Akkad assembled his army and went to Hattu. He encamped against the city of Judah, and in the month of Adar, on the second day, he took the city (and) captured the king. A king of his own choosing he appointed in it. He took its abundant tribute and brought it to Babylon. (*ABC*, chronicle 5, reverse, 11–13)

One imagines that the chronicle's compiler found these events to be significant for some reason, especially since no other events of that year are mentioned, but he or she never explains what that reason is. There is no indication as to what caused Nebuchadnezzar to move against Jerusalem or what resulted from the change of king there. Readers receive no explanation as to why the event was significant or meaningful, but significance and meaning and explanation are precisely what we expect histories to provide, and they need narrative to do it; it is because histories are more than simply lists of chronological events that true narrative is the preeminent characteristic of history. It is not simply the questions of what and when that matter to historians, but also the multifaceted question of why. While annals and chronicles can answer the first two questions, histories also answer the third, something they cannot do without narrative. Yet, as we discuss, narratives are not inherent in past events themselves but are creations of historians. Not only does the creation of the past in a history reflect the historian's own interests, it reflects the historian's culture, which

---

6. E. D. Hirsch (see, e.g., 1984) sees meaning and significance as two different things: the meaning of a text corresponds to an original authorial intention in history and so is fixed, while significance refers to the present uses of the text, which need not focus on what the author is trying to say. This raises a number of interesting hermeneutical questions that are outside the scope of this work to engage, but it should suffice to say here that we are generally interested in the ways that people encounter narratives of the past produced by their contemporaries and that we consider the two terms as synonyms, as historians explain what past events mean and simultaneously explain their significance to a contemporary audience.

leads historians to be interested in particular things, limits the ways they can conceive of dealing with those things, and provides them with standards and norms to follow as they create their narratives. The histories a culture produces, in fact, create the past insofar as it exists and is meaningful for that culture, and, as we see later in this chapter, the creation of collective trauma is, just like the creation of history, a narrative reflection of a particular social worldview.

In order to explain and provide significance, a history writing must contain a narrative that links together facts about the past, which is to say that it must provide a story that explains the relationship of these facts to one another, describing how some caused others and why they are significant. Sometimes a historian will explain the significance of facts by discussing the causal relationship of past events to one another, or by arguing that they are excellent examples of a certain phenomenon or an odd exception to a general rule. Other times a historian will explain the significance of certain facts or events by indicating that they provide important context for understanding the discussion of other events in the history, or for understanding the reader's present, or will argue that they are important for some other reason. At a minimum, a narrative provides causation that links events, which is to say it has a plot. There is no plot in the sentence "The king died and then the queen died," writes E. M. Forster (1927, 86), but there is in the sentence "The king died and then the queen died of grief," because the latter includes causality and thus plot. Forster calls the former sentence "story," but I will use the term *story* as a synonym for *narrative*, something with a beginning and an end that both describes and explains change (Danto 1965, 233–35). So even if we could go back in time and precisely reproduce the past events that populate a history we are writing, that in itself would not be fulfilling the complete function of historians, writes Arthur Danto (112–17), because histories must also include explanations of these events that speak to their significance. Insofar as historians create narratives that explain and provide significance, they produce meaning (White 1987, 42–43), and a history cannot exist without this.

The alternative to the view that the significance and meaning of the past is created by historians' narratives is to say that meaning and significance are inherent in those events, but this seems like an unlikely conclusion. What, for example, is the inherent or natural meaning of Nebuchadnezzar's capture of Jerusalem in the seventh year of his reign, the meaning the Neo-Babylonian chronicle fails to provide? According to 2 Kgs 24:13, this event happened "just as YHWH had spoken," so perhaps the meaning of the event is that it proves YHWH's control of history.[7] Since 24:9 refers to the evil of Jehoiachin, the Judean king of the time of Jerusalem's capture, perhaps the significance of the event is that it is an important example of a key aspect of history, namely, that YHWH punishes evil Judean and Israelite kings, something that certainly coheres with the larger pattern of the book of Kings, as we discuss in the next chapter. I do not know, however, how one could prove that this is significance inherent in the event itself rather than significance produced by the Deuteronomist. One imagines that the compiler of the Neo-Babylonian chronicle, if pressed for the event's meaning, would come up with a different explanation, since not one known Mesopotamian writing explains events by referring to the power of the God of Israel and Judah[8] (excluding, of course, any writings produced by Judeans who were living in Mesopotamia). Modern historians, who refrain from attributing divine causation to events, are more likely to conclude that Nebuchadnezzar's capture of Jerusalem in 598/7 BCE was the result of Judah's failure to remain a loyal client to Babylon (see 2 Kgs 24:1). For someone whose worldview is largely in accord with that of the Deuteronomist, the explanations 2 Kgs 24 suggests make sense. Modern historians, whose field prohibits them from explaining events by means of divine causation, could not assent to that explanation. The case seems to be that interpretations of events that determine their significance and meaning and define causation depend on one's worldview; it is not clear to me how to make the argument that

---

7. Unless otherwise noted, all translations of biblical texts are my own.

8. To be fair, Mesopotamian empires had been attributing at least some of their victories to the decisions of their enemies' gods to abandon their cities and lands because of their people's evil since the Tukulti-Ninurta Epic of the thirteenth century BCE (Machinist 1976), and this notion of divine abandonment played an important role in the Neo-Assyrians' explanations of their imperial victories (see Oded 1992, 121–22; Holloway 2002, 145–46). It is not impossible, then, that a Neo-Babylonian scribe could also have explained Nebuchadnezzar's defeat of Jerusalem as a result of Yhwh's decision to abandon his people because of their sin; on the other hand, Assyrian claims of divine abandonment also included the assertion that the gods of the defeated peoples wanted to submit to Aššur and to travel to his temple (Cogan 1974, 20–21). Moreover, when Neo-Babylonian texts discuss divine agency for the destruction of Assyria, they refer to anger on the part of Babylon's gods, not divine abandonment on the part of Aššur (Machinist 1997, 186), so it seems unlikely that a Mesopotamian scribe and the Deuteronomist would be in complete agreement as to the explanation for and significance of the fall of Jerusalem.

one of the explanations mentioned above, or some other explanation, is inherent in the event itself.

This means, then, that historians create plots or narratives that seem to best explain the facts of which they are aware.[9] Historian David Carr makes the point that we narrate our own lives as we live them so that they make sense to us (1991, 21–30, 55–65), but this is simply a recognition that we individually have a need to apply narratives to our personal pasts, not evidence for narrative as inherent in events, present in them without humans putting it there.[10] But Carr is correct to assert that narrative is the way that we make sense of things; Aristotle, writes Paul Ricoeur, realized that we need narrative to experience temporality (1984, 1:41–42; see also Mink 1987, 186). Our own lives, or any series of past events, have no story at all until we give them one, until we impose the plots that have beginnings, middles, and ends, all of which are arbitrarily assigned. Past events are meaningless until we give them meaning in narrative, but there are no natural beginnings and endings when it comes to such narratives.

A history of the postexilic period, for example, might begin with Cyrus's destruction of Babylon, but a historian might view that as inadequate, depending on his or her purposes in writing the history. If the focus of the study is to be on the postexilic Judean temple assembly, then the historian might decide that something should be said about Judah before Judean immigrants from Babylon began arriving in the late sixth century BCE, so that he or she could explain why there may (or may not) have been conflict between the groups. In that case, should the historian begin with Nebuchadnezzar's destruction of Judah, in order to explain how there came to be Judeans in Babylonia in the first place and how their identity was formed by their life there? Should he or she begin with a narrative of the situation in Judah during the Neo-Babylonian period in order to discuss the relationship between the immigrants from Babylon and the population already present in Judah? Or would it make more sense to begin with Judah in the late monarchic period in order to demonstrate how the populations and polities in and around Judah changed from the late Neo-Assyrian period and on? There is no place that is natural to begin a history

---

9. For a longer explanation of this point, see White 1973, 6–13.

10. Moreover, historians qua historians do not narrate their own lives, points out Frank Ankersmit (2012, 34–40); they write about individuals who have experienced things, and they say things about individuals and whole societies that those individuals and societies did not know.

of the postexilic period; the beginning of the narrative is determined by the kind of story the historian wants to tell.

Louis Mink is right to claim that "stories are not lived but told. Life has no beginnings, middles, or ends; there are meetings, but the start of an affair belongs to the story we tell ourselves later, and there are partings, but final partings only in the story.... So it seems truer to say that narrative qualities are transferred from art to life" (1987, 135). We need narratives in order to make sense of past events, to see them as meaningful and significant in some way, but these narratives are our creations. We have to choose among the infinite number of past events for places to begin and end as we write histories, and we have to write stories that supply the events we discuss with meaning. Without narrative we can know that past events happened—or so I assert now, at any rate, although I point out in the next section of the chapter that the matter is more complicated than this—but we cannot explain them or locate their significance, so without narrative they are meaningless. Narrative, to quote Mink once more, is "the primary cognitive instrument," that which makes relationships comprehensible (185–86); narrative replaces a mere copy of events with meaning (White 1987, 1–2).[11] So one of historians' chief jobs is emplotment, as their narratives fit past events into plots as syntax fits individual words into a sentence, and once readers understand the plot then they understand the significance of the events (White 2010, 122–24).

The emplotment is done, of course, by historians with particular interests and worldviews, and these shape the stories they tell.[12] This is why it is the historian's interests that determine where he or she decides to begin the history of postexilic Judah, as we discussed above, and the historian's worldview that determines how that story gets told. Is the decisive factor in the history of the postexilic period the economic situation of a struggling immigrant community in Judah, or is it Persia's political interest in maintaining a secure link with—and sometimes secure border against—Egypt, or the struggles for political influence within the community itself? For a historian convinced that macroeconomic factors are the driving force behind history, a focus on the community's internal and external economic relationships best explains what really happened. For someone

---

11. This is why it is not terribly helpful to distinguish between history and narrative history—contra Barstad 2008, 13–23—for a history cannot be a history without narrative.

12. History, as Keith Jenkins puts it, is always history for someone (1999, 1–2).

convinced that God controls all important events in history, then a focus on events as manifesting the working of the divine might be best.

As part of our discussion concerning the creation of the past in narrative, it is worthwhile considering what might allow someone to recognize a particular writing as history rather than fiction. Based on my argument so far, it may sound as though I believe that historians can write whatever story they want, but that is not the case. If they are intellectually honest then they must adhere to the standards and norms determined by the worldview of their intellectual culture, the kind of thing Davies discusses in regard to modern historiography, an intellectual culture shaped by the Enlightenment. These standards, however, are culturally dependent, and a modern scholar providing a narrative to explain postexilic Judah could not invoke divine causation, whereas an ancient Judean author likely would, at least given what we know of ancient Judean culture, since this is what their respective belief systems would lead them to conclude. Ancient Judeans, like ancient Near Easterners in general, believed the divine world was active in shaping historical events, whereas the modern field of history has developed in such a way that it is illegitimate for modern historians qua historians to refer to divine causation.[13] This is an important reason why, for modern historians, Kings is not a history. Even if they may not doubt, for example, 2 Kgs 25's assertion that Nebuchadnezzar besieged and destroyed Jerusalem, in their roles as modern historians they cannot believe the explanation for this event that Kings provides, one that is based in divine intervention in history, so Kings is not a historical narrative from the vantage point of the modern historian. To discuss what really happened, histories have to provide explanation and significance in narrative; it is the narrative and not simply the events they explain that make a history a history, and from the perspective of modern historians the Deuteronomist did not create acceptable narrative explanation. To say that Kings contains records of events that really happened is not enough, even though that is true (e.g., Halpern 1999; Long 2002a; Millard 2010); this in itself does not make it a history, since chronicles and annals can also contain accurate records of events, yet they are not histories either. To be considered a history, a writing must provide narrative explanation that for the most part, at least, appears to be rational, but for one's community, rational

---

13. So, for example, David Law's (2012, 20–23) description of the presuppositions with which historical criticism functions includes antisupernaturalism, the assumption that the laws of nature can never be violated.

behavior is simply what parallels group behavior (Rorty 1991, 199–200), and as rational as Dtr's explanation of events may have seemed to some ancient Judeans, divine direction of history is not a rational explanation of things as far as modern historians are concerned.

Because the standards historians follow are dependent on their culture, historians can only produce histories that are in accord with their cultures' worldviews, worldviews that limit the kinds of things that historians can think about investigating and the kinds of explanations that they can think about proposing, just as it is the worldview of one's culture that limits what sorts of narratives one is willing to accept as history. Historians rarely find a need to justify the standards and norms that they follow, since such things are grounded in their intellectual culture. Modern scholars do not need to explain why they do not invoke divine action to make sense of Nebuchadnezzar's destruction of Jerusalem, despite the fact that a key source for their construction of the event, the book of Kings, insists that this was ultimately the result of God's will, because their intellectual culture excludes this as part of any explanatory device. And this is why a modern scholar such as Ernest Nicholson, to take simply one example, can state that "there is no intellectually serious conception of history that resorts to divine agency as a mode of explanation" (2014, 140), while having virtually no need to provide a defense of this position, since modern historians take it for granted.

Iain Provan complains about precisely this rejection of divine causation as an explanatory device in regard to the modern study of the history of ancient Israel but says that "it is simply how modern scholarship is. If you do not like it, find a game of your own" (2000, 284). Even though he does not appear happy to arrive at this conclusion he is exactly right, just as he is right when he says that another scholar's rejection of divine causation in explaining past events is a statement of faith, understanding faith in this context as referring to an unproven assumption (315). Frank Ankersmit makes a more general point that echoes Provan's observation in regard to the standards and norms historians follow when he writes that "there is no point outside historiography itself from which rules for the historian's method of work can be drawn up: if historians consider something to be meaningful, then it is meaningful and that is all there is to it" (1998, 177). The standards and norms historians follow and the breadth of their interests when it comes to creating narratives that construct and explain what really happened are grounded in cultural worldviews, and this is why what is widely regarded as a history in one culture can be viewed as fiction by readers within a different one. So when Philips Long writes that it is "less acceptable" for a historian who is a theist to reject divine causation as an explanatory category because the field's norms reject it (2002b, 9–10), he misses the first point Provan makes: the field or language game is what it is, and to consistently violate one of its important standards is to begin to move into a different field altogether. Scholars such as Provan and Long encounter difficulty in entirely agreeing with the standards and norms of modern historiography because they are convinced that God acts in history and are also part of a field that rejects this as a possible way to explain things. Their particular situation, being part of different groups with incompatible worldviews and conflicting standards of behavior, is precisely the sort of thing that tends to produce moral dilemmas (Rorty 1991, 200–201). At points where those worldviews come into conflict it may not be clear how to act, and creative moves to ameliorate the disjuncture may be taken by staunch adherents of one or both worldviews as an abdication of one's duties.

Since it is the wider culture of which historians are a part that provides the worldviews that produce the standards and norms they follow as they create their narratives, then they must practice "ascetic self-discipline" and put the field's demands over their own desires if they wish their work to be understood as histories by this culture (Haskell 1998, 301–2). The past cannot be explained in ways unsanctioned by the field, for historians' work is read by others in the field and the intellectual culture of which they are a part, and it can only be taken seriously as history if it reflects the worldview and concerns of that social group. The culture of which one is a part limits the ways in which one can see and explain the world, and it limits the kinds of explanations that are accepted by others in that culture. One could argue, as Provan does, that the historian's duty is to the truth and not to the field's method, and that "epistemological openness" to any method that leads us to the truth should be the historian's goal (2000, 301–8). The problem with this claim, however, is that it assumes there is some way to judge the truth of historians' work that exists outside any method, outside the standards and norms developed by any intellectual culture to evaluate evidence and create true narratives, for it assumes that truth exists independently of what anyone thinks.[14]

---

14. I do not mean to argue, however, that we should never violate a field's standards and norms; such violations are the ways fields change over time and, as their practitioners eventually see it, progress (see, e.g., Feyerabend 1975), and certainly a

Perhaps truth does exist in such a way, although it is not clear how we could ever know it, because all we can do to arrive at truth is to think about things and use language to describe them. We have to use language—talk, write, and think—as we describe what really happened and why, and we can only use the language and syntax that are available to us. We can learn new languages and play new language games, which is to say that we can adopt new standards and norms that develop out of different worldviews, but there is no standard that exists outside these language games themselves that tells us whether one method is better suited than another to correspond to the truth of the past, because that would demand using non-linguistic means to judge language. That may be possible for God, writes Richard Rorty, but it is not for humans, and there is no point in asking questions that we would have to step outside our own minds to answer (1991, 6–7). History does not exist on its own terms; it exists on ours (White 1978, 116–17), and since these terms vary from culture to culture, so do cultural understandings of the truth of the past (see Mink 1987, 35–41).

Part of the point of this section of the argument is to explain that histories cannot exist without narratives, and this is why trauma, which is antinarrative, is also antihistory, the issue we examine in chapter 4. Yet another point of this section of the chapter is to lay the basis of my claim that ancient Judeans could have legitimately seen Dtr as a history that describes what really happened—a matter we explore in chapter 3—even though that view would not seem to be a viable option for modern historians, since readers can understand creations of the past in narrative to be true only insofar as such creations reflect their worldviews. We know something of the larger cultural context in which Dtr was produced, and we know that Judeans believed that the divine world directed history. Given that this appears to have been a widespread belief, it would have been negligent for an ancient Judean who wrote about the past to fail to

---

failure to interrogate and be willing to challenge these standards and norms can lead to failures to confront oppressive worldviews. My discussion of Provan's concept of epistemological openness, however, deals with the fact that only fields or discourses or language games ground concepts of truth. The field of biblical history will change over time, because that is what fields tend to do, but it will only change because of internal debates in regard to its standards and norms, not because it moves closer to truth or meaning inherent in past events themselves, since past events have no meaning until humans say they do. For more on the concept of change in a professional field, see Fish 1989, 141–60.

refer to God's will as manifested in historical events.[15] This certainly does not mean that all ancient Judeans agreed on the reasons for divine intervention; in Kings, for example, monarchs can be punished by God after their deaths as their royal houses are annihilated for the king's sin (e.g., 1 Kgs 11:9–13; 14:6–16; 21:20–29), whereas, according to Chronicles's well known doctrine of immediate retribution, God punishes evil kings during their lifetimes, and this difference in worldview causes the Chronicler to alter stories adopted from Kings.[16] Yet both writings violate an important standard of the modern field of history in referring to divine causation as an explanatory principle. This is not a rational explanation of historical events for modern scholars, although it is for ancient Judean writers, so for modern historians Kings and Chronicles are not histories. A community can only recognize a work as a history if the group accepts that it is a rational presentation and explanation of what really happened.

2.3. Historiography's Narrative Creation of Past Events

I have been arguing that historians create the past insofar as they are responsible for creating the narratives that explain past events, narratives that provide readers with the significance of those things, and thus we could say that they create the meaning of the past. What I have said up to this point could be understood as implying that past events can have some sort of reality for us independently of narrative, but that is not really true. Insofar as events can exist or be real for us, they are themselves constructed through narratives that are also our creations, and to say that historians' narratives must be faithful to the events they are explaining is only to say that they must be faithful to other stories that they or their cultures or other historians have created. If this is correct, then while some modern historians argue that Kings and the Deuteronomistic History as a whole is not a history in part because it refers to events that did not occur, ancient Judean readers could not make that argument unless they, like the modern scholars, believed they had sufficient warrant to doubt enough factual

---

15. The author of Esther, though, avoids referring to divine intervention, and if this is the exception that proves the rule it also suggests that at least some intellectuals in ancient Judah at some point in time did not see it as mandatory to refer to divine causation in an explanation of historical events.

16. For some relevant discussions and examples of this issue in Chronicles, see Kelly 2003; Japhet 2006; Ben Zvi 2006; Galil 2010; Janzen 2017, 86–90.

claims made by the Deuteronomist. In that case their cultural narratives would have provided them with different facts from those the Deuteronomist maintains are true. The work of historians, then, involves not only writing stories that connect and explain facts, but also creating the facts through other narratives. Any facts they do not create they access from cultural narratives that have formulated ones the historians assume to be true, so this section of the chapter is simply part of the larger argument that narrative is history's essence. Moreover, as we discuss here, since it is our worldviews that allow us to discern whether a narrative has correctly created and explained the facts of the past, histories reinforce those worldviews; in our upcoming examinations of psychological trauma, however, we see that trauma cannot offer such support, so histories tend to repress it.

The assertion that historians create past events, personages, and so on does not intuitively appear to be correct, since some facts seem to be true apart from what anyone thinks. We can say, for example, that it is a fact that the book of Kings is a part of the Bible; surely no narrative or interpretation is necessary to arrive at that conclusion. This seems to be something different from the narratives that link and explain facts, narratives that are guided and limited by one's culture and interests as a historiographer. When we refer to the year Erasmus was born, writes Frank Ankersmit, we do not look for explanatory power or comprehensiveness, for our reference is either true or false, and apparently no interpretive narrative is needed (2001, 55–56). Some past events seem to be so obviously true that it is appropriate to refer to them as facts. A fact is something that is true—no one would in good faith refer to something as a fact if one believed it to be false—so we can say it is a fact that Kings is a book in the Bible and that Nebuchadnezzar captured Jerusalem in the early sixth century BCE and deported some of its population. A fact is not only something that is true, though; it is also something that is widely accepted within a group, something on which a group has reached consensus. I am less sure that I am entitled to refer to King David's existence as a fact rather than as an invention of the traditions that biblical authors drew on, even though I am fairly sure that David did exist, for David's existence is a contested matter in the field of the history of ancient Israel. No one in the field contests that Kings is a book of the Bible or is remotely interested in doing so, and Nebuchadnezzar's destruction of Jerusalem is basically uncontested. For example, even Lemche, a scholar who is often quite skeptical that biblical books provide us with accurate information about the eras they purport to describe, states in regard to this event that "it is more than likely that the second capture of Jerusalem really took place and resulted in the destruction of the temple" (2008, 115–16; and see Thompson 2000, 214). By describing this event as "more than likely," Lemche indicates to readers that he is interpreting evidence at his disposal. In fact, 2 Kgs 25 describes an event like this, and although the Neo-Babylonian sources known to us do not, there is enough archaeological evidence for a siege and destruction of Jerusalem in the early sixth century BCE that Dan Bahat refers to this evidence as "among the most dramatic at any biblical site" (1993, 709). The Babylonian capture of Jerusalem would appear to be a fact as far as the field is concerned, but it is not clear that we could refer to the existence of David as a fact. For historians of ancient Israel like Lemche, who are often called minimalists, despite a plethora of stories about David in Samuel, Kings, and Chronicles, and references to him in Psalms and other biblical texts, it seems more likely that he is an invention of ancient Judeans. This is true even despite the appearance of the word *bytdwd*—translated by most scholars (although generally not minimalists) as "house of David"— on the Tel Dan stela of the late ninth or early eighth century BCE. The appearance of the word might seem to indicate that a figure called David did exist before the inscription was carved and that he was a founder of a royal dynasty, but minimalists argue that it is unlikely the word should be understood in this way (e.g., Thompson 2000, 203–5; Lemche 2008, 113–15; Davies 2014, 36–39).

If a fact depends on consensus within a group, then things can be facts at one point in time and at another point lose that status. Apparently, to arrive at the conclusion that David existed is something that demands interpretation, but so, for that matter, is the conclusion that Nebuchadnezzar captured Jerusalem and exiled some of its population. While both of these things may seem different from claiming that the book of Kings is part of the Bible, that also is something that demands interpretation, even though no one who studies the Hebrew Bible makes arguments for or against it or feels the need to say that it is "more than likely" that Kings is part of the biblical corpus. The difference is simply that we almost never think about the interpretation that has gone into arriving at this conclusion. Merely to assert that it is a fact that Kings is a part of the Bible is to assert that this is true, and truth value is bestowed by interpreters on things, not inherent in the things themselves. Humans do not naturally know, without teaching or context, what the Bible is and what Kings is. Those with absolutely no knowledge of Judaism or Christianity, for example, could not in good faith assent to the statement "It is true that Kings is a book in the Bible," because the sentence would be meaningless for them. Given the opportunity to learn about these religious traditions and their sacred texts, however, they would absorb a narrative that would allow them to make sense of that sentence and to agree that it states a fact. But for those of us who study the Hebrew Bible, this fact seems so obvious that we pay no attention to the interpretation that allows us to assign truth value to it. What seems to be most obviously true, least in need of justification, seems that way because we are held tightly in the grip of a worldview that has already done the work of interpretation for us, that has ingrained such knowledge in our basic understanding of the world (Fish 1980, 268–92).

The result is, then, that many aspects of the past can seem as if they are self-evidently true and in no need of interpretation and that to write about them is to represent rather than to construct a past (Mink 1987, 93–94). But narratives are also needed to construct facts in regard to past events, which means that facts are as much linguistic constructions as the narratives historians create to explain them. Since we are unable to judge the truthfulness of a statement by comparing the statement's language to something that exists outside language (White 2010, 313), facts about the past are facts and have truth value for us because we believe and assert and argue that they are true. To designate something as a fact, or as evidence, or as an archaeological artifact, one must designate, which is to say that one must use language and decide that something is one thing and not another. Past events and evidence for them have no meaning for us until we make such decisions by clothing things in language; when things are "linguistically naked, they are unintelligible" (Danto 1965, 219). Historians thus create worlds just as fiction writers do, and just like fiction writers they create the past events and figures that populate these worlds, or at least they and their intellectual cultures do, so it is no wonder that even people in the same intellectual culture can disagree as to whether a given work is history or fiction, especially when they might simultaneously be members of other cultures with competing worldviews. Historians do indeed need to discuss facts and are under a different obligation in this manner than fiction writers are, but the facts they discuss have also been created by stories. When it comes to events that are so widely accepted by a culture that no one disputes them, then there is no need for historians to tell stories about those particular facts because they are so firmly ingrained in their minds and those of their readers; when discussing the year of Erasmus's birth or Kings' status as a canonical writing, historians do not need to provide narratives of explanatory value, because these things appear to authors and readers within the same culture as self-evidently true.

Yet this means that historiography is, from beginning to end, a genre that involves the creation of narratives, so on this level there is no inherent difference between it and fiction. "Western historiography struggles against fiction," as Michel de Certeau puts it in a discussion of why it does not intuitively seem correct to make this claim (1986, 200). History does seem to provide us with a truth and reality that fiction cannot, and to have a "special relationship" to the real (201)—Ranke understood the past that historians construct to be "a replica of the real," according to Stephen Bann (1990, 39)—but this is simply because we are culturally conditioned to accept some renderings of the past as believable and others as unbelievable. Both history and fiction hope to mimic reality (Partner 1998, 75–76), but Roland Barthes writes that history, unlike fiction, has managed to confuse the signified with the referent (1981, 17). Barthes uses the language of structuralism here, in which the word *signifier* refers to a "sound-image," as Ferdinand de Saussure calls it, which is to say the words we speak. Signifiers, as the term suggests, signify something else, the "signified" in structuralist terminology, which is itself a linguistic concept; the sound-image *cat*, or *chat*, or *gato*, depending on what language one speaks, signifies to speakers their understandings of a cat (Saussure 1983, 65–67). But while words can bring concepts to mind, they cannot provide access to referents, things in the world unclothed by language, since it is not possible to think about (or apply language to) things that exist outside our linguistic context until they are mediated by the culture's language.[17] So, writes Barthes, when historical discourse convinces us that the signified is the referent—when it convinces us that it merely reflects rather than creates the past, in other words—it has been "very crafty" (1981, 17). Sometimes in this discourse even the narrator seems to disappear and the past seems to tell itself, Barthes claims (11); at the least, we could say, in a history the narrator is present to communicate but appears to be absent in the sense that the narrator does not seem to block the truth the history relates (White, 2010, 119–20).

To be clear, I am not arguing that past events did not happen—Caesar did cross the Rubicon, Margaret Thatcher was the prime minister of Britain, Nebuchadnezzar did capture Jerusalem—just that we can know about

---

17. For the "fallacy of representation," see White 2010, 198.

these events only through the stories we and our cultures and our historians tell. These facts do not exist for us, nor are they meaningful, in any other way, so what a past event was is what we now say it is (Bennett 1990, 48–49), and the same is true for the narratives that connect and explain those facts. Every time we recognize a particular narrative as a history, as a true story that provides us with the real past and not some kind of fictional account, we do so because it reinforces things we already know to be true or are willing to accept as such, since it proceeds from a worldview we already believe.[18] These histories thus reinforce our worldviews and their understandings of the true and real, just as our worldviews vouch for the truth and reality of these histories. Every time we come across a piece of fiction the author of which we believe means us to understand it as a history, our rejection of what we see as its truth claims reinforces our worldview's boundaries concerning the limits of our beliefs. In the field of the history of ancient Israel, for example, some scholars worry in print that the discipline is being corrupted by those with ideological goals, where ideology is understood as an agenda imported from some different worldview—evangelical Christianity, for example, or Zionism, or anti-Semitism—that undermines the field's standards and norms that are supposed to produce a true picture of the real (e.g., Garbini 1988, 14; Dever 2001, 31, 44; Lemche 2005; Dever 2012, 20; Davies 2014, 28). In making these sorts of claims, scholars reject competing works by labeling them as ideologies—fictions, in other words—rather than histories, thereby reinforcing the boundaries of the true as far as their own worldviews are concerned. There are, of course, institutions and organizations and other groups of people who are invested in understanding one particular kind of discourse as providing a transparent medium to truth, and when we assume that histories or some other kind of writing provide us with access to a prelinguistic referent we reinforce for ourselves and others the claims of the worldview that predispose us to see the writing as true, and thus the authority of the institutions whose legitimacy depends on this worldview

---

18. Altering one's beliefs and views of the world is obviously possible; if a new experience throws existing ones into question, or if we realize that some of our existing opinions contradict each other, or if we encounter facts that challenge them, we modify our beliefs—although as few as possible, so as to keep our existing worldview largely intact—to deal with the new situation (see James 1910, 58–60). If, however, the ideas we encounter disagree too radically with the worldview we hold, we are not able to assimilate them and do not recognize them as true (201).

(Foucault 1971). Because our worldviews commit us to particular ways of understanding things, we can neither accept nor write contradictory histories if we are to be intellectually honest,[19] unless, of course, our beliefs and worldviews radically shift.

In the next chapter our focus turns to the Deuteronomistic History, and we ask what worldview it reflects and supports as it creates and explains the past of the sixth-century disaster for its readers. Ancient Judean readers would have possibly understood the work to be historiography, as we discuss there. Insofar as the Deuteronomist writes history, he or she defends and promotes particular ways of understanding the world and bolsters the claims of a group whose authority is rooted in an acceptance of the legitimacy of a particular worldview. The history (and collective trauma) the Deuteronomist creates, however, is different from the psychological trauma that we discuss in chapter 4, and in chapter 5 we see that trauma in Lamentations abandons and rejects the claims of history, reacting to the disaster of the sixth century in an extremely different way. In doing so, of course, Lamentations cannot offer any sort of support for a worldview and the communal unity and the authority of particular institutions that might depend on a broad acknowledgment of a particular belief system, precisely the sort of failure that leads historians and cultures to repress trauma, as we discuss in chapter 4.

2.4. History and Collective Trauma

Having argued that histories create pasts, we are now in the position to show that collective traumas do the same thing, an important part of our discussion, since collective trauma enters into our analysis of Dtr in chapter 3, and it receives even more emphasis in our examination of Lamentations in chapter 5. Collective trauma is trauma as it is often understood in the field of sociology,[20] and sociologist Jeffrey Alexander refers to it as

---

19. Relativism in the sense of accepting the equal value of contradictory statements and worldviews is thus not a tenable position. See, e.g., Rorty 1982, 160–75; Fish 1980, 302–21.

20. Not all sociologists who study groups in the aftermath of traumatic events focus their work on collective trauma; Kai Erikson (see, e.g., 1995) is an example of a sociologist who is interested in examining how groups that are full of survivors of traumatic events deal with their trauma, without necessarily privileging a search for group narratives that act to reshape social identity.

something that, just like a history, has been constructed by a social group, emerging from its worldview (2012, 6). Collective traumas in this sense are not "naturally occurring events"; groups view particular events as traumatic because they have decided to view them that way (7–8). The traumatizing events may not even have occurred, writes Alexander (13–15), but what matters for sociologists is the existence of specific claims that a group has undergone great suffering, how these claims came to be made, and how they affect the society in question.

There are a number of things to consider in regard to this understanding of trauma. The first is that collective trauma is not naturally occurring but is part of a past that a group creates, just as all of history is. When a trauma exists for a community, the community has decided to create the past as traumatic. To clarify Alexander's point that the traumatic events might not even have occurred, I do not understand him to mean that the group that creates the traumatic past does not believe it to be true, but rather that modern historiographers might argue that there is little or no good evidence that the traumatic events actually took place. If the group is successful in its creation of trauma, however, then it will have created a narrative that, as far as its members are concerned, relates what really happened. Just as historians create meaning as they create pasts, trauma in this sociological sense is "meaning making" (Alexander 2012, 16), an active negotiation of the meaning of an event that affects cultural identity for the social groups who believe in its reality (Smelser 2004, 48–50). The existence of collective trauma is dependent on carrier groups, a concept Alexander borrows from Max Weber that refers to groups that may consist of elites or the marginalized or those in between (2012, 16–17). The group aims to persuade the larger society to accept its master narrative that a particular event was traumatic. This narrative explains what happened, who was victimized, and who was responsible for the trauma; it can be created in different institutional and social arenas, including religious, artistic, legal, and governmental ones (17–25); and it will involve "storytelling of all kinds" (Alexander and Breese 2011, xiii). This collective trauma, writes Ron Eyerman, grounds the identity of a people (2001, 1–2). He refers to the work of the early twentieth-century sociologist Maurice Halbwachs, who pointed out that individual memory is a function of group memory, since individuals exist as members of groups. Individuals remember particular things because they are significant, and it is the group that informs individuals which things meet that standard (Connerton 1989, 36–38). As a kind of collective memory, collective trauma is thus a creation and interpretation of past events that the group has determined are significant because of the great collective suffering involved, and the collective interpretation of these events meets particular needs the group has (Eyerman 2001, 5–10).

Collective trauma as these sociologists understand it is more or less what history is, except that traumatic histories always focus on collective suffering. This kind of trauma is created through narratives or stories, whether written or oral, stories that create a past, just as histories do. One does not necessarily need collective trauma to ground the identity of a group, and while, as chapter 3 discusses, the Deuteronomist does create collective trauma, this is not the focus of Dtr, not even at the end of Kings, where the destruction of Jerusalem and the exile are created for readers. If collective trauma is "meaning making," as Alexander puts it, that is because it is a kind of history, and as such it is a narrative that creates meaning. In history of any sort, the past that a writer creates derives from the writer's worldview and so functions to draw or reinforce allegiance to that worldview and to the groups whose authority is grounded in it. We can see why a group within the exilic Judean community might have felt it was necessary to draw attention to and reinforce its worldview: survivors of the eighteen-month siege of Jerusalem, of the starvation, slaughter, and rape that assumedly accompanied it, and of the forced migration to Babylonia might well have had their worldview and collective identity shaken. If the worldview held by the Deuteronomist and the Deuteronomist's elite carrier group (we discuss their identity in the next chapter) is unable to explain the community's suffering, then it would have been difficult for the exiles to believe in its validity. In that case, members of the community might conclude that the worldview is not trustworthy, that there is no legitimate basis for the authority the elite claim, that a competing worldview that vouched for the authority and leadership of a different group more correctly explained past and present, or even that they should abandon the community altogether. The creation of history and collective trauma in Dtr draws on the worldview of one group among the Babylonian exiles—although, as we discuss in the next chapter, aspects of it seem to have been widely accepted by Judeans—and in using it to explain what really happened, the Deuteronomist demonstrates that it is a valid way to conceive of reality, at least to those predisposed to accept the kinds of truth claims Dtr makes.

In reinforcing or perhaps reforming social worldviews through a creation of the past, a work such as Dtr does what all histories do as they create pasts by emplotting facts that their authors and societies have created. The process of the creation of a history, writes Hayden White, has something in common with psychotherapy, in which patients know the facts of their lives but need therapists to help them reemplot those facts to change the meaning and significance of them (1998, 20–21). Dominick LaCapra also turns to psychotherapy to create a metaphor to make sense of the creation of history, but he refers to Freud's concept of transference, in which the relationship between child and parent is repeated in the relationship between analysand and analyst, as patients compulsively relive their symptoms (1998, 93). This is a way of talking about the formation of a past by means of a group's understanding of the world: in its creation of the past in its stories and histories, a society repeats its present concerns as well as its overall understanding of the way the world is or should be, so just as historiographic narratives give the past coherence, they also make it desirable. To put this another way, as we create pasts, we create narratives that supply coherence and causation, and beginnings, middles, and endings, and these narratives shape pasts that reflect our own worldviews. To that extent, when we function as historians we can be said to be moralizing the past (White 2010, 20–24), because the past we have created reflects the values and morals of our worldviews. This past, moreover, justifies our present or the present we would like to have because our understanding of the present is based on the same worldview that creates our understanding of the past (126–35), and we find this past to be desirable because it reflects the group's present or the present it wants to see. Insofar as history or collective trauma expresses the needs and desires of the carrier group, insofar as it is a narrative that portrays the world as the group believes it is or should be, history allows societies to write their present concerns on the past. The Deuteronomist, then, not only reinforces or perhaps even draws readers' allegiance to a worldview and the authorities associated with it, but the Deuteronomist also alludes to the present that they should want to see, as we discuss in the next chapter.

If history has something in common with fiction, it also has something in common with law, and this is perhaps especially noticeable when the past that a group creates in its histories is a collective trauma that identifies victims and assigns guilt. Mark Cousins (1987) writes that legal trials, like histories, are interested in establishing whether particular past events really took place and in issues of causation and guilt. Trials, like historiographies, claim that all the evidence available and necessary to explain an event has been accounted for in narrative, and, like historiographies, they render verdicts based on a socially sanctioned set of standards and norms. In the fields of both law and history the truth of the past serves to bolster the desires of present institutions and the worldviews that they produce and that in turn support them. Trials produce justice, that which is right, and histories produce the past, that which is true, and when the verdicts each manufactures are widely acclaimed within a group, then the institutions that have created them are affirmed, for the group then accepts that the institutions' standards and norms render the authoritative voice of the real. Geoffrey Hartman claims that the point of a history is actually a little different from the point of a legal trial, since the latter determines guilt while the former is forensic, producing meaning "to make a case for what should be remembered and how it should be remembered" (1991, 148). Yet Alexander and other sociologists' understanding of collective trauma includes both the production of meaning and the assigning of guilt and victimhood. As chapter 3 discusses, Dtr is an example of a work that does these things. As chapter 3 also points out, as Dtr does this it also works to tacitly support one particular institution, the authority of which was rooted in the worldview on which the Deuteronomist drew to create the history that he or she did.

3
Kings, the Deuteronomistic History, and the Creation of History and Collective Trauma

3.1. Kings and Dtr as History

As the first of our two studies of works that respond to the sixth-century disaster, we examine how Kings and the Deuteronomistic History as a whole creates this event for its readers and provides an explanation that at least some of them could have understood to be true, thus allowing them to view the writing as a history. As the discussion of chapter 1 suggests, for them to read Dtr as history rather than fiction, their worldviews would largely have to overlap with that of the Deuteronomist, or the work would have had to persuade them to adopt the author's worldview, and in this chapter we discuss the ways in which Dtr reflects the belief system of the author and the author's community. As far as we can tell based on other biblical literature, much of the Deuteronomist's thought derived from widely accepted Judean beliefs, a focus of the first part of the chapter, but in the following sections we turn to the author's beliefs concerning God's support for the Davidides and the inherent sinfulness of the people. The Deuteronomist's pro-Davidic worldview means that, by the time the Deuteronomist reaches the end of the narrative at the sixth-century disaster, his or her focus on the Davidides and their successes and failures causes him or her to elide or simply not to see the great suffering of the people; in other words, what we find at the end of Kings is history (as far as some ancient Judeans would have been concerned) that explains the disaster, but not collective trauma, since the account of 2 Kgs 25 almost entirely avoids references to widespread suffering among the people. The Deuteronomist does create collective trauma elsewhere in the work, as we discuss in the third section of the chapter, and even implies that it is related to the sixth-century disaster, but, shaped as Dtr is by the Deuteronomist's belief in the inherent sinfulness of the people, the collective trauma we do encounter makes the people and not the kings the perpetrators of their suffering. The Davidides may have had something to do with the fall of Jerusalem, according to Kings, but the suffering endured by the survivors was their own fault. To put this in the terms used in chapter 2, historians can only create histories that correspond to their worldviews; the authority of particular institutions is grounded in those belief systems, and the most important of such institutions for the Deuteronomist is Davidic rule. The past of Davidic rule is thus made desirable, since that is what the Deuteronomist believes readers should want to see in the present.

So as not to draw our attention from the study of the Deuteronomist's worldview and the ways in which it shaped the work's creation of the past, an explanation as to why we may assign virtually all of the material in Deuteronomy and the Former Prophets—and all of the material from Kings— to a mid-sixth-century BCE author who lived among the Judean exiles is found in the appendix of this volume. Many of those exiles survived an eighteen-month siege of Jerusalem, which 2 Kgs 25 briefly describes, the rape and slaughter that assumedly accompanied the fall of Jerusalem and of other Judean settlements,[1] and the forced migration to Babylon. Insofar as readers could understand Dtr to be a history, it explains these events, and modern summaries of the work sometimes describe it as an exilic confession of sin, a justification of God's work in history that explains the great suffering of the group (e.g., von Rad 1962, 337, 342–43; Noth 1981, 89–92; Nelson 1981a, 123; Kaiser 1993, 128–30; Albertz 2004, 282). Dtr and Kings create a "logic of history," as Martin Rose (2000, 447–48) puts it: the exile has meaning, Dtr explains, because it is punishment that manifests divine power and justice exercised against Israel's disobedience. Dtr has this meaning, that is, if one accepts its logic, which is to say if one accepts the worldview of the writer who produced it, so we explain in the first section of the chapter why some Judeans could have understood Dtr to be history rather than fiction.

As we discuss in chapter 2, if Judeans in Mesopotamia or anywhere else were to see Dtr as a history, then they must have been able to see it as relating events that they believed really happened, and their worldviews must have been similar enough to the Deuteronomist's that they could

---

1. I say "assumedly" because Kings actually says nothing about rape and slaughter inflicted on the population of Judah. Lamentations does, however, as we see in chapter 5.

have believed his or her explanations of events. To begin with the first point, readers who trusted Dtr's veracity would not have understood the work to be relating events that they saw as contrary to fact, and we have reason to believe that at least some exilic readers would have generally assented to the reality of the events Dtr includes. The work closes with a description of destruction and exile that we have no reason to doubt actually happened,[2] so that was part of the experience of the exilic community itself. In 2 Kgs 24:8–17 we read of an earlier wave of exile in 598/7 BCE, one that removed the Davidide Jehoiachin to Babylon; it is corroborated by a Neo-Babylonian chronicle, as seen in chapter 2, and as a result neither we nor the first readers of Dtr have reason to call the reality of that event into question, for it too was part of the experience of the exilic community. The Deuteronomist says little about events between the end of Josiah's reign and this earlier wave of exile, and the narrative of the Deuteronomist creates focuses almost entirely on the religious reforms he is said to carry out. Modern scholarship does not entirely agree as to whether Josiah actually enacted these reforms, but it is certainly possible that he did. Those who argue that Josiah truly reformed the religion of late seventh-century Judah can point to an aniconic movement in Judean seals from the late eighth to early sixth centuries (see, e.g., Finkelstein and Silberman 2001, 288; Uehlinger 2005, 292–95; Grabbe 2017, 256) and argue that, as external forces caused the Assyrians to end their centuries-long dominance of Judah and the Levant, Josiah eliminated cultic imagery that reflected Assyrian and Aramean religious influences, an assertion of his independence (e.g., Spieckermann 1982, 245–51; Taylor 1993, 176–82; Arneth 2001; Uehlinger 2005).

The fact of the matter, however, is that we do not have anything like detailed archaeological evidence to support the reality of the reforms Dtr describes as taking place not only in Judah and Jerusalem but in the old Northern Kingdom as well. Of course, writes Rainer Albertz, parents and grandparents of some of the exiles would have worked in Josiah's court, and we would not expect Kings simply to lie about events that would contradict their cultural memory (2005, 40–41). Yet 2 Kgs 23:15–20 describes Josiah's destruction of a northern high place at Bethel, as well as of "all the

---

2. As the discussion in chapter 2 notes, the archaeological evidence for the destruction of Jerusalem supports the account of Kings. For inscriptional evidence of a Judean community in Babylonia in the sixth century BCE, see Joannès and Lemaire 1999; Pearce 2006; 2011.

temples of the high places that were in the cities of Samaria," and while it is widely acknowledged that Josiah certainly could have expanded his borders a bit further to the north to include Bethel (e.g., Lipschits 2004a; Na'aman 2005, 215–19; Koch and Lipschits 2013), something that became possible as Assyria withdrew from the region and Egypt concentrated its attention on the Palestinian coast (Na'aman 2005, 216–17), it does not seem likely that he took possession of the entirety of the old Assyrian province of Samerina, and we do not have archaeological evidence for the widespread dismantling of shrines that 2 Kgs 23 attributes to Josiah (Fried 2002, 450–61). Simply because we see aniconic seals around the time of his reign does not necessarily mean this was the result of reforms the king enforced (e.g., Pakkala 2010, 217–19; Lemche 2010; Davies 2010, 53–54), and perhaps there were exiles whose parents and grandparents had told them rather different stories about Josiah's religious proclivities; they might have been suspicious that Dtr relates what actually happened when it talks about the king's reign. On the other hand, the case may well have been that most of the exiles had only vague cultural memories of Josiah's rule—Dtr, as the appendix discusses, was written about fifty years after his death and more than sixty years after Kings says he carried out his reforms—and so were willing to accept the causation and events the writing describes. The account 2 Kgs 23 portrays a reform at the Jerusalem temple that emphasizes, among other things, an elimination of images associated with the heavens (23:4, 5, 11), and whether or not Josiah enforced a politico-religious reaction against Assyro-Aramean astral cults, these images, writes Boyd Barrick, were the sorts of things Judeans would have imagined were associated with foreign worship (2002, 159–72). For readers to believe Dtr's account of Josiah's reforms, Kings merely needs to describe the kind of things readers would believe to have been likely to have happened. In the same way, exiles may have heard stories from their parents or grandparents about Josiah's expansion of his borders, but most, if not all, were likely unclear as to how much land that truly encompassed. To be fair, 2 Kgs 23:15–20 does not claim that Josiah incorporated Samaria into his kingdom, merely that he destroyed high places there, so if readers were told by their parents or grandparents that Josiah had managed to expand his kingdom only slightly to the north, perhaps some would have found it believable that he had made a brief military incursion farther into the old kingdom of Israel following the Assyrian withdrawal.

    Our informed guesswork suggests to us, then, that it is quite possible that at least some of the exilic community was willing to see Dtr as relating events that actually happened, since they could have found plausible its account of things within the span of their memories and those of their parents and grandparents. We can easily imagine as well that exilic readers were willing to accept on principle the basic explanatory link that Dtr provides between cultic failure and national disaster, a theme that works its way through the entire writing and culminates in 2 Kgs 21–25. This theme includes some of the most basic aspects of Deuteronomistic theology, for example, the importance of the worship of YHWH alone, an emphasis on covenant and cult, and the promise and endangerment of the land (Lohfink 1999, 40–42)—and these aspects, the connections between them, and some of the language the work uses to discuss them seem so fundamental to ancient Israelite and Judean thought that deuteronomistic editing is seen in many places in the Hebrew Bible outside Deuteronomy through Kings,[3] particularly in the Latter Prophets.[4] These basic aspects of Deuteronomistic theology are so pervasive, in fact, that it seems that they were simply a part of widely accepted religious thought in Israel and Judah, at least in the circles responsible for producing the society's literature (Coggins 1999; Wilson 1999, 82). The notion that God intervenes in history to punish the people and their kings for their cultic infidelity in ways that dramatically affect their life in the land is hardly an idea confined to Deuteronomy and the Former Prophets, suggesting that the causal explanation Dtr offers for events the exiles and their recent and distant ancestors experienced was hardly revolutionary, and so would have fit a Judean worldview, making it more likely that Judean readers would accept Dtr as a history.

Nor was this sort of historical cause and effect unique to Judean thought in the ancient Near East, for important Deuteronomistic ideas, such as the understanding that national disaster is a punishment for straying from cultic norms, are well known in ancient Judah's cultural milieu. A writing as early as the late third-millennium Curse of Agade links the destruction of a city to its king's cultic failings; the Weidner Chronicle (*ABC*, chronicle 19), known from Neo-Assyrian and Neo-Babylonian copies (*ABC*, pp. 43, 145), appears

---

3. I use *Deuteronomistic* when referring to the work produced or adapted by the Deuteronomistic Historian in Deuteronomy through Kings but *deuteronomistic* when referring to material outside these books understood to mirror their ideology and/or language.

4. For a summary, see Coggins 1999. Marttila 2012 provides a more in-depth summary of deuteronomistic influence in the Psalms.

to explain that kings who do not uphold the cultic norm are punished with national disasters;[5] and the Cyrus Cylinder and the Verse Account of Nabonidus both explain the destruction of the Neo-Babylonian Empire as the result of Nabonidus's failure to properly venerate the gods of Babylon (Schaudig 2001, K2, P1).[6] A common Neo-Assyrian explanation for that empire's conquests was divine abandonment, the notion that the gods of a land become so disgusted with their peoples' moral and cultic behavior that they cease to defend it and abandon it altogether, leaving the Assyrian king to enact their punishment.[7] Some scholars go so far as to argue that there is so much similarity between Kings and Mesopotamian writing about the past that the author must have worked in Babylonia or had direct access to Neo-Babylonian royal inscriptions,[8] but regardless of whether this is true, the action of closing rival shrines attributed to Josiah was known elsewhere in the ancient Near East (Scurlock 2006), and the claim in 2 Kgs 22 that his reform was prompted by the discovery of an ancient book in a shrine was also a broadly accepted Near Eastern explanation for cultic reform (Na'aman 2011). We cannot know what individual Judean exiles thought of Dtr's overall explanation for events such as Judah's destruction, but what we do know of the generalities of Judean and ancient Near Eastern worldviews suggests that they would not have found it to be prima facie implausible.

Simply because the Deuteronomist relied on well-accepted historical explanations and tropes, however, does not mean that every Judean exile would have believed the particulars of the Deuteronomist's appropriation of them. We turn in the next sections of the chapter to other important aspects of the Deuteronomist's worldview—specifically, the belief in God's eternal covenant with the Davidides and the inherent sinfulness of

---

5. Insofar as the Weidner Chronicle actually provides explanation, then, it could not really be said to belong to the genre of the chronicle, regardless of the title modern scholars have given to it.

6. The Nabonidus Chronicle (*ABC* 7) also refers to Cyrus's defeat of Nabonidus, and to the failure of the Akitu festival to be performed at points during Nabonidus's kingship (7.ii.5–6, 10–11, 19–20, 23–24), but because it is a chronicle it never actually provides a causative or explanatory relationship between these two things.

7. For the place of divine abandonment in Neo-Assyrian explanations of victory, see Oded 1992, 121–22; Holloway 2002, 145–46. For a broader discussion of Mesopotamian texts that use divine abandonment as historical explanation, see Block 2000, 114–42.

8. So Wissmann 2008, 213–23; Liverani 2010, 178, but see the argument against this idea in Van Seters 1983, 356–58.

the people—that shaped the Deuteronomist's history, and if some readers could not accept these beliefs then they would have read the work as fiction. Yet the fact that, as I argue in the following sections of the chapter, Dtr is a pro-Davidic work points to the elite group that it supports. In neither Samuel nor Kings does the Deuteronomist refrain from criticism of the Davidides, and the Deuteronomist does not deny that they bear some responsibility for the exile, but the writer manages to compose a conclusion to Kings that explains this event as taking place with virtually no suffering at all. In the end, for the Deuteronomist, it is not the people's suffering that really matters; it is the past and present of the Davidides. As we discuss in the next section, the end of Kings may be a history for readers who believe its explanatory narrative, but we cannot call it collective trauma, since there is virtually no suffering to explain. The pro-Davidic lean of the work suggests it was written to promote the Davidides' return to power as a client monarchy for the Babylonians (see Janzen 2013a), so we imagine that promonarchic factions among the exiles would have been most readily convinced that Dtr presented them with a true explanation of events. The Deuteronomist likely had the exilic Judean elite—the elders of the ancestral houses that formed in Babylonia as the basis of the exilic community's social organization[9]—in mind as he or she wrote, hoping to win these community leaders to the Davidic cause. One result of the Deuteronomist's worldview, in which the Davidides are the most important human figures in any discussion of Judah/Israel, is that, by Kings, the narrative has become so focused on royal activities that the tribulations of the people are rarely of major concern. This is not to say that there is no collective trauma in Dtr, but when readers encounter the great suffering narrated in Deut 28 that they could easily associate with the sixth-century disaster, they find a passage shaped by the Deuteronomist's belief that the people are inherently sinful and the ones responsible for their own suffering, as we discuss below.

3.2. The Pro-Davidic Worldview and the Creation of the Sixth-Century Disaster in Kings

Given that Dtr was composed for a community that had survived the destruction of Judah and forced migration to Babylonia, the description of

---

9. For the development of the בית אבות, "ancestral house" (as distinct from the preexilic בית אב), as the basis of the social organization within the exilic Judean community, see, e.g., Williamson 2003; Faust 2012a, 106–7; Janzen 2017, 39–46.

these horrific events at the end of the reign of Zedekiah in 2 Kgs 25:1–12 seems remarkably laconic:

> In the ninth year of his reign, in the tenth month, on the tenth day of the month,[10] Nebuchadnezzar the king of Babylon and all his army came against Jerusalem and he encamped against it, and they built a siege wall around it, and the city was besieged until the eleventh year of King Zedekiah. In the fourth month,[11] on the ninth day of the month, famine had seized the city, and there was no food for the people of the land. The city was breached, and all the soldiers went out[12] that night by way of a gate between the walls that were near the King's Garden, although the Chaldeans were around the city. He went on the road to the Arabah, but the army of the Chaldeans pursued the king and overtook him on the Plains of Jericho, and his army was scattered. They arrested the king, brought him up to the king of Babylon at Riblah,[13] and judged him. They slaughtered the sons of Zedekiah in front of his eyes,[14] blinded Zedekiah's eyes, and bound him in bronze fetters and brought him to Babylon.[15] In the fifth month, on the seventh of the month, which was the nineteenth year of King Nebuchadnezzar the king of Babylon, Nebuzaradan, the captain of the guard, the servant[16] of the king of Babylon, came to Jerusalem and burned the house of YHWH and the house of

---

10. LXX 2 Kgs 25:1 omits "on the tenth day of the month," as does the parallel text of Jer 39:1.

11. 2 Kgs 25:3 omits "in the fourth month," although the parallel text of MT Jer 52:6 has it; LXX Jer 52:6 reads the same Hebrew text as 2 Kgs 25:3, however. The Peshitta of 2 Kgs 25:3 begins, "In the eleventh year of the reign of Zedekiah, in the fifth month." Given the passage's close attention to dates, it is likely that "in the fourth month" was an original part of 25:3 but fell out early in the process of transmission.

12. MT 2 Kgs 25:4 contains no verb that explains what "all the soldiers" did. LXX 2 Kgs 25:4 makes them the subject of ἐξῆλθον, likely reading Hebrew יצאו, which corresponds to the Hebrew text behind LXX Jer 52:7. MT Jer 52:7, however, says יברחו ויצאו מהעיר, "they fled and went out from the city," a text close to MT Jer 39:4. The Vulgate of 2 Kgs 25:4 has *fugerunt* here, although that may be influenced by the *fugit* that appears later in the verse as a translation of וילך.

13. MT Jer 39:5 and 52:9 add בארץ חמת, "in the land of Hamath," at this point in the story. LXX Jer 39:5, however, says that Zedekiah was brought to Babylon.

14. MT and LXX Jer 52:10 and MT Jer 39:6 add that כל-שרי/חרי יהודה, "all the officers/nobles of Judah," were slaughtered along with Zedekiah's sons.

15. Jer 52:11 adds to the end of 2 Kgs 25:7 that "they put him in prison until the day of his death."

16. LXX 2 Kgs 25:8 has ἑστὼς ἐνώπιον in place of MT's עבד, likely reading עמד לפני, which is the text of MT Jer 52:12.

the king and all the houses of Jerusalem; every great house he burned with fire,[17] and all the Chaldean army who were with the captain of the guard tore down the walls around Jerusalem.[18] Nebuzaradan, the captain of the guard, exiled the rest of the people who were left in the city, and the ones who had surrendered to the king of Babylon, and the rest of the multitude,[19] but the captain of the guard left some of the poor of the land as vinedressers and tillers.

The account then goes on to narrate in 2 Kgs 25:13–17 the Babylonians' removal of the temple vessels and the execution of other officials from the city, including the high priest Seraiah. As a whole, this appears a most restrained portrayal of the unimaginable devastation and slaughter to which contemporary archaeology points, as chapter 1 discusses. The Deuteronomist says nothing about the deaths of anyone in Jerusalem or Judah, except for a few figures among the elites. To take 2 Kgs 25 literally is to conclude that an eighteen-month siege of the capital that ended only when the Babylonians starved Jerusalem into submission ended with virtually no Judean casualties at all, despite the fact that the archaeological evidence points to a vast decline in Judah's population in the sixth century BCE, something most easily explained through the war and the famine and disease that likely accompanied it. Lamentations, as we see in chapter 5, devotes the majority of the material in its five chapters to describing the horrific suffering that accompanied the annihilation of Jerusalem. Despite a brief reference to the siege, the Deuteronomist obviously did not want to pause at much length here to consider or create a vast collective suffering. Rather, the Deuteronomist simply seems to want to acknowledge an unfortunate event in the people's past and move on. A description of 2 Kgs 25 as a creation of collective trauma may seem somewhat questionable, and while it is fair to describe the destruction of Jerusalem and the exile that we see in 2 Kgs 25 as a disaster as far as the Deuteronomist is concerned, the vast slaughter to which modern archaeology points is

---

17. LXX and Vulgate of 2 Kgs 25:9 omit both "great" and "with fire," following a Hebrew text that read only שרף בית כל ואת. MT Jer 52:13 has הגדול בית-כל-ואת, "and every house of the great," in place of גדול ואת-כל-בית in MT 2 Kgs 25:9, while Targum 2 Kgs 25:9 has רברביא בתי כל וית, "and all the houses of the nobles," suggesting it is following a Hebrew text like that of MT Jer 52:13.

18. The OG omits almost all of 2 Kgs 25:10.

19. LXX 2 Kgs 25:11 has στηρίγματος here, reading Hebrew אמון, "craftsmen," the text of MT Jer 52:15, while MT 2 Kgs 25:11 has המון, "multitude."

notably absent here. Lamentations, in contrast with Kings, focuses on the famine (1:11, 19; 2:12, 19–20; 4:4, 8–10) that Kings passes over in a few words; refers to the slaughter of Judah's army (1:15), of which Kings says nothing at all; describes killing in Jerusalem's streets (1:20; 2:21), an idea also absent in Kings; and refers to the rape of the city's inhabitants (1:8, 10; 5:11), concerning which Kings is silent.

We discuss all of those issues when we turn to Lamentations in chapter 5, but the failure of the Deuteronomist to create collective trauma in 2 Kgs 25, we see in this section of the chapter, is the result of his or her pro-Davidic worldview that focuses the narrative on the fate of this royal house while largely ignoring the damage inflicted on their subjects. In the collective trauma the Deuteronomist does create, the people and not the kings are the real perpetrators of the community's suffering. As we turn now to consider the creation of the past in Kings, we certainly see why scholars might describe it as an explanation of destruction and exile, even though one might expect a more forceful description of the great suffering the Judean community in Babylonia underwent rather than the understated picture readers actually encounter in 2 Kgs 25, which avoids the creation of collective trauma. Volker Heins and Andreas Langenohl (2011), however, describe a situation rather like this in Germany in the post–Second World War period, arguing that the massive Allied bombing of Germany that killed about six hundred thousand civilians did not become part of a cultural trauma because it would have contradicted the construction of a German identity in the postwar context that focused on the nation's own guilt. Great suffering on the social level, in short, does not always result in collective trauma, and 2 Kgs 25 was not composed to reflect or create it, even if it is present elsewhere in Dtr. We expect collective traumas to create victims and perpetrators and to assign guilt, and while Dtr is full of references that establish those latter two issues, it is somewhat more circumspect in referring to victims.

Unless we believe the Deuteronomist was lying and deliberately creating a work of fiction that stated things that he or she did not believe to be true, the author seems convinced that God had given the Davidides an eternal covenant to rule and so believed that, regardless of what sin the members of the house had committed, they were destined to return to power. The Deuteronomist portrays Davidic rule as God's desire and so implicitly urges readers to desire it as well. The carrier group of which the Deuteronomist was a part was obviously an elite one closely associated with the Davidides, guided by a worldview that obviously privileged

Davidic authority. As discussed in chapter 2, however, it is readers' reception rather than authorial intention that determines whether they understand a work to be a history, and so long as readers' worldviews largely overlapped with that of the Deuteronomist—or at least that which the text suggests the Deuteronomist held—then they would have understood Dtr to relate what really happened.

As the first section of this chapter discusses, some aspects of the Deuteronomist's worldview, such as the importance of the worship of YHWH alone, were ones that were broadly accepted within ancient Judean society, but in the rest of this chapter we focus on two particular aspects of his or her worldview that resulted in the Deuteronomist's specific creation of the sixth-century disaster: God's consistent allegiance to the eternal Davidic covenant, and the inherent tendency of the people to sin and thus anger YHWH. These two ideas, along with the others we have already mentioned, explain why the Deuteronomist created the sixth-century disaster in the way that he or she did, why the Deuteronomist avoids collective trauma in 2 Kgs 25, and how that disaster is related to the earlier sections of Kings and Dtr as a whole. Presumably, of course, only those Judeans who belonged to a pro-Davidic party or parties would ultimately have seen Dtr as a history, for they would have been most likely to have shared all or most of the author's worldview, and for them the sixth-century disaster mainly was what the Deuteronomist created, an unfortunate event for which the people and Davidides shared responsibility, a creation that keeps virtually any picture of great communal suffering at arm's length. Other Judean groups in Babylonia, however, may have had serious doubts that Dtr truly explained what really happened and may have believed in the truth of different sixth-century disasters from the one the Deuteronomist created, perhaps ones that prominently featured the suffering of collective trauma.

The most obvious reason to see the Deuteronomist's worldview as pro-Davidic is Dtr's inclusion of a story in 2 Sam 7:4–17 of an eternal covenant made with David, a covenant that is never annulled (readers may also consult the appendix for further discussion of the issue). The narrative of Athaliah in 2 Kgs 11 demonstrates the Davidides can be temporarily removed from the throne for cultic infidelity, so it provides a model for the exilic punishment of the house and reflects the Deuteronomist's certainty of their restoration (see McKenzie 2000, 139–43). In 2 Kgs 8:16–29, two Davidides in a row are said to act like the kings of "the house of Ahab," and at this point all but one of the Davidides are assassinated (11:1–2), and

Athaliah, a member of the northern royal family (10:26), usurps Davidic rule in Jerusalem for seven years (11:1–16). For the Deuteronomist, the Babylonian exile is simply a longer version of this punishment, for here also only one Davidide (Jehoiachin) seems to survive into exile, but this punishment is already on its way to ending, given the Babylonian treatment of Jehoiachin (see below), for Dtr provides no indication that the eternal covenant with David is not still in effect. The worldviews that shape authors' understandings of the past also shape their understandings of the present, so it is no wonder the work concludes with the restoration of Jehoiachin to a throne, as we discuss below: if YHWH has chosen the Davidides to rule forever, then it stands to reason that this is where Jehoiachin belongs; and the Deuteronomist almost certainly believed that the Davidides would return to power in Judah, even if only as clients to the Babylonians, which would have been no different from the dynasty's position between 605 BCE, when Nebuchadnezzar forced Egypt out of Palestine, and the exile.

If Dtr reflects a pro-Davidic worldview, it might seem counterintuitive that its author would place any responsibility at all on the house for the sixth-century disaster that the Deuteronomist creates, yet the Deuteronomist's worldview likely left him or her with no option but to do so. The sons of Zedekiah, the last Davidide to reign in Jerusalem, were executed, and he was blinded and made a prisoner as the house was removed from power. His predecessor, his nephew Jehoiachin, had been made a Babylonian prisoner eleven years earlier (2 Kgs 24:10–12), and in an ancient Near Eastern context these were not the sorts of events that an author could let pass without some kind of indictment of the house. So, for example, some decades after 706 BCE, when the Neo-Assyrian king Sargon II was killed in battle, his grandson Esarhaddon produced the Sin of Sargon, a text that explains his grandfather's untimely demise as the result of his failure to properly venerate the gods of Babylon.[20] The Sin of Sargon is not the only ancient Near Eastern document that explains a disaster such as this as befalling a king due to his cultic failures; the first section of this chapter refers to the Mesopotamian texts that link the destruction of the Neo-Babylonian Empire to Nabonidus's cultic faults, as well as the Weidner Chronicle, which connects the sicknesses and deaths of some kings

---

20. SAA 3.33. For a discussion of the text, see Tadmor, Landsberger, and Parpola 1989.

and others' loss of rule to their failures to properly provide for Marduk's temple. A sixth-century Judean audience and author, even a pro-Davidic author, would likely have found it difficult to explain the destruction of Jerusalem, the execution of Zedekiah's sons, and Jehoiachin's imprisonment without some kind of reference to Davidic cultic sin, and this had to become part of the sixth-century disaster the Deuteronomist created.

Notably, however, the Deuteronomist places blame for the destruction neither on the exiles themselves nor on Jehoiachin, the Davidide in Babylonia who has already been restored to a royal throne at the end of the work, but on Manasseh, Jehoiachin's great-great grandfather, and his subjects. The Deuteronomist, in fact, refers to Manasseh's sin as an explanation for the disasters that strike Judah on three separate occasions (2 Kgs 21:1–16; 23:26–27; 24:2–4), so that readers are clear that the Davidide who bore some responsibility for the destruction of Judah was not Jehoiachin but a king who died more than half a century before the catastrophe. Manasseh's sin is entirely cultic, according to Dtr: he causes Judah to abandon cultic fidelity to YHWH and to worship Baal, Asherah, and idols; in short, he causes Judah to sin, and Dtr uses the verb חטא in the *hiphil* in regard to Manasseh's sin in 2 Kgs 21:11, 16. By 2 Kgs 21, Dtr has already used the verb חטא in the *hiphil* repetitively to explain the destruction of the Northern Kingdom. The first action Jeroboam undertakes upon the north's independence from the Davidides is to construct idols in the form of calves for his subjects to worship and to appoint a non-Levitical priesthood (1 Kgs 12:25–33). God soon refers to this as "the sins of Jeroboam" that "he caused Israel to sin" and that will result not only in the annihilation of Jeroboam's house but in the exile of the north (14:6–16). References to "the sins of Jeroboam" and the use of חטא in the *hiphil* appear in the evaluation of almost every northern king, since none of his successors ever removes his cultic innovations, and one after another the northern dynasties are condemned to the same decimation as Jeroboam's house.[21] The summary explanation of the north's destruction and exile in 2 Kgs 17:7–23 concludes with a reference to Jeroboam's action of causing Israel to sin, and, as I have just mentioned, as soon as Jeroboam begins to cause the people to sin God announces the north's coming exile. By this logic of history, then, it makes some sense that the same announcement would

---

21. For a detailed discussion of these phrases as appearing in the evaluations of the northern kings, see Janzen 2008, 44–49. See nn. 16 and 17 on p. 45, which list the verses where each of these phrases appears in the evaluations of the kings.

come in reference to Judah as soon as a Davidide causes them to sin, and Manasseh is the first and only Davidide whom the Deuteronomist makes the subject of חטא in the *hiphil*. The kings may establish the cult their subjects follow, but in the end the punishment visited on the people is the result of their sin, even if the kings have caused them to commit it. So if the Deuteronomist had no way to create the sixth-century disaster without referring to Davidic sin, the Deuteronomist does manage to place the blame for it on a king who was long dead and on the people he caused to sin. Zedekiah and Jehoiachin are hardly sinless (2 Kgs 24:9, 19), but they are also not to blame.

At this point in Dtr's construction and explanation of the disaster, we see the influence of the Deuteronomist's belief that the people are inherently sinful, something we discuss in more detail in the next section of the chapter. Some ancient Judeans might have read as theological hairsplitting the Deuteronomist's claim that the people are to blame for the exile because of sin that someone else causes them to commit, but the Deuteronomist's worldview leads him or her to split precisely this hair. In 1 Kgs 14:15–16, announcing the coming destruction of the north as punishment for the sins of Jeroboam, the prophet Ahijah says, "YHWH will uproot Israel from the good land that he gave to their ancestors and scatter them across the River because they made their Asherim, vexing YHWH" (14:15). While this is immediately followed by a reference to the sins of Jeroboam that he caused the people to sin, 14:15 is a direct indictment of the people's cultic actions, of what "they made," and not of what the king had done (see Sweeney 2005, 268). In Dtr, the cultic sin of Jeroboam and his successors is no different from what Israel has habitually done since the inception of the nation. In the same way, when the prophets first announce divine judgment on the sin of Manasseh in 2 Kgs 21:10–15, YHWH states that YHWH will "uproot" what is left of the people—Judah, in other words—"because they did what was evil in my eyes and they vexed me from the day their ancestors went out from Egypt until this day" (21:14–15).[22] Manasseh has caused Judah to sin, but Judah/Israel has always sinned, and Dtr says that this proclivity is not incidental to their punishment. Readers, moreover, encounter the same mix of blame directed against people and monarchs in 2 Kgs 17:7–23, the summary of the sin and punishment of the

---

22. Instead of MT's יצאו אבותם, "their ancestors went out," the LXX has ἐξήγαγον τοὺς πατέρας αὐτῶν, "I brought their ancestors out," reading something like הוצאתי את אבותם.

north. The conclusion of this passage may refer to the sins that Jeroboam caused the people to sin, but 17:7–18 discusses what Israel had done since coming out of Egypt, with no reference to royal leadership in cult, while 17:19–20 points ahead to the coming punishment of Judah for their sin without saying anything about their kings. In a discussion that refers to the sin of the people, 2 Kgs 18:9–12 briefly returns to the reasons for the exile of the north, and here also there is not a single mention of royal leadership in that cultic wrongdoing.

Guided as the Deuteronomist is by the beliefs inherent in his or her worldview, he or she concludes that the Davidides cannot avoid blame for what happened, but neither can the exiles' ancestors. Dtr does not claim that any king after Manasseh caused the people to sin, although his son Amon "did evil in the eyes of YHWH just as Manasseh his father did" (2 Kgs 21:20), and assumedly his grandson Josiah did likewise before he began his cultic reforms in the eighteenth year of his reign (Janzen 2013b, 355–59; and see Ben Zvi 2008, 198), and this implies that Manasseh's two immediate successors also caused the people to sin, although the Deuteronomist does not explicitly make that point. All four of Josiah's successors are said to imitate all the evil of their ancestors,[23] but Dtr does not actually specify that they imitated Manasseh's cultic failure of causing the people to sin. Perhaps the Deuteronomist simply could not convince himself or herself that ultimate blame belonged with Jehoiachin, and perhaps it was just easier—or, to put this another way, simply felt more correct—to conclude that responsibility belonged with a king and a Judean population who were long dead. So there is no specific record here of the people sinning since the time Josiah undertook his reforms in the late seventh century BCE, more than half a century before the mid-sixth-century composition of Dtr (see the appendix for the date of the work), meaning that virtually no one among the exiles is directly accused of cultic infidelity, except for Jehoiachin, who "did evil in the eyes of YHWH" (24:9). Jehoiachin may have been no paragon of virtue according to Dtr, but it was his great-great-grandfather and the Judeans of his generation who were responsible for angering YHWH and causing the destruction of Judah.

---

23. Jehoahaz and Jehoiakim each "did evil in the eyes of YHWH like all that his ancestors had done" (2 Kgs 23:32, 37), while Jehoiachin "did evil in the eyes of YHWH like all that his father had done" (24:9), which equates his sin with Jehoiakim's. Zedekiah too "did evil in the eyes of YHWH like all that Jehoiakim had done" (24:19).

Of course, it may simply have been more convenient for the Deuteronomist to decide that the current Davidide and his Judean contemporaries did not cause the sixth-century disaster: this lessens Jehoiachin's guilt and makes him seem a more appropriate figure to continue Davidic rule, and it does not antagonize readers and potential converts to the Davidic cause. We have no way of knowing whether the Deuteronomist truly believed Manasseh and his generation were responsible for the disaster rather than Jehoiachin and his generation, but the narrative of Kings is true for readers so long as they believe it. It would make sense, however, that the author actually believed that Jehoiachin was sinful: he was in power the first time Nebuchadnezzar took Jerusalem, and that surely pointed to some sort of guilt in ancient Judean and Near Eastern worldviews—but we should also remember that he receives this evaluation after only three months in office (24:8), which means there is still time for him to change. Josiah continued Manasseh's great sin for eighteen years before enacting his reform, and his evaluation—"he did what was right in the eyes of YHWH and walked in all the way of David his ancestor" (22:2); "there was no king like him before him who repented to YHWH with all his heart, self, and might according to all the law of Moses, and none after him arose like him" (23:25)—is exemplary, with no mention at all of the sin he committed before his reforms, so nothing would prevent Jehoiachin from earning such an evaluation as well should he be returned to power and decide to act just like Josiah (Janzen 2013b, 359).

Jehoiachin thus has a chance to redeem himself in a newly restored reign as a client king, a reign that the Deuteronomist suggests is imminent. Blaming Manasseh for the sixth-century disaster does not make "utter nonsense of Josiah's reform" that follows Manasseh's sin and yet fails to prevent Judah's destruction (Halpern 1998, 486), but it is a way of distancing the exiles, their parents, and the last few Davidides from responsibility for it. Blaming Manasseh for the exile only makes nonsense of Josiah's reforms if we must assume that the Deuteronomist believed that those reforms would inevitably cause God to alter the earlier decision in regard to the punishment for Manasseh's sin, but it is possible to see the point of those reforms in Dtr's narrative as a model for Jehoiachin to imitate, and such imitation would assumedly win him the same kind of exemplary evaluation that Josiah received. Josiah is rewarded for his pious attitude that leads to the reforms that garner such lavish praise from the Deuteronomist, who interprets his death through Huldah's oracle: "Your eyes will not see all the evil I am bringing upon this place" (22:20). This allows Dtr

to make sense of his death—it is a mercy killing (Janzen 2013b, 365–69)—
and if this does not seem like much of a reward, recall that the last thing
Zedekiah's eyes saw before Nebuchadnezzar had them torn out was the
slaughter of his own sons, while Jehoiachin was in a Babylonian prison for
thirty-seven years (25:27). From the standpoint of Jehoiachin and his sons,
a thirty-one-year reign in Jerusalem like Josiah's (22:1), even as a Babylonian client, would seem an enviable fate.

The concluding reference to Jehoiachin's release from prison in 2 Kgs
25:27–30 may not appear to signal an overly promising future, but the
Deuteronomist claims as well that the Babylonian king places him on a
כסא above those of all the other client rulers in Babylon, and as a group
they are referred to as מלכים, "kings," making it clear that the כסא is a
"throne" and not merely a seat.[24] His situation may not sound much different from the fate of Mephibosheth, Jonathan's grandson and a survivor of the Saulides' failed war against David, for Evil-merodach provides Jehoiachin with royal rations just as David does for Mephibosheth
in 2 Sam 9 (e.g., Granowski 1992; Ceresko 2001, 24; Schipper 2005, 523;
Sweeney 2005, 273; Janzen 2008, 55), but the fact that Jehoiachin's seat is
an exalted throne, even if it is one of a client ruler, is not a minor point
(contra Murray 2001, 261–62), and Mephibosheth is certainly never said
to sit on such a thing. Placing Jehoiachin on a throne is a way of concluding the narrative with a virtual restoration of the preexilic *status quo ante*
in which the Davidides were clients of the Babylonians; all that is needed
is the final geographic movement to Judah. The restoration for which the
Deuteronomist hoped may only have been one in which the Davidides
functioned as clients to Babylon, but when we realize that Kings only
refers to a royal throne in the context of rule over all Israel and not just
Judah,[25] we can see that the Deuteronomist is suggesting that Jehoiachin
or one of his sons could end up ruling the north as well as Judah. As
far as the Deuteronomist understands things, God took the rule of the
north away from the Davidides because Solomon built high places where
his foreign wives could worship their gods (1 Kgs 11:1–13), but Josiah

---

24. כסא appears thirty-four other times in Kings, and only in 1 Kgs 2:19 (where
it refers to a seat for Bathsheba beside the כסא of Solomon); 22:19 (where it refers to
God's throne in the divine council); and 2 Kgs 4:10 (where it refers to a chair on which
Elisha is to sit) does it signify something other than a royal throne.

25. There is no "throne of Judah" in Kings, only a "throne of Israel" that the Davidides lose because of Solomon's sin (Nelson 1981a, 99–105; Halpern 1996, 157–74).

destroyed them during his reforms (2 Kgs 23:13–14) and so prepared the way for a restoration of Davidic rule in the north as well as Judah (Knoppers 1994, 195; Halpern 1998, 488–89).

3.3. The Davidides, the Sinfulness of the People, and Collective Trauma in the Deuteronomistic History

The Deuteronomist's pro-Davidic worldview in part explains why the Deuteronomist constructed the sixth-century disaster that he or she did, for the real lesson to learn from 2 Kgs 21–25 is that, while God has punished the people and royal house for their joint sin, God is committed to supporting Davidic rule, as Jehoiachin's restoration to a throne above those of the other Babylonian clients demonstrates. Given the way the Deuteronomist sees things, it is the punishment as an abstract concept rather than the horrific specifics of the destruction of Judah that matters, so it seems to occur without great communal suffering, although this does not mean that we cannot locate any collective trauma in the work. Like any other historian, however, the Deuteronomist constructs such trauma in a way that made sense to him or her, and when Dtr does explicitly point to perpetrators and guilt in the context of narrating a great suffering that sounds like the sort of thing the exiles and their parents might have experienced, it is the people alone who are to blame. This is best explained by turning our attention to another important aspect of the Deuteronomist's worldview, the inherent evil of the people, something related to the pro-Davidic aspect of the Deuteronomist's worldview, since the Deuteronomist believes that the Davidides are the best possible leadership option for Israel/Judah, even if they are not perfect. Indeed, to turn to the Deuteronomist's beliefs concerning the nature of the people merely leads us back to our earlier discussion of God's choice of the Davidides. The larger history the Deuteronomist constructs ultimately grounds Davidic privilege in the people's failure as well as divine choice, a choice so unwavering that no Davidic sin is too great to cause God to permanently oust them from power. What really matters in Judah's history is God's choice of the Davidides, their deeds, and even their errors, and what is important about the sixth-century disaster is their fate. That is not to say that the Deuteronomist writes the suffering of the disaster out of history altogether; the Deuteronomist implicitly admits great suffering was associated with the exile but does not involve the Davidides in the guilt for this collective trauma, which is the fault of the people alone.

We know that Dtr does not blame the Davidides alone for the exile, and a king was necessary in the preexilic period according to Dtr because the people were unable to keep from angering their God. Since the moment of Israel's inception, says Moses near the beginning of Deuteronomy, Israel has been קְשֵׁה-עֹרֶף, "stiff-necked, stubborn," and YHWH gave them the land of Canaan only because the previous inhabitants were so evil (Deut 9:4–6). Indeed, Israel was so stubborn that their first act upon leaving Egypt was to worship an idol, almost causing God to destroy them at Horeb (9:7–10:5). Israel's natural stubbornness and rebelliousness becomes an important theme in Deuteronomy (e.g., 1:26–33; 4:3–4, 25–28; 31:16–21), something often linked to the threat or certainty of destruction and/or exile (e.g., 4:26; 7:1–10; 8:11–20; 9:7–14; 31:16–21; see Janzen 2013a, 77–85). Israel does not appear in a markedly better light upon settling in the land. Judges is devoted to a portrayal of a people who repetitively worship foreign gods and who learn nothing from the inevitable punishment of foreign invasion that consistently accompanies such evil. Already in Judg 1 the tribes are presented as less and less willing to exterminate the Canaanites as God commands in Deut 7:1–4 and 20:16–18 (e.g., Younger 1994, 216–20; Wong 2006, 149–52), and this deterioration of the people's character continues throughout the book. By Judg 10:6–7 Israel is not merely worshiping the Baals and Asherahs, as had been the case at the beginning of their cultic failures in the land in 3:7, but also the gods of Aram, Sidon, Moab, and Philistia, showing that repetitive punishment has not taught them anything about the error of their ways or about how God directs history (Assis 2005, 175–76). The judges God sends to save the people after they cry for help become progressively worse. Gideon, for example, leads national worship of an idol (8:27–28);[26] Jephthah, a bandit by profession (11:1–3), sacrifices his daughter (11:29–40), despite the prohibition on child sacrifice in Deuteronomic law in Deut 12:29–31 (Janzen 2005); Samson does not lead Israel in battle at all, thus becoming a link between the time of the judges and the leaderless anarchy of Judg 17–21 (Amit 1996, 288–89, 307–8). There is a message about leadership here in the midst of Judges' repetitive recounting of the people's sin, for, the narrative implies, even when God chooses and

---

26. Israel is said to "prostitute itself after" the ephod Gideon makes (Judg 8:26–27), and the only metaphorical sense in which Dtr uses the verb זנה is in reference to improper worship (Deut 31:16; Judg 2:17; 8:33), a fact emphasized when the same verb appears six verses later to refer to Israelite worship of the Baals (Judg 8:33). The Deuteronomist clearly envisions Gideon's ephod to be some kind of idol.

supports the judges, this form of leadership is not a real solution to Israel's desperate need for guidance.

These are not stories that focus on the people's suffering, however, so we are not faced with a narrative of collective trauma in Judges. Foreign invasions are certainly not presented positively here but are instead the punishment earned by a stubbornly sinful people; there is explanation, that is, but not explanation of great social suffering. The explanation involves a failure of leadership, and if the judges are not the solution to the problem Israel's character poses, then, the narrative suggests, some other office of leadership must be found. By Judg 17–21, in fact, once the leadership of the judges has disappeared, the people are so morally lost that one man believes his idol will please YHWH (17:1–13), while people from Dan steal it so the whole tribe can turn to idolatry (18:14–20). Israel then collapses into civil war, something that follows on the gang rape and murder of a woman and concludes with the kidnapping of women at YHWH's annual festival at Shiloh (21:15–21). "In those days there was no king in Israel," the Deuteronomist informs readers here on four occasions (17:6; 18:1; 19:1; 21:25), and if the judges are failures as leaders, the people clearly cannot govern themselves, something that is as true for Judah as it is for the other tribes,[27] and royal leadership would appear to be the solution to which history points. The story of the priestly house of Eli in 1 Sam 1–4 demonstrates that priestly leadership is not the answer, for the Elides' cultic failures cause God to announce their removal from the priesthood and replacement by a different house that will enact the cult under royal supervision (1 Sam 2:27–36), and Eli is the last and only priest said to have judged or ruled Israel (4:18). Samuel's attempt to turn the ad hoc office of judge into dynastic succession fails as his sons are so bad at their job that they cause Israel to demand a king "like all the nations" (8:1–5), echoing the language of the law of the king in Deut 17:14–20, which permits just such a request. Israel, YHWH says to Samuel upon hearing the demand, is habitually rebellious and has constantly rejected divine leadership (8:8), and assumedly this is why he tells Samuel on three occasions to listen to the people's request and to appoint a king (8:7, 9, 22),[28] something that might put a stop to this rebellion.

---

27. The point is often argued that Judges condemns the northern tribes but not Judah (e.g., Dumbrell 1983; Brettler 1989; Tollington 1998), but Judah's portrayal in Judges is not entirely positive either (see Webb 1987, 201–2; Wong 2005).

28. In 1 Sam 8:7–8, YHWH seems to imply that even the act of requesting a king

From this point on, the Deuteronomist largely turns his or her attention to the monarchy and dynastic succession. Yet, as we discuss above, not even in Dtr's portrayal of the siege and destruction of Jerusalem is there enough emphasis on the community's suffering that we could refer to the narrative in 2 Kgs 25 as collective trauma. The Deuteronomist has emphasized the people's inherently sinful nature and their need for leadership, and Dtr has closed off alternative avenues of leadership to the monarchy, part of the way the Deuteronomist links his or her dual beliefs concerning the divine choice of the Davidides and the sinfulness of the people, but this is still not an explanation of great communal suffering, for there is little suffering of the people on display in Samuel and Kings. Without a king, the Deuteronomist explains in Judges, the people are doomed to invasion and foreign oppression, but not just any royal leadership will do, readers learn in Samuel, for YHWH simply seems to prefer David to Saul. Saul loses the kingship almost as soon as he is anointed, and whatever his faults in 1 Sam 13 and 15 that result in this loss,[29] God will treat David and his descendants differently. God promises David in 2 Sam 7:11–17 that his house and throne will be established forever, and that his descendants will never be treated as Saul was, even if they can be punished, and the stories about David the Deuteronomist chooses to include make it clear that God is serious about this eternal covenant. Even the sort of abuse the founder of the dynasty visits on two of his subjects in 2 Sam 11 by committing adultery with Bathsheba and then murdering her husband, Uriah, in an attempt to cover up the crime does not cause God to strip his house of the covenant. God does not apply the law to David in regard to the adultery and murder, for both are crimes that demand the death penalty (see Exod 21:12; Lev 20:10; Num 35:31–34; Deut 22:22); in the divine judgment of David in 2 Sam 12:1–14, God appears far more concerned instead that David has taken from his subjects—specifically, he has taken Bathsheba

---

is some sort of rejection of divine leadership, but given that Israel's request mimics language from the law of the king in Deuteronomy, it is assumedly not the request in and of itself that leads YHWH to this conclusion but Israel's belief that a king is necessary to fight their battles (8:20). In this they demonstrate they have failed to learn a key aspect of history as the Deuteronomist understands it, which is that cultic fidelity alone guarantees divine protection in warfare.

29. The discussions concerning Saul and the reasons for his removal from power are many, but see Gunn 1980; Nicholson 2002, 36–112; McKenzie 2006; Heller 2006, 121–30.

from Uriah—without explicitly asking for the divine permission that would have been forthcoming, thereby making the murder unnecessary (Janzen 2012a). "I anointed you king over Israel," God tells David, "and I rescued you from the hand of Saul, and I gave you the house and wives of your lord into your bosom, and I gave you the house of Israel and Judah, and if this be too little, I will add even more to you" (2 Sam 12:7–8). God, apparently, would have been happy to have given Bathsheba to David, a far smaller gift than the rule over Israel and Judah that had already been bestowed on him, had he simply asked.

God does not annul the eternal covenant for this act, nor for Amnon's rape of Tamar in 2 Sam 13, which imitates his father's sin, nor for David's failure to punish Amnon, nor for any other sin committed by David and his descendants. David, adulterer and murderer though he is, claims in 2 Sam 22 that God has rewarded him because of his moral perfection (22:21–25) and can say in his "last words" of 23:1–7 that his eternal covenant from God is the result of his just treatment of his subjects. Seemingly, as Antony Campbell writes, these sorts of claims "would be embarrassing to any Davidic chronicler" and "would rightly bring a blush to the Davidic cheek," but to some degree David has a point (2010, 353–54). As hard as it seems to apply words such as צדיק ("righteous"), צדקה ("righteousness"), and תמים ("moral perfection"; 2 Sam 22:21, 24, 25; 23:3) to David's reign after readers have encountered the story of Bathsheba and Uriah, let alone David's claims concerning "the cleanness of my hands" (22:21, 25), God did make an eternal covenant with David and never annulled it, regardless of what he and his sons have done, and certainly seems to treat him as if these descriptions of ethical perfection applied to him. Nor does God seem to exhibit any qualms concerning what appear to be rather obvious violations by David and Solomon of the law of the king, which limits the monarch's ability to multiply horses and wives. David has no lack of the latter (2 Sam 3:2–5; 5:13; 15:16),[30] and the law of the king might seemingly have been written to condemn Solomon's actions. The law of Deut 17 does not just prohibit royal acquisition of wealth, something that 1 Kgs 5:1–8 [4:21–28] and 10:11–25 assure readers Solomon has in vast quantities, but proscribes acquiring many wives so that the king ולא יסור לבבו, "does not turn his heart aside" (Deut 17:17), while Solomon's wives, הטו את־לבבו

---

30. This would appear, then to be a violation of the law of the king (Steussy 1999, 84–85). For arguments that the stories of David's acquisition of wives chart a decline in his character and actions, see Nicol 1998; Kessler 2000.

אחרי אלהים אחרים, "inclined his heart after other gods" (1 Kgs 11:4). The report in 1 Kgs 10:26–29, meanwhile, focuses on Solomon's acquisition of many horses.[31]

One could simply argue that the law of the king (or Deut 16:18–18:22 as a whole) and the so-called succession narrative of 2 Sam 9–20 and 1 Kgs 1–2 were later additions to Dtr and so preserve blameless portrayals of David and Solomon (apart from 1 Kgs 11) in an original edition of Dtr (see the appendix for the arguments of some scholars who make these arguments), but as we look at the narratives of the various members of the Davidides in Kings we can see that the Deuteronomist is not interested in a blameless portrayal of the house. For the Deuteronomist, the fates of kings such as Jehoiachin or Zedekiah obviously point to some sort of guilt on their parts, as we discuss above, yet the eternal covenant with the house remains in place, and there is no indication that the Deuteronomist can conceive of a world where that would not be the case. The explicit and implicit condemnations of David and Solomon simply set the stage for what we see in Kings: while the Davidides might be punished, the covenant with the house will not be annulled no matter what they do to their subjects, even if they cause the people to worship foreign gods, the sin that repetitively results in the annihilation of the northern dynasties. The eternal covenant means that the Davidides end up being above the law, no matter what Deut 17 says, just as David is in the story of Bathsheba and Uriah, the story that sets the stage for future Davidic violations of torah. The divine decision to make an eternal covenant with his house, valid no matter what David or his descendants do, leads to a conflict with the dictates of the law that is decided in the house's favor. Monarchs are not to multiply wealth and wives, says the law of the king, but, on the other hand, God does not object when the Davidides do so. God might hold a king such as Saul accountable to divine command, but David and his dynasty are treated differently. God is quick to remove Saul from power and destroys the northern dynasties that cause Israel to sin (see 1 Kgs 14:10–11; 16:2–4; 21:20–24) but is specifically committed to treating the Davidides differently, as God says in 2 Sam 7:15, and nothing in Kings indicates that this far more favorable treatment has been abandoned, even in the punishment of exile. Both Athaliah's usurpation of the Davidides

---

31. For discussions of Solomon's violations of the law of the king and implicit critiques of him in 1 Kgs 1–10, see, e.g., Brettler 1991, 90–93; Parker 1992, 83–86; Sweeney 1995; Scheffler 2007, 133–34; Nicholson 2009, 52–53.

and the exile show that the house can be punished for its cultic abuses, as does the Davidides' loss of the north for Solomon's sin of constructing foreign high places (1 Kgs 11:9–13). Yet these high places are not removed until Josiah's reform (2 Kgs 23:13–14), and Dtr provides positive evaluations for some Davidides between the time of Solomon and Josiah, saying that they "did what was right in the eyes of YHWH," even while noting that they tolerated the existence of the high places,[32] despite the fact they are in obvious violation of the command of Deut 12:2–3 to destroy foreign places of worship. In Kings, only the worst Davidic cultic violations meet with punishment, and even Ahaz, whom the narrative says in 2 Kgs 16:3 acts like the kings of Israel (thus implying but not explicitly stating that he caused the people to sin) and whose narrative in 2 Kgs 16 is dominated by descriptions of his apostasy, suffers only the loss of the city of Elath to Edom (16:6), while Jerusalem is saved from destruction (16:5). David is not the only king in the dynasty whom God treats as if he were righteous and morally perfect even when he is not.

This sort of concentrated focus on the monarchy, particularly on the Davidides, however, means that there is simply far less space devoted to the concerns of the people. The narrative has little to say about their suffering because that is not the main issue the Deuteronomist wishes to address with the explanations of events we find in Samuel and Kings, so we do not encounter collective trauma here. Instead, the Deuteronomist emphasizes what for the Deuteronomist is the fact that God regards the Davidides with such great favor that not only do they have an eternal covenant, but even important violations of the law on their part are overlooked, and only their worst infidelities are punished. The people cannot rule themselves, and the only kind of leadership that appears to meet with any success is the Davidic monarchy, a monarchy that, the Deuteronomist believes, history has demonstrated will rule forever. In Deut 30:1–10, Moses says that the

---

32. This is the situation for Asa (1 Kgs 15:11, 14), Jehoshaphat (22:43), Jehoash (2 Kgs 12:3–4 [2–3]), Amaziah (14:3–4), Azariah (15:3–4), and Jotham (15:34–35). Iain Provan has argued that the high places to which Kings refers up until the time of Hezekiah's reforms—2 Kgs 18:4 refers to his removal of high places—must be Yahwistic, since Dtr would not have given positive evaluations to kings who supported foreign cults, and that references to them as foreign are exilic insertions (1988, 57–90), but the evidence is not as clear as he makes it out to be (see the critiques in McKenzie 1991, 119–21), and 2 Kgs 23:13–14 is clear that Solomon's foreign high places are not destroyed before the time of Josiah. Moreover, even the toleration of Yahwistic high places violates the laws of cultic centralization in Deut 12 and 16.

people will repent in exile and that God will then return them to the land,[33] but even more important than that in the Deuteronomist's eyes is the restoration of the Davidides, something already begun in the final verses of Dtr, and Jehoiachin or one of his sons will return to power even if, like Ahaz or Jehoiakim or Zedekiah, he reigns as a client within a larger empire (2 Kgs 16:7; 23:34; 24:17).[34]

The worldview that informs the Deuteronomist's history suggests that the Deuteronomist simply cannot imagine a future without a Davidic king, since God has chosen David's house to rule and allowed the house to do so even when members of it openly disobeyed aspects of the law, something that points to a divine privileging of the dynasty. The Deuteronomist's creation of a past reflects a worldview that cannot conceive of things without Davidic rule, even if, when the Deuteronomist was writing, it had been temporarily suspended, and the result is that the Deuteronomist cannot be intellectually honest without constructing a history of Israel and Judah that is dominated by a history of the Davidides, the central figures of the work beginning in the book of Samuel. There are other kings in the narrative—Saul and the kings of the north, mainly—but they are all held to a different standard from the Davidides, for despite all of their misdeeds Davidic suffering in 2 Kgs 25 has come to an end by the chapter's conclusion, and their eternal covenant remains intact.

This is what is most important to know about history for the Deuteronomist, and this is one reason why vast social suffering is written out of the work's conclusion. In fact, 2 Kgs 25 devotes more space to describing the suffering of Zedekiah than that of the people during the entirety of the siege. So focused is the Deuteronomist on tracking the fate of the Davidides

---

33. Deut 30:1 begins with a temporal clause: והיה כי־יבאו עליך כל־הדברים האלה, "When all these things happen to you...," a reference to the disasters of destruction and exile discussed in Deut 28–29. The next clause continues the idea begun with the imperfect verb יבאו in the opening clause with a consequential *wqtl* or converted perfect: והשבת אל־לבבך, "you will turn your heart...." The train of thought is then continued with other converted perfects in the following verses. Moses thus describes a situation in which the people will turn their hearts in exile to YHWH and will repent and will listen to YHWH's commands (30:2) so that God will return them from exile (30:3). All of these are things that will happen, according to the syntax Moses uses. For the consequential *wqtl*, see *IBHS* §32.2.1d.

34. Judean monarchs from the time of Ahaz to Josiah were clients to the Assyrians even though the text says nothing about that for a figure such as Josiah; see the discussion in Handy 2007.

at this point that there is virtually no space devoted to the people's suffering, and as a result it is difficult to describe the end of Kings as collective trauma, since the end of Kings does not describe the people as suffering at all. Perhaps yet another reason why there is so little evidence here of the people's suffering as a result of the sixth-century disaster is that when the Deuteronomist does create collective trauma, the Deuteronomist prefers that such pain be closely linked to the people's sin, so it is simply easier to create collective trauma before the Davidides appear on the historical scene. In fact, were it not for Deut 28:15–68, we would have to conclude that Dtr has created virtually no collective trauma at all. Deuteronomy 28, however, dependent as it is on the Neo-Assyrian treaty format,[35] provides a long list of curses for Israel should the people disobey any aspect of Deuteronomic law, including plague and epidemic (28:21–22, 27, 35, 60), invasion and defeat in battle (28:25, 47), loss of land and possessions to foreigners (28:30–34, 51), a siege and resultant famine so severe it results in cannibalism (28:52–57), and exile (28:64–67). We cannot vouch for the cannibalism, part of the repertoire of the curse sections of Assyrian treaties (2.2.iv.8–11; 2.6.449–450, 547–555), but the other aspects of the curse enumerated above were part of the experience of the Judean community forced to migrate to Babylonia, as far as archaeological evidence suggests. Insofar as exilic readers could see in Deut 28 a foreshadowing of what they and their parents suffered in the Babylonian destruction of Jerusalem and Judah, they would have encountered a curse that lays this suffering at the feet of the people who have disobeyed the law, a curse that does not even mention royal leadership. As Deut 28 presents matters, the people are both the perpetrators and victims of this suffering, but the chapter has nothing to say about monarchs. In our study, we see that Kings blames the people as well as Manasseh for the destruction and exile, and if Manasseh's sin was to cause the people to engage in apostasy,

---

35. Carly Crouch rightly argues that Deut 28 reflects a broad tradition of ancient Near Eastern curse material rather than that found specifically in a single known Assyrian treaty such as the Vassal Treaty of Esarhaddon (2014, 108–17). Her point that there is not enough evidence to argue that the chapter is subverting that particular treaty is well taken and an important corrective to arguments such as that of, for example, Hans Steymans (1995), who sees 28:20–44 as a translation of parts of the Vassal Treaty of Esarhaddon. Yet Judah was a client to Assyria for about a century and would have been sworn to such a treaty. Deut 28 certainly reflects aspects of known Assyrian treaties, especially in its extreme length of curses, so it makes sense that its composition reflected knowledge of the format.

it would appear that, in the Deuteronomist's worldview, the Judeans of Manasseh's day could be convinced to do this because of Israel/Judah's natural inclination to stubbornness and rebelliousness, which the Deuteronomist carefully documents throughout the work. Insofar as there is any collective trauma in the community's past, it is something for which the people bear responsibility, and thus the great suffering described by Deut 28, which mirrors the experience of the exilic community, a suffering that results from lawbreaking, is linked directly to the sin of the people, not the sin of the Davidides.

4. Conclusion: The Deuteronomistic History's Fetishistic Narrative

This nod to the reality of the suffering of the exilic community near the end of Deuteronomy is not repeated at the end of Kings, and one gets no real sense that there was any suffering that continued beyond the end of the siege of Jerusalem. Even the horrors narrated in Deut 28 are soon followed by Moses's comforting words in 30:1–10 that, after the people have undergone this suffering, YHWH will place the curses of Deut 28 on the people's enemies "who persecuted you," and that the exiles will repent and God will return them to land, at which time "YHWH your God will circumcise your heart and the heart of your descendants" so that Judah will faithfully follow the law. Although 30:1–10 is full of Deuteronomistic language, writes Marc Brettler (1999), this message of divinely ensured fidelity does not seem to cohere with the rest of Dtr's understanding of how history works, where Israel/Judah must choose to keep the law. But there is no reason why the Deuteronomist could not envisage a postexilic future that in at least one respect would be radically different from the past, and the Deuteronomist would not be the last author who wanted to create a happy ending for figures in a narrative. Closure for readers, the Deuteronomist suggests, is near at hand.

The Deuteronomist's own worldview, which appears to have reflected that of an elite Judean group who believed God had made an eternal covenant with the Davidides, causes the Deuteronomist to avoid portraying the Judean kings as perpetrators of collective trauma, if only because the Deuteronomist is so focused on the fate of the Davidides by 2 Kgs 25 that the people's suffering is of little concern. While the Deuteronomist avoids portrayals of great suffering in Judah during Davidic rule, even in the narrative of the siege and destruction of Jerusalem, the Deuteronomist is not so circumspect in the narratives of the northern monarchy, and in 2 Kgs 6:24–31, for example, we see the realization of Deut 28:49–57's curse of cannibalism of one's own children as famine takes hold of Samaria during an Aramean siege. The author of Lamentations, however, is under no such compunction when it comes to describing the vast suffering of the people of Jerusalem during the kingdom's final days, as we have already mentioned. Lamentations says that Jerusalem "weeps" (Lam 1:2, and see 3:38–49), "the roads of Zion mourn," the priests "groan," and the young women "grieve" (1:4) as the children and elderly starve to death (1:19; 2:11–12, 19–20; 4:4), mothers eat their own children (2:20; 4:10), and slaughter and rape invade the streets and houses of the city (1:8, 10, 20; 2:21; 5:10). As we will discover in chapter 5, there is some reference in Lamentations to Judah's sin, but the work fails to definitively create or accept collective trauma and so has nothing coherent or conclusive to say about perpetrators and guilt. Speakers in Lamentations can blame YHWH for the vast suffering the community has experienced, and at points it is not clear there that the pain God has caused is related to just punishment, but the Deuteronomist's worldview does not seem to permit ideas like that in his or her construction of the past. For the Deuteronomist, YHWH's actions are understandable, predictable, and rational, and this is why the Deuteronomist has confidence that the royal house God chose to rule forever will rule forever, despite the situation in which the exiles currently find themselves. History has proven this, as far as the Deuteronomist is concerned, so the past our author has created validates the present that the Deuteronomist desires and the future that the worldview of the Deuteronomist's carrier group understands to be inevitable. In our analysis of trauma in Lamentations in chapter 5, however, we see that Lamentations rejects the kind of creation of the past that Dtr provides, so that there is no sixth-century disaster for the victims of trauma in that book, let alone any rational explanation of it.

The Deuteronomist, on the other hand, has produced a fetishistic narrative. Dominick LaCapra describes fetishistic historical narrative as closely related to totalizing narrative, a creation of history that attempts to explain everything, that tends to involve a sovereign who does not make mistakes, certainly not judicial ones, and in which mourning is always overcome (1994, 190–91). Dtr would certainly seem to qualify as a totalizing narrative since, from the standpoint of sympathetic readers, it provides a full explanation for destruction and exile, presenting it as punishment from a perfectly just sovereign God, and what little collective trauma that is actually permitted entrance into the past the work creates is immediately followed by Moses's promise of an end to suffering. Fetishistic narrative is much like totalizing narrative, writes LaCapra (1994, 192–93), but beyond its totalizing aspect it also marginalizes psychological trauma. Eric Santner (1992) discusses fetishistic historical narrative in the context of the Freudian concept of the pleasure principle and says that narrative fetishism is an avoidance of psychological trauma in the creation of a narrative that produces pleasure through its repression of trauma. Even if Dtr does create some collective trauma, the work appears to disavow psychological trauma altogether, allowing no space for it.

As we see in the next chapter, however, psychological trauma is antinarrative and antihistory, something that history cannot comprehend or encompass, so one could conclude that it is not realistic to expect a historian creating an explanatory narrative to incorporate such trauma, since no narrative could do so. But a history's acknowledgment that individuals suffer from such trauma saves historical narrative from totalizing and fetishistic impulses, and recognizes that it can never give a complete account of the trauma or the past in which it occurred, can never fully explain the present in which it continues to occur in the lives of survivors. A history like that is not totalizing because it admits this sort of trauma cannot be explained and accounted for; it is not fetishistic because it cannot provide closure or a happy ending for readers insofar as it acknowledges the psychological trauma that continues to intrude into the lives of those who survived the horrific events narrated in the history. By acknowledging the trauma that continues into the present in survivors' lives, neither the past nor the present can seem desirable in such narratives. We turn now to discuss psychological trauma and to investigate why it cannot be explained by histories, but at this point it is enough to say that, even if the Deuteronomist were willing to create collective trauma in Deut 28, this is something the historian constructs on the terms of the worldview of the Deuteronomist's carrier group. The psychological trauma to which we now turn our attention has been repressed and overwritten in Dtr, but as we learn in chapter 5, Lamentation's reaction to the same events is a rejection of the sort of historical project that we see in Dtr.

4
Trauma as the Failure of History

4.1. Introduction: Trauma as Failure of Experience

The psychological trauma to which we now turn our attention is so different from the collective trauma we have been discussing that the two things are not really related at all. Narrative is the essence of collective trauma, since it is a kind of history, but narrative is precisely what this other kind of trauma resists. Trauma's essence, we could say, is a failure of narrative because trauma victims have "registered rather than experienced" the traumatic event, and it is precisely this failure of experience, as we discuss in this chapter, that makes it impossible for trauma to be narrativized (Hartman 1995, 537). Without the explanation that narrative can provide, there can be no understanding of the past, and we are left instead with a list of unrelated and unexplained events; this is what annals and chronicles look like, as discussed in chapter 2, but at the center of history is explanation, significance, and meaning. So Elie Wiesel, a Holocaust survivor and perhaps the best-known author of Holocaust literature, says in regard to the Holocaust, "I do not understand. And if I write it is to warn the reader that he will not understand either" (1978, 203). This is why, he says, "There is no such thing as literature of the Holocaust, nor can there be. The very expression is a contradiction in terms" (quoted in Rosenfeld 1978, 4). Massive psychological trauma, Wiesel is saying, cannot be understood by victims or nonvictims and thus cannot be written about. As we explain in the first part of this chapter, this is rooted in the failure of experience and thus of memory and narrative in regard to psychological trauma, which therefore falls outside the scope of history.

Psychological trauma is rooted in an individual's exposure to a traumatic event, which can be caused by being a victim of or witnessing horrific violence, such as that of warfare, rape, torture, or other events that threaten life and safety (Briere 2004, 10–26, 30–32). To explain why this can result in a failure of experience of the traumatic event, it is perhaps most helpful to begin by referring to trauma as a neurobiological phenomenon. This chapter is not a discussion of posttraumatic stress disorder,[1] although it describes the neurological basis of the disorder in order to help us better understand why we can refer to trauma as a failure of history. Individuals exposed to a traumatic event, especially if the violence is particularly severe and/or of long duration, may not actually experience the event, at least in the way that *experience* is commonly understood. Bessel van der Kolk, a psychiatrist who specializes in the study and treatment of posttraumatic stress disorder, writes that in normal situations of danger the amygdala signals the hypothalamus and brain stem, which release stress hormones that aid the ability of the organism to fight or flee, but there are times when violence overwhelms the individual, who then becomes incapable of doing either (2014, 54–55, 60–62). At the root of psychological trauma, writes van der Kolk, is this immobilization in the face of grave danger. In such situations, the dorsal vagal complex, part of the parasympathetic nervous system, is activated, and it shuts down awareness, closing off experience of the event (80–84).[2]

Linked to this failure of experience is a failure of memory, writes van der Kolk. In normal experience, sensory information goes to the thalamus, which passes it on to the amygdala and frontal lobes, but in situations of overwhelming violence this processing of sensory information can break down and be encoded as dissociated fragments rather than memory as we normally understand the term. Traumatic "memories" are really traces of sensations, images, and sounds associated with the traumatic event that do not change over time, as normal memories do; since they have not been stored as normal memories, trauma victims do not feel as if they have truly experienced the traumatic events, so traumatic memories do not form part of the sense of self at all (van der Kolk 2014, 175–76). This dissociation of traumatic memories from the self, writes van der Kolk (66), "is the essence of trauma. The overwhelming experience is split off and fragmented, so that the emotions, sounds, images, thoughts, and physical sensations take on a life of their own. The sen-

---

1. A definition of posttraumatic stress disorder and a list of its symptoms appear in DSM-5 (271–80).

2. Judith Herman (1992, 52–53) also describes this immobilization or violation of autonomy, this inability to react to danger, as the essential aspect of trauma.

sory fragments of memory intrude into the present, where they are literally relived." The result, then, is that trauma victims do not remember
the events but relive them, often in fugue states, hallucinations, and other
kinds of flashbacks, as the brain secretes stress chemicals in response to
a danger that is no longer present, so that for the survivor in the thrall of
such flashbacks there is no distinction between past and present (66–69).
Most Holocaust survivors, for example, "know" of their trauma as fragments in which parts of the traumatic experience have been retained, but
only in a decontextualized way that is not meaningful to them (Auerhahn
and Laub 1998, 29–31),[3] reflecting the original failure of experience of
the traumatic event and consequent failure of the trauma to form normal
memories and so to form part of the self. Other Holocaust survivors can
encounter their trauma in fugue states in which they relive and reenact
the traumatic experience without remembering it (28–29).

Memory—at least normal memory—and sense of self are closely
linked, as van der Kolk acknowledges, drawing from the work of Pierre
Janet, a psychologist who studied trauma in the early twentieth century.
Memory, wrote Janet, is in essence the telling of an autobiographical story,
and as we have new experiences and so create new memories our sense
of self changes; as that happens, older memories change as well, in order
to adapt to the changing self, for our past must fit our current sense of
self, the narrative we tell ourselves about who we are, something that we
are constantly constructing. But Janet noticed that those exposed to traumatic events are unable to associate them with their sense of self and experience exactly the sort of dissociation van der Kolk describes, in which
they cannot assimilate the traumatic events, so traumatic "memories" do
not change over time. Like van der Kolk and others, Janet observed that
trauma victims cannot remember the traumatic events but can only relive
them because of trauma's dissociative nature (1925, 1:660–63).[4]

Sigmund Freud came to a similar conclusion in regard to the "traumatic neurosis" he observed in those exposed to combat in the First World
War. Trauma victims, he concluded, were unprepared for the vast violence

---

3. Auerhahn and Laub, to be specific, conclude that these fragments can also be
"known" as transference phenomena, in which they can be grafted onto current situations. So, for example, the self-discipline necessary for survival in the camps can still
be enacted by victims as a life-or-death matter in the present.

4. For Janet's conclusions in regard to traumatic memory, see also Perry and Lawrence 1984, 28–34; van der Kolk and van der Hart 1995, 159–64.

to which they were exposed and so were overwhelmed by it, respond-
ing with "fright" (*Schrek*) rather than "anxiety" (*Angst*) (1955a, 12–13).
Dreams of trauma victims, Freud noted, do not function like normal ones,
which are governed by the pleasure principle, a psychological tendency
toward pleasure, but are literal repetitions of the traumatic event (7–11).
The trauma, Freud concluded, must have broken through the shield of
the pleasure principle, with the result that the individual was not able to
master or integrate the experience into the ego, and the literal repetition of
the traumatic event in dreams points to an unconscious attempt to create
retroactively the anxiety that would have prepared the victims for the traumatic event and so have psychologically protected them (18–27). Patients
are not remembering their trauma in these literal dreams of the events,
but rather they are reliving it (30–33), and the "war neuroses" that Freud
observed in combatants were not assimilated into the ego; he referred to
them as the ego's "parasitic double" (1955b, 209).

So Freud also concluded that an essential aspect of trauma is its dissociation from the self, something rooted in the missed experience of the
traumatic event. A failure of experience means the event is not remembered, or at least not in the normal sense of that term, so it fails to become
part of the self. Yet trauma remains a powerful force in the life of survivors, and in Freud's discussion of trauma as a parasitic double of the self
that repetitively returns in literal dreams of the events, one is reminded
of his description of the uncanny in an essay he published in 1919, soon
after the First World War. The uncanny, Freud writes, is something that
is dissociated from and stands over against the ego, something that victims are helpless to prevent from repeating in their psychological lives
(1955c, 234–38). Psychological trauma is not the experience of horrific
violence, nor a memory of it; it is the lack of experience that involuntarily
and repetitively recurs in the psychological lives of victims who can only
relive but not remember the event (Caruth 1996, 1–6). Trauma as psycho-
analysis understands it is the Lacanian real, the missing encounter that has
not lodged in consciousness, and as chaos beyond the signifier it can only
be inferred through symptoms (Hartman 1995, 539; Flanagan 2002, 389).
Insofar as trauma involves intrusive returns into victims' lives as they are
forced to relive an event they did not experience and so do not know, it is,
as Cathy Caruth puts it, "intricately bound up with its refusal of historical
boundaries" (1995a, 8). A traumatic flashback is "a history that literally
has no place, neither in the past, in which it was not fully experienced, nor
in the present, in which its precise images and enactments are not fully

understood" (Caruth 1995b, 153, emphasis original). As far as victims are concerned, their trauma is not about history or the past, for they do not have memories of a past experience of it but relive trauma currently as it repeats into their psychological lives.

From a psychological standpoint, then, the most basic explanation for why trauma cannot be narrativized is that it has no place in the self; it does not form part of victims' autobiographical narratives that they rely on to make sense of who they are, because it has not been experienced as a past event and is not really a memory. This is why, as we discuss in more detail in the next section of the chapter, trauma lies outside language and chronology. Caruth may refer to a traumatic flashback as a "history," but since trauma cannot be narrativized and is not experienced as something from the past, it is not really a history at all, and this is why she says that it has no place in the past. Perhaps just as importantly when examining the nonhistorical nature of trauma, it also lies outside morality. As we examine in chapter 2, histories are shaped by the worldviews that have formed the thought of the authors who produce them, and the past that historians create reflects the truth of their present, or at least the present the historians and their cultures would like to see, so insofar as readers acknowledge a given history to be true, they validate the worldview of the culture that has produced historian and history. Morality is similarly a production of a cultural worldview, reflecting its understandings of good and evil and right and wrong, and without the limits it places on the behavior of a society's members, the group would collapse. So as histories and collective traumas reinforce or draw readers' allegiance to a particular belief system, they reinforce their allegiance to the morality that accompanies it. But trauma can offer no validation for the worldview that forms the past that a particular culture has created, since it cannot be narrativized, nor, as we discuss later in the chapter, can it offer validation for the moral categories associated with that belief system. Writers' worldviews have no place for traumas that cannot be narrativized, understood, or explained, and as the final section of the chapter notes, we would expect histories to repress trauma and erase it from the historical record, which is what Dtr has done.

4.2. Trauma as Failure of Narrative

The failure of victims to experience traumatic events results in their failure of memory, and this results in the essence of trauma as far as psychologists are concerned, its dissociation from the self. Trauma cannot be part of victims' history because it has not been experienced as a past event, only as a powerful force that is constantly and currently present to them. In this section we turn from a psychological explanation of trauma to a discussion focused on the failure of literature and testimony to represent trauma. From a literary perspective, the essence of trauma is the failure of narrative that results from the failure of experience, so we move to delve further into our explanation of why trauma is a failure of language and chronology and thus a failure of narrative and history. History is the use of narrative to create chronology and a past, and this, as considered in chapter 2, results in our experience of the past. We cannot have awareness of the world without language and narrative, as we also discuss there, and things and events can only become things and events for us as we put them in language and so comprehend them, precisely what cannot happen with trauma (Alphen 1999, 24–25; Gana 2014, 81). This means that trauma victims cannot form a history of the traumatic events that so deeply affect them, and as a result these events cannot be part of the past as they understand it. Psychologist Henry Greenspan refers to conversations with a Holocaust survivor who tells him that his story about the Holocaust "is *not* a story. It has to be *made* a story. In order to convey it. And with all the frustration that implies" (2010, 3, emphasis original). This is why Wiesel can say that "there is no such thing as literature of the Holocaust," so trauma remains a "not-story," as Greenspan puts it (4), even as survivors try to put it into words. So while we can refer to "trauma literature," this is a term of convenience, and we must remember that trauma testimonies do not convey the truth of trauma as histories are understood by their readers to convey the truth of the past. Our historical narratives create the past and thus become equivalent to it, but there is no such equivalence between trauma testimonies and trauma. We can find narratives or stories in trauma testimonies because survivors create stories out of not-stories, but trauma itself remains a not-story, something that cannot be narrated,[5] and this results, as we discuss here, in the failure of language, chronology, and belief that we see in trauma testimony and literature. It results, ultimately, in the failure of history, since unnarrativizeable trauma cannot become part of the past, the existence of which (for us) is dependent on narrative.

---

    5. As Robert Eaglestone notes, we should not see trauma testimonies as trauma itself, since that would confuse the suffering of trauma with the testimonies (2004, 31–33).

To begin with the failure of language at the edge of trauma, we could discuss this by means of a neurobiological explanation; van der Kolk describes a malfunctioning of the Broca's area, one of the regions of the brain linked to speech production, during traumatic flashbacks, making it impossible to put thoughts and feelings into words, as well as a decrease in the functioning of the left hemisphere of the brain, which translates perceptions into words and organizes thoughts into logical sequences (2014, 43–45). But here, in our turn to a study of trauma literature and testimony, we can see that we need not refer to neurobiology to explain why trauma is not amenable to language. This, for example, is how Jean Améry, who survived Auschwitz and torture by the SS, discusses his inability to explain the suffering of his trauma in his testimony:

> It would be totally senseless to try to describe here the pain that was inflicted on me. Was it "like a red-hot iron in my shoulders," and was another "like a dull wooden stake that had been driven into the back of my head"? One comparison would only stand for the other, and in the end we would be hoaxed by turn on the hopeless merry-go-round of figurative speech. The pain was what it was. Beyond that there is nothing to say. Qualities of feeling are as incomparable as they are indescribable. They mark the limit of the capacity of language to communicate. (Améry 1980, 33)

This is not a unique observation on the part of a trauma victim.[6] Primo Levi, for example, says the same thing about words such as *hunger, fear,* and *pain,* which, he writes, simply do not mean the same thing to nonvictims as they do to Holocaust survivors (1996, 129). And this is also why Wiesel says that the Holocaust cannot be understood and Holocaust literature cannot be produced: "We all knew that we could never, never say what had to be said, that we could never express in words, coherent, intelligible words, our experience of madness on an absolute scale.… All words seemed inadequate" (1978, 201).

So as victims create stories that might reflect traces of the not-story of trauma, what they relate cannot be knowable to readers. They use words such as *hunger, fear,* and *pain,* even while readers cannot know what these words mean, since there cannot be a link between the signifier and signified for them that would be remotely equivalent to the one trauma

---

6. See other examples that make the same point in Eaglestone 2004, 16–19.

survivors are futilely attempting to express. Ferdinand de Saussure referred to the sign as that unity in which a signifier or "sound-image" conjures up the meaning associated with it (1983, 65–67), but since the mental image that trauma victims might associate with the word *hunger* is utterly different from that their readers might associate with it, there is no sign to express what they mean. One of the ways in which trauma literature reflects this problem, writes Walter Kalaidjian, is through writing that mirrors the gaps in awareness and the failure of language. In a discussion of the poetry of Peter Balakian on the Armenian genocide, Kalaidjian refers to the catachresis (contradictory metaphors or "verbal 'breakdown,'" as Kalaidjian calls it), aposiopesis (ellipsis), and anacoluthon (non sequiturs and logical incoherence) appearing throughout his work (2006, 36–37, 42). Ellipsis, which points to an absence of meaning, as well as contradictory metaphors and the logical incoherence of anacoluthon, are not helpful rhetorical devices if one wants to convey the truth of a historical event such as the Armenian genocide, but Balakian's poetry does not do that. In a poem titled "Geese Flying over Hamilton, New York," in which news reports of slaughter in other regions, and even the landscape and animals around his American home, return Balakian to the genocide that killed members of his family, he writes,

> then the light came and the branch
> of a sycamore on the wall
>   was the menorah
> on the arch of Titus.
>
> I was thinking like
>
> the cows by the paddock in a peel of sun
>
> when they cut a wide arrow
> their feathers oily with tundra
> the gabbling like field-holler. (1996, 11)

The poet's thought cannot settle on any set of traumatic events, whether those undergone by his own family or those to which the Arch of Titus alludes, and cannot explain them. His family's nonmemories are not accessible in this way but recur seemingly at random and with no clear relationship to what triggers them, and ideas end without conclusion or clear connection to what precedes or follows, as "truncated thoughts trail off into the aposiopesis of lines that fall silent and bleed eerily into the white space of the page" (Kalaidjian 2006, 42). There is no logical progression from thought to thought or image to image—there is only verbal breakdown, logical incoherence, and ellipsis—and the extra spaces between some of the lines mirror visually absences of thought and language and the impossibility of connecting those disparate images into a coherent narrative.

Trauma is not history; it is the intrusion of the unknowable event into the victim's present, so trauma literature cannot point to meaning, only "to an understanding of what it means that meaning is absent" (Ramadanovic 2001, 115). A history, we could say, represents the past insofar as those who understand it to be a history see it as providing the truth of what happened and why. For sympathetic readers, the narrative of a historiography is like a mirror that truly reflects the past. Trauma testimonies cannot act in this way in regard to trauma, because the language for trauma does not exist, and the testimonies cannot function as mirrors that reflect the truth. Unexplainable trauma is thus "a hole in the fabric of language" (Fridman 2000, 132); it can mirror only the failure of language and the absence of truth, and no words will be able to make it part of a narrative that could create and control its meaning. So it is not a metaphor to say that trauma cannot be expressed (contra, for example, Lang 2000, 17–19; Stampfl 2014, 21–22); this is literally true.

Since narrative is history's essential aspect, creating causation and meaning, narrative is also wholly reliant on temporality; if, after all, one thing causes another, then we must be clear as to the order of events, and our narratives must have beginnings, middles, and ends as they describe significance in their creations of the past. Trauma, however, resists chronology as it resists language, because it is the repetition of events not experienced, known, or integrated into the self, and it is something with the power to convert the present into the failed experience of the traumatic events. Because these events took place outside experience, they are not structured by causality or time, and in their uncanny repetitions into victims' lives they remain "current in every respect" (Laub 1992a, 69). So the irony in the title *Auschwitz and After*, Charlotte Delbo's Holocaust trilogy, is that the author experiences no difference between Auschwitz and after (Langer 1995, 18). This is trauma time, as Jenny Edkins calls it, something immune to the concept that the past precedes the present, that life is a chronological series of individual and interconnected nows that each fade into the past (2003, 29–42). For Delbo, as for other trauma victims, trauma converts the present into what a nonvictim would recognize as the past, shattering any kind of chronological certainty. After Auschwitz, "I was unable to get reaccustomed to myself," she writes. "How could I reaccustom myself to a self which had become so detached from me I was not sure I ever existed? My former life? Had I had a former life? My life afterwards? Was I alive to have an afterwards, to know what afterwards meant? I was floating in a present devoid of reality" (Delbo 1995, 237). These words do not only express the dissociation of trauma—"a self which had become so detached from me I was not sure I ever existed"—they also provide no sense of chronology at all, no clear awareness that there was a pre-Auschwitz time followed by Auschwitz and then an after. In *Auschwitz and After* it is repetitively clear that there is no "after" as far as Delbo is concerned; the reality she can conceive of is the reality of "Auschwitz," which seems far more real than her present: "I'm not alive. I died in Auschwitz and no one knows it" (267). "I'm not alive," she writes again. "I'm imprisoned in memories and repetitions" (261). The most important aspect of her reality is the past of her trauma that repeats over and over, and her present has been colonized by the trauma caused by past events she does not truly know and did not truly experience. She died, metaphorically speaking, in Auschwitz, and now repetitively relives that time. In this sort of not-story, "chronology disappears from consciousness" (Langer 1995, 17). Narrative is impossible here, for there is no end to trauma time as the trauma continually intrudes into and overthrows the present, and as a result the chronological beginnings and endings so necessary to narrative are simply foreign to trauma (Laub 1992a, 65–67; Alphen 1999, 34–35; Luckhurst 2008, 80–81).

Yet another reason why trauma cannot form part of narrative and history is the impossibility of truth claims in regard to it. Again, from a psychological standpoint, the essence of trauma is its dissociative aspect, the original failure of experience that causes trauma in the first place. Because of this failure of experience and memory, trauma exists as a "parasitic double" of the self, as Freud put it, something that does not really seem like an experience and thus something that is not truly part of the victim's sense of self. The result, then, is that it can be hard for even the trauma survivors themselves to believe in the reality of events they might associate with their trauma, which results in an inability to make any kind of truth claims about them. Holocaust survivors interviewed in Claude Lanzmann's film *Shoah* frequently refer to their inability to believe what happened during their time in the camps. Simon Srebnik, for example, one of a handful of survivors of Chelmno, where as many as two hundred thousand Jews were murdered, said, "It was terrible. No one can describe it. No one can recreate what happened here. Impossible? And no one can understand it. Even I, here, now ... I can't believe I'm here. No, I just can't believe it" (quoted in Lanzmann 1995, 3). In Srebnik's interview he refers both to his lack of belief, the result of the dissociative aspect of trauma, and the concomitant impossibility of describing and understanding the traumatic events in testimony, and if one cannot believe one has undergone a traumatic event, one can hardly make the sort of truth claims that historiography does. The creation of truth claims about the past is the whole point of historiographies, but as the epigraph for *None of Us Will Return*, the first volume of her Holocaust trilogy, Delbo writes, "Today I am not sure that what I wrote is true. I am certain it is truthful" (1995, 1). This, it is fair to say, is not the sort of epigraph one would expect to see in a historiography; this failure of belief, the result of trauma's failure of experience, results in a "crisis of truth," as Caruth writes, for one can hardly make truth claims about what one cannot really believe, so trauma cannot be true in the way that history is (1995a, 8).

This contrast between trauma and history is not due solely to the failure of the victims to experience traumatic events, but also to the fact that these events are so far outside the range of everyday human experience, at least as far as those who have not been traumatized are concerned,[7] that it is virtually impossible for anyone to believe them. Much of the first part of Wiesel's *Night* reflects the inability of the narrator's Jewish community to believe what the Nazis were about to do. They do not believe the first witness who tells them of Nazi atrocities, they do not believe the Germans will reach their town in Hungary, and, once they do arrive, they do not believe the Nazis will do anything terrible to them. "Was he [Hitler] going to wipe out a whole people? Could he exterminate a population scattered throughout so many countries? So many millions! What methods could he use? And in the middle of the twentieth century!" (Wiesel 1981, 18–19). So survivors can fail to believe these events even as they occur, and Levi writes that, upon arrival at Auschwitz, "We looked at each other

---

7. Laura Brown (1995) makes an important point, however, when she argues that rape, which is well-known as something that causes posttraumatic stress disorder, is common enough that it is really not outside the range of everyday experience. For those who have not been victimized in this way, however, this trauma is not something they can imagine, so it remains outside the range of their experience.

without a word. It was all incomprehensible and mad" (1996, 26). Filip Müller, another survivor of Auschwitz, recalled in his testimony the story of a woman in the camp who tried to warn others about the gas chambers: "Mothers carrying their children on their shoulders didn't want to hear that! They decided the woman was crazy. They chased her away" (quoted in Lanzmann 1995, 116). Victims are not the only ones on whom this crisis of truth descends, for those who listen to trauma testimonies also find them difficult to believe. The failure of language and of the victims' own belief in the not-stories that exist for them only in a fragmented manner make trauma testimonies difficult for listeners to accept, especially when they reflect events so alien to normal experience that emotional comfort is destroyed, and listeners can even find it easier to side with the perpetrators of the trauma (Herman 1992, 7–8) or can act to avoid or impede the testimony (Laub 1992a, 72–73).

In this failure of language, chronology, and belief, it is no wonder that trauma tends to silence; as her epigraph for *Useless Knowledge*, the second book of her trilogy, Delbo (1995, 115) quotes Paul Claudel: "We came from too far to be believed." There is nothing like this in normal experience, and it is easier for listeners to deny victims' testimony than to believe it. It is easier even for survivors to see themselves as guilty, and survivor guilt is "ubiquitous" following traumatic events (Speckhard 1997, 92); it has been documented as an aspect of the response of victims to such massive traumatic events as the Holocaust (Niderland 1968), the Armenian genocide (Kupelian, Kalayjian, and Kassalian 1994, 194), the atomic bombing of Hiroshima (Lifton 1991, 494–95), and the South Asian tsunami of 2004 (Boss 2006, 165). Such blame and guilt would appear to be entirely misplaced since, as we have discussed, at the root of trauma is the victim's inability to act and so to make any sort of moral choice. Guilt is a reflection of morality and of the worldview that grounds an ethical system with basic understandings of good and evil, and just as it can be easier for listeners to side with perpetrators and blame the victims than to accept the not-stories of trauma, it can be easier for victims to accept blame and look for meaning in the belief system that supplies their guilt, as we will discuss in the next section of the chapter. Groups have no way to make sense of trauma, so it might seem inevitable that they would repress and overwrite it with histories and collective traumas, things to which even trauma victims often wish to give their assent, since histories at least provide one with truth and are things that others in one's society are willing to hear and believe.

4.3. History's Repression of Trauma

Because psychological trauma cannot be contained in narrative, it is something that the social worldview cannot explain, so it is clear enough why the narratives of histories and collective traumas might omit this sort of trauma entirely and so repress it. Chapter 2 compares history to the field of law, for histories, like trials, assemble all known and relevant evidence to render a true verdict. Our deliberations in this study show why trauma cannot be accounted for in narrative, as it resists the totalizing impulse of historical and legal accounts. In fact, Dori Laub, a Holocaust survivor and psychiatrist who has worked with other survivors, writes that because the Holocaust "had no witness to its truth" it "essentially did not exist" (1992b, 83). The trauma of the Holocaust cannot exist in histories that create the truth of what really happened because there are no truth claims that can be made about it. But as trauma resists the narrative of history, it also threatens history's truth and the comprehensiveness of the worldview that forms it. When readers assent to the truth of the past created in a history, as examine in chapter 2, they tacitly affirm the worldview that sits behind it and that has formed or limited what it can say, and their own belief in the worldview is reinforced. Exilic readers who accepted the truth of Kings and Dtr, for example, did so because they believed that the divine power that controls history punishes the people for their cultic unfaithfulness but is also unfailingly loyal to the Davidides, even in their sin, and will return them to power. Dtr, then, reinforced their belief in this understanding of the way the world is, or perhaps convinced some readers with somewhat different worldviews that this was the way they should see things. Trauma, however, permits no such affirmations; since it cannot be known, there is nothing to learn from it, no moral to draw from it (e.g., Langer 1991, 77–120; Agamben 2002, 27–28). Auschwitz provided no wisdom, writes Améry, made no one better or more humane (1980, 19–20). The impulse of both trauma victims and those who listen to their testimonies to blame them for their suffering—and this is certainly the approach of Dtr, as we have seen—is one that necessarily reflects a moral system rooted in some worldview with particular concepts of right and wrong. Trauma, though, in its failure of belief and truth, can provide no such support for moral claims, and at this point it would seem to threaten and throw into question important aspects of the victims' culture itself. While histories cannot comprehend trauma, that does not mean that they must ignore and repress it, as we analyze in chapter 6, but the threat trauma poses to historians' cultures and ethical systems gives them an incentive to do so.

A group deeply affected by great suffering has a need to explain it in order to demonstrate that it can be understood within the worldview that holds the community together and that undergirds its morality and the authority of its ruling groups. It is possible, as chapter 2 notes, that if the community's worldview cannot account for the suffering, then community members may begin to believe that the worldview, or at least some important part of it, is not correct, that it provides no legitimacy for the authority their rulers claim, that there is no validity to the culture's moral system, or even that they should abandon the group altogether. The Deuteronomist certainly made an effort to explain the exilic community's situation and, as we saw when discussing Dtr, the understanding of morality in the work was an integral part of this explanation and thus reflected the worldview of the pro-Davidic carrier group to which the Deuteronomist belonged. Since God exists in a particular way for the Deuteronomist, a way that demands Judah's complete cultic loyalty, the result of this is that the community must act in a particular way. But the Deuteronomist's understanding of God proceeds from a worldview that reflects Davidic interests and in which God privileges the Davidides, providing them with their past and future authority to rule, no matter how poorly individual members of the house conduct themselves. Morality is an integral part of the worldview readers encounter in Dtr, as is its assertion that the Davidides, the chief members of the Deuteronomist's social group, are to some degree beyond the moral strictures that apply to other Judeans and even to Saul and the northern dynasts. The history created by the Deuteronomist reinforces important lessons about how God responds to the people's actions, how readers should act, and how they should regard the Davidides, or at least it did for readers who saw Dtr as a true account of what really happened. The work validates the authority of the Davidides and the present the Deuteronomist and his or her community saw as true because that is the only way that the group could conceive of the past as existing; this past is desirable for the Deuteronomist's pro-Davidic carrier group because it reflects the present and future the group wanted to see.

Writers explain past suffering through whatever means their worldviews allow, and in fact they have to explain suffering in such ways if they wish to be intellectually honest, for the only alternative is to lie and explain things in a way that authors do not believe to be true. In some cases historians might have a need to justify great suffering undergone by their communities; Edkins, for example, writes that in modern societies, where the military is composed not of subjects but of citizens who themselves are understood to make up part of the state, the government has a particular need to envelop the dead in a national narrative that presents them as willing sacrifices and martyrs (2003, 93–95). But the modern state is not the only kind of social group that finds a need to justify suffering, for there were groups who were in a position to affect the political order in the ancient world also, such as the Judean elite in Babylonia for whom Dtr was written. In such cases, it is easy to see why historians' worldviews might leave them no space to acknowledge the reality of psychological trauma, for since trauma cannot be narrated it cannot be understood and cannot be a part of a history that validates Davidic rule. Moreover, a difficulty that could arise in a community where many members suffer from massive psychological trauma is that the not-stories of the traumatic events could alienate a significant part of the population from the narrative truths that writers such as the Deuteronomist were attempting to advance. Should this happen, then there might be significantly fewer people who would be willing to believe the history and so to affirm the worldview and morality of the social group, and it is thus in the interests of the carrier groups creating collective trauma to portray victims as martyrs and heroic adherents to the culture's moral system, or even as the ones responsible for the trauma itself because of their moral failings. This does not mean that historians who create pasts that affirm their belief systems and concomitant moralities are deliberately misleading readers; it means they are shaping the past in ways their worldviews mandate, ways that repress trauma. Historians do not need to to repress trauma, as we discuss in chapter 6, yet by doing so they evade any challenge to the worldviews that undergird their histories and to the ethical systems and social hierarchies that correspond to them.

Trauma survivors might publicly assent to the truth of a history's creation of the past and thus to the validity of the historian's belief system and attendant morality, but the result, writes Lawrence Langer, is that survivors will simultaneously inhabit two worlds: that of trauma, which is based in the original inability to react to horrific violence and so in a situation without ethical choice, and that of a present that demands moral evaluations of actions, even as it is impossible to integrate these two worlds (1991, 83). The inability to react to traumatic violence is not always a matter of being unable to fight or flee but sometimes simply the result of existing in a context so horrific that there are no good or moral choices to make.

Langer refers, for example, to the testimony of a Holocaust survivor who, upon arrival at Auschwitz, was sent to the right with his younger brother, while his parents were sent to the left to die. Not knowing what this separation meant, he sent his brother after his parents. "I feel like I killed him," he said in his testimony, simultaneously relying on an ethical system and demonstrating the futility of such reliance (Langer 1995, 29–30). When Langer discusses the example of a Jewish doctor poisoning the children in a hospital in the Warsaw Ghetto before the Nazis could remove them to Treblinka, he concludes that the act was not one of heroism; even though it had been described with such language of morality, says Langer, that sort of depiction simply manifests "the poverty of traditional moral vocabulary when we address the subject of human conduct during the destruction of European Jewry" (32). In such a setting, Langer is arguing, morality simply fails to help us distinguish between the doctor's choices of acting and not acting, because in such a context there are no good choices to make, yet individuals must continue to choose.

Trauma is unavailable to moral evaluation because it is rooted in victims' inability to act and in their situatedness in contexts where no moral choice was possible. A massive trauma such as that of the Holocaust, writes Jean-François Lyotard, impugns historical knowledge (1998, 57–58), and it does so because it impugns the worldviews and associated moral systems in which histories are based. A history can only comprehend things that the historian's narrative can comprehend, and it only creates a past that is explainable on the historian's terms, as discussed in chapter 2 above. The historian uses the same worldview to understand both past and present, so if the historian believes God acts in history in certain ways for certain reasons, then the historian likely believes that history always has and always will be shaped by such action. This is why, again, histories validate historians' worldviews. The difficulty, then, with noticeable gaps in a historical narrative, anything that might seem to make it less than totalizing, is that they throw the historian's worldview into question and so are potentially damaging to the social group, its leadership, and its morality. In chapter 6 we address the possibility of historians allowing trauma testimony to parallel and question their narratives, something that would prevent a history from taking on a totalizing nature, though on the face of it this might seem a counterproductive move for a historian, since it seems natural to conclude that a good history is one that avoids gaps in explanation, while trauma is a lacuna in history, something that worldview and morality cannot account for.

Communities and their leadership depend on widespread acceptance of worldview for their existence, as chapter 2 explains, and histories tend to repress trauma precisely because historians have no way to make sense of it and to try to create some sort of room for it beside the history would throw into question the historical explanation and the worldview that grounds it. The absence of narrative explanation that is trauma is thus not acceptable for history as we normally conceive of it, and this means that we would expect trauma to be repressed and overwritten as groups create their pasts in the stories they tell.

So trauma testimonies are likely to be misunderstood as listeners attempt to make sense of them through their worldviews; even therapists who treated American veterans of the Vietnam War, writes Kalí Tal, had a tendency to overwrite and so repress their patients' testimonies by grafting them into a narrative that presented the patients as successful warriors, thereby creating stories on their behalf that conformed to an American myth (1996, 147–53). This is an example of the fetishistic narrative that the end of chapter 3 discussed: a narrative that represses trauma, that eliminates the gaps trauma creates that threaten totalistic narrative coherence and truth, and that thus constructs a past governed by the pleasure principle that allows for no challenge to the cultural worldview at all. History cannot comprehend trauma because there is no truth or understanding for it, merely the same unexplainable suffering over and over.

Walter Benjamin seems to get at this distinction between trauma and history in his description of "the angel of history," who, Benjamin says, faces the past but is inexorably blown backward into a future he cannot see. "Where we perceive a chain of events," he writes, "he sees one single catastrophe which keeps piling wreckage upon wreckage and hurls it in front of his feet." The storm that blows the angel backward, says Benjamin, is what we call progress (1968, 257–58), but trauma is the wreckage of the past from which victims, like the angel, cannot avert their gaze, while the creators of histories describe chains of explainable events. Like the Deuteronomist, writing from a pro-Davidic worldview, historians can have the tendency to see history as progress; for Dtr there is a progression toward the Davidides in Deuteronomy through Samuel, and a progression back to Davidic rule at the end of Kings. The chaos of not-story is something that historians like the Deuteronomist ignore because they have no way to make sense of it, since they have created an ordered and understandable past that reflects the present and future they believe should exist. Trauma is instead fixated to the chaotic, unordered wreckage of the past, and to make any attempt to include it beside the narratives such historians create would result in a challenge to the fetishistic and totalizing impulses of those narratives. "Only things that move in the direction of history [*le sens de l'histoire*] have historical meaning [*sens historique*]," writes Jean Baudrillard (1994, 17), and for one seeking to understand the past, things that do not make sense and that cannot be accounted for by one's worldview— things that do not have meaning, in other words—simply do not exist, which is precisely what Laub says about the trauma of the Holocaust and what Wiesel says about Holocaust literature.

Because historians must create narratives if they are to write histories, trauma cannot, by its nature, be included in them. This does not, however, condemn all histories to be fetishistic narratives that repress trauma, and Dominick LaCapra argues that histories are closest to fiction when they provide "unproblematic closure" and "a sense of an ending," closing off any reference at all to trauma that would throw a narrative's conclusions and worldview into question (2001, 15–16). Historians can, however, acknowledge that their narratives cannot ever be totalizing or comprehend the suffering of trauma and to insist that readers not be misled into thinking that a history provides them with a final and ultimate account of traumatic events (Hilberg 1988, 25). If historians claim that they know and can explain trauma, then they are overwriting and repressing it, claiming that it is comprehensible and can be appropriated into someone else's narrative. Yet historians can "brush against the grain," as Benjamin puts it (1968, 256–57), although this means questioning the validity of the narratives they create and being willing to doubt the worldviews that shape their consciousness. This is a matter we take up again in chapter 6, but we turn first to the struggle between collective and psychological trauma in Lamentations.

5

Lamentations and the
Failure of Collective Trauma

5.1. Introduction: Lamentations and the
Struggle Surrounding Collective Trauma

Current scholarship almost universally sees Lamentations as composed in the wake of Jerusalem's destruction in the early sixth century BCE. Discussions of its date often refer to the general agreement among scholars concerning its composition in the wake of that event (e.g., Westermann 1994b, 54–55; Joyce 1999, 247; Middlemas 2006b, 177–84; Boase 2006, 3–4), and there is good reason for this consensus. Throughout the work, Lamentations obviously seems to reflect the suffering of the people from warfare and its attendant horrors, as well as the destruction of Jerusalem and Judah (2:2, 5, 8–9), the enemy's entry into Jerusalem and its temple (1:10; 2:1, 6, 7; 4:12), and the exile of the people, nobility, and king (1:3, 5, 6; 4:15–16, 20), issues that appear to reflect the specific event of the sixth-century disaster.[1] Unsurprisingly, then, a study of the language of Lamentations concludes that it shares features of both pre- and postexilic Hebrew and is thus a product of the transitional linguistic stage of the exilic period, most closely comparable to the Hebrew of Ezekiel (Dobbs-Allsopp 1998). Scholars also widely agree that the exilic author of Second Isaiah knew Lamentations and responded to the work;[2] we consider a few instances of that response in the next chapter, but the point here is simply

---

1. Contra Provan 1990b. For more discussion of the ways in which Lamentations reflects the early sixth-century destruction of Judah and Jerusalem, see Parry 2011, 66–78.

2. The most detailed study of Second Isaiah's response to Lamentations appears in Willey 1997, but the conclusion that Second Isaiah knew the work is widely accepted;

that Lamentations must have been written earlier in the exilic period than Second Isaiah. Despite some references to Judah and its people going into exile, there is not so much emphasis on exile in Lamentations that the book could not have been written in or around Jerusalem. The suffering of the inhabitants of the city is the focus of the work, and Zion is even personified as a female voice, so Lamentations, unlike the Deuteronomistic History, may well have been composed in or near the ruins of the city.

While Lamentations responds to the same disaster as Dtr, the specifics of its response are different, since it privileges repetitive articulations of the survivors' suffering and rejects history and collective trauma. In the following sections of the chapter we examine each of the five poems that make up Lamentations to demonstrate how such rejection is manifested, and we do something similar in this first section as we discuss aspects of voice and poetry in regard to Lamentations as a whole. In Dtr, an authoritative narrative voice creates a past that is an unfolding of Moses's warnings and instructions in Deuteronomy and that thereby explains the sixth-century disaster. In Lamentations, however, numerous voices speak, and there is no agreement as to precisely how many should be identified. The following sections of the chapter return to the question as to who speaks where in these poems; it is enough to note here that there is no authoritative narrative voice in Lamentations, as there is in Dtr, and that the multiplicity of voices with different and changing perspectives on the disaster is an important difference between the two works.

There is a speaker in Lam 1–2 who is often described as a narrator, and in the opening verses of the book he[3] begins to create history and collective trauma, but by the following chapter he abandons this attempt,

---

besides the scholarly works Willey discusses on pp. 4–6 and 48–50, see also, e.g., Seitz 1998, 130–49; O'Connor 1999; Linafelt 2000, 62–79; Tiemeyer 2007.

3. No gender is specified for the narrator, and if we were to understand this speaker to be a professional lamenter—although that is not clear—then we might expect this figure to be female, since lamenters in ancient Israel often were women (Goitein 1988, 23–27; Bergant 2013, 145). Since the narrator's voice alternates in Lam 1–2 with that of Zion, who is portrayed as a woman, it is somewhat simpler to use male pronouns for the narrator in descriptions of the chapter. But it may also be helpful for readers to think of a male narrator who begins his speech by blaming a female victim for the suffering she has endured and witnessed, a narrator who, as a male and so as inherently more privileged in Judean society than a woman, represents the status quo that benefits the more privileged, just as the Deuteronomist promotes a *status quo ante* that privileged the elite among the exiles.

as we discuss below. The narrator's voice alternates with Zion's in the first two poems of the book, but these speakers are replaced by an entirely different one as Lam 3 opens, and a communal voice that first appears in Lam 4 exercises a monopoly over the speech in Lam 5. These voices do not all speak of Zion's trauma in the same way, and without a guiding narrator who articulates one perspective throughout the work, and without any divine speech at all,[4] there is no single response in Lamentations to the vast suffering the community has undergone. This has not stopped some scholars from arguing that the book produces a unified evaluation of the disaster—and such arguments often make the case that Lamentations advances collective trauma and thus is a theodicy that explains and justifies the community's suffering[5]—but these are not really arguments that take the basic structure of Lamentations seriously, for we encounter different voices articulating different responses to Jerusalem's disaster, and sometimes even the same speaker changes his or her opinion. There simply is no stable narrative explanation in Lamentations, where, unlike Dtr, trauma refuses to be repressed by history.

We certainly cannot maintain, however, that Lamentations makes no attempt to create a history or collective trauma that explains the devastation of Judah and Jerusalem, that it does nothing to justify divine actions in this regard. The narrator, the first speaker of the book, initiates an attempt to do this, and in the context of describing Zion's suffering and mourning refers to her "iniquities" in 1:5 and says she sinned in 1:8. Zion even seems to accept this explanation, at least in Lam 1, as we discuss further below, and there are attempts to create collective trauma in other chapters as well.[6] Yet none of these attempts goes without challenge or contradiction, and if we see efforts in the book to create a history that explains the readers' pain, which is in part what collective trauma does, they are tentative and thrown into irresolvable doubt. These movements toward explanations that provide totalizing histories ultimately fail, as each explanation

---

4. The man who speaks in Lam 3 does quote God in 3:57, although he does so either in reference to an event unrelated to the sixth-century disaster or in referring to divine speech that the man wishes God would utter. See the analysis of Lam 3 below.

5. Bier 2015, 12–19, refers to such readings of the book as "theodic." For some examples of interpretations of Lamentations that view the book in this way, see Johnson 1985; Krašovec 1992; Berges 2000; House 2011; Conway 2012.

6. So readings of Lamentations that Bier (2015, 19–24) refers to as "anti-theodic" do not by themselves entirely explain what we see in the book.

is abandoned, or contradicted by a competing voice, or even challenged by the original speaker. At points Lamentations can seem to approach what we refer to in chapter 3 as a fetishistic narrative, something that provides closure and avoids the ongoing suffering of psychological trauma, but closure is never fully reached in the book, mourning is never quite overcome, and at places where fetishism seems about to triumph readers are returned to the community's suffering yet again, and history's repression of trauma fails. Lamentations is, in the end, a conflict around collective trauma, a struggle to create, accept, and finally to reject it. Unlike Dtr, Lamentations passes no final verdict on the truth of the history and explanation of the sixth-century disaster, for there is no authoritative or divine voice to pass it,[7] and in the end the repetition of the victims' suffering does not accept any of the attempts to explain and so to repress their trauma. Narratives of collective trauma and thus of history are not absent here, but they fail to silence the uncanny repetition of psychological trauma, and they hardly meet with universal acceptance among the competing voices in the book. Similarly, we see a desire for closure on the part of some of the voices in Lamentations as they attempt to account for everything and to move toward an end to mourning, only for the suffering to repeat as closure collapses. We can say, then, that Lamentations witnesses to the failure of collective trauma and history to repress the voices of the traumatized.

One of the formal aspects of Lamentations that lends itself to the insistent repetition of psychological trauma, repetition that throws the various attempts at creating collective trauma into doubt and unresolved trial, is the structuring of each of the first four poems by alphabetic acrostic. The first word of every verse of Lam 1, 2, and 4 begins with a consecutive letter of the Hebrew alphabet, starting with *aleph* in verse 1 and ending with *tav* in verse 22, while in Lam 3, another acrostic, each line for three consecutive verses begins with the same letter, while the following three verses begin with the next letter, and so on, until the final three verses (3:64–66) each begin with *tav*.[8] The significance of this acrostic form for the first four poems of the book is debated: some have proposed that it acted as an aid

---

7. In trauma testimony, writes Shoshana Felman, "language is in process and in trial, it does not possess itself as a conclusion, as the constatation of a verdict or the self-transparency of knowledge" (1992, 5).

8. In 2:16–17; 3:46–51; and 4:16–17, *ayin* and *pe* appear in the reverse order of their normal positions in the alphabet. This happens also in the alphabetic acrostic that structures the poem of Pss 9–10, and it may simply reflect two accepted orders of

for memorization, although this seems unlikely,[9] that it creates a sense of completeness for each poem, that it was purely an aesthetic device (e.g., Westermann 1994b, 99; Salters 2011), or that it has some other purpose (Pyper 2001, 62–63). To argue that the author intended it solely as an aesthetic device, or even as an aid in memorization, does not deal with the question as to what effect it has on readers. The acrostic might obviously seem to signal completeness, because once the twenty-second and final letter of the alphabet is reached at the beginning of the final verse, then each of the four alphabetic acrostics is complete. The notion that the acrostic signals completeness, perhaps of explanation or perhaps of the articulation of the community's suffering (e.g., Gottwald 1954, 30; Johnson 1985, 60–61; Owens 1990, 77; O'Connor 2002, 13), however, would appear to be undercut by the fact that one acrostic poem follows another, so one complete picture of suffering or one complete sense of explanation would only seem to be displaced by another somewhat different and yet supposedly equally complete account.

What the acrostics suggest is not completeness but repetition; with the acrostic structure, the community's suffering repeats over and over, from beginning to end, from *aleph* to *tav*, as psychological trauma repeats into the lives of survivors, making the trauma continually present. If readers are led by one acrostic poem to believe they have encountered the totality of explanation and/or suffering, the move to the next subverts that conclusion, for repeated and somewhat different attempts to explain the traumatic events of Jerusalem's destruction, attempts that are then followed by voices that ignore or contradict what has preceded, merely make any step toward collective trauma seem like a futile endeavor to deal with a problem that cannot be resolved. If the alphabetic acrostic was a conscious attempt to create formal order that structures chaotic thought (Assis 2007, 714), then it is significant that it is absent in the final poem of Lam 5.[10] At the end of

---

these letters in the alphabet (Giffone 2010, 55), although for another explanation see Koptak 2014.

9. For arguments that the acrostic functioned as a mnemonic device, see, e.g., Assis 2007, 712–13; Thomas 2008, 137. But as Norman Gottwald (1954, 26–27) points out, it is difficult to see how someone reciting the book would be aided by knowing that the first word of an upcoming verse began with a particular letter. Since there are four acrostics in the book, and since three verses in Lam 3 begin with each letter, that means that six verses in the book each start with the same letter.

10. Although some see the poem, or at least parts of it, as structured by other kinds of acrostic (Bergler 1977; Guillaume 2009; Rong 2013, 42–43).

the book, there is no attempt on a formal level to signal a complete account of Zion's pain and no formal sense that a complete explanation has been offered, merely a repetition of the same suffering that has been voiced in the previous poems, that is still present to Zion's victims of trauma, and that seems as if it will go on forever.

Narratives can be told in poetic meter, but Lamentations does not leave readers with a sense of a coherent story that begins in 1:1 and concludes in 5:22. Unlike Dtr, Lamentations as a whole has no plot and tells no story, contains no unified train of thought even within the individual poems, let alone from the beginning to the end of the work, and it presents readers with "a seemingly haphazard movement between ideas and images" (Boase 2008a, 34; see also Westermann 1994b, 64; Salters 2000; O'Connor 2002, 1–2). Shifts of perspective from speaker to speaker, and even by the same speaker, disorient and unsettle, and to some degree the only constant among the poems is the repetitive return of suffering and the continual competition between and rejection of attempts to explain it. Sixth-century readers may even have found the mix of genres in the poetry disorienting. The poems contain formal elements of the *qinah* or dirge tradition mixed with those of the lament psalms (Westermann 1994b, 1–11; Middlemas 2012, 43–44), but Lamentations belongs fully to neither tradition. The three-plus-two meter of the dirge does not appear consistently throughout the poems and is virtually absent in Lam 5 (Shea 1979, 103), and while lament psalms typically end with or at least include thanksgiving, this is absent in Lamentations (Mandolfo 2007, 70–71). Lamentations 4 and 5 contain aspects of the communal lament genre seen in the Psalms, yet such psalms always open with direct address to the deity, which is absent in Lam 4, and include an appeal for restoration, also absent there (Salters 2007, 327*). The complaint section in Lam 5 (5:2–18, 20) is extremely long and its turn to God (5:19) extremely brief, and there is no expected vow of praise (Williamson 2008, 73). Lamentations 3 contains elements of both individual and communal laments (Bier 2015, 7–8). Lamentations 1 and 2 reflect aspects of the *balag* and *eršemma*, types of Mesopotamian city laments (Gwaltney 1983; Dobbs-Allsopp 1993), but the Mesopotamian poems do not blame the city, its population, or its gods for its destruction, whereas Lam 1–2 does all three, and Lamentations does not refer to restoration and the return of the divinity to the city, unlike the Mesopotamian laments (Gwaltney 1983, 207, 209; Dobbs-Allsopp 1993, 52–55, 92–94). Lamentations does not so much imitate as vaguely echo ancient Judean/Israelite and Near Eastern poetic genres (e.g., Salters 2007,

328*; Middlemas 2006b, 225; Boase 2006, 37; Mandolfo 2007, 65–68), and where readers might expect particular movements of the poems to restoration or praise or divine return to Zion based on the poetry's genre (or quasi-genre), these hopes are repetitively dashed.

So the poetry of Lamentations follows no predictable tracks and arrives at no comforting conclusions or attitudes, as readers might initially expect. Expectations raised by the poems' generic aspects that a totalizing explanation might be established, or that trauma may be avoided in a fetishistic narrative that closes off mourning, remained unfulfilled, and readers are uncannily returned to the same suffering over and over. As a result, the acrostic structure might suggest that the totality of pain has been covered in each chapter, yet readers encounter the same suffering anew in each poem, so the acrostic points not to completeness but to the repetition of suffering. While explanation is offered in some of the poems, later ones simply ignore or contradict these explanations, so the acrostic does not signify completeness of explanation but points only to the attempt to establish it as an endless and irresolvable problem. While we cannot argue that the explanation of collective trauma is absent from Lamentations, it never manages to fully repress or drown out the voices that bear testimony to psychological trauma, which constantly repeat their suffering, trauma's uncanny return, and which struggle with and ultimately reject the various creations of collective trauma offered by some of the speakers. We now begin to trace this conflict around collective trauma and its ultimate failure in Lamentations to repress testimonies of psychological trauma as we move through the book's poems.

5.2. The Creation, Acceptance, and Rejection of Collective Trauma in Lamentations 1–2

Both Lam 1 and 2 are, as mentioned above, structured by alphabetic acrostics, and while each poem can be regarded as complete in and of itself because of this structure, they contain the same speakers, the narrator and Daughter Zion, who is a personification of Jerusalem.[11] Consequently, we can examine them together, especially because the speech of each of the

---

11. Some scholars understand the word בת in the phrase בת ציון to mean "fair" or "dear" rather than "daughter" (see Stinespring 1965). When בת appears in construct with a geographical name, however, it draws from the Akkadian divine title *mārat GN*, "daughter GN." The use of the title in the Hebrew Bible does not imply reference to a

voices appears to be affected by that of the other throughout the two chapters. The narrator's speech opens the first poem, and in 1:1–9 he emphasizes Zion's suffering and her change in status: she was full of people but is now like a widow; she was great among the nations but now is forced labor; she had lovers (אהבים) and friends (רעים), which is to say political allies,[12] but they have become her enemies (1:1–2). People once honored her but now despise her, and Zion can do no more than remember her מחמדים, "precious things," that she had in the past (1:7–8); her downfall, says the narrator, was "extraordinary" (1:9) and involved the exile of her children and princes (1:3, 5–6). With no מנחם, "comforter" (1:2, 9), Zion and her people can only mourn (1:4). So while the narrator's opening speech mainly focuses on Zion's suffering, he does create chronology and change and makes some minimal attempt to explain it: "YHWH made her suffer [הוגה] for the greatness of her iniquities" (1:5); "Jerusalem sinned greatly,[13] therefore she has become a lament"[14] (1:8). If Zion is a suffering victim, according to the narrator, then she is not a guiltless one. Her former allies certainly are also not blameless—"they acted treacherously" (1:2)—and while YHWH inflicted her suffering, it was a punishment for sin. This is not as detailed an explanation for the readers' pain as that provided by Dtr, but we do see the start of a narrative here, and the narrator looks back to Zion's glorious past and says that the change that led to her current suffering can be explained through her sin. We could say that the explanatory narrative so far has a beginning and a middle section, for the end of the poem of Lam 1 directs readers to a potential end to this story.

---

goddess, as it does in the Mesopotamian texts, but it does reflect a personification of a city (Dobbs-Allsopp 1995).

12. For the political significance of these words, see Olyan 1996, 215–16; Parry 2011, 85–86.

13. Reading חטוא חטאה with 4QLam instead of חטא חטאה, "sinned a sin," with the MT and Versions; see Cross 2000, 233.

14. נידה, translated here as "lament," is a *hapax legomenon*, and the Versions largely connect the word to the root נוד, understanding it to refer to Zion's wandering or exile (σάλος in the LXX, *instabilis* in the Vulgate, טלטיל in the Targums). The verb נוד is also used in the context of shaking that appears as a kind of lamenting (e.g., Isa 51:19; Jer 15:5; 16:5; 22:10; Job 2:11), so perhaps Zion has become a "lament" here, something done or said as a kind of mourning. It is also possible that the word derives from the root נדד, like the noun נדה used to describe Jerusalem in 1:17, so it is possible that it refers to Zion's impurity (so, e.g., Renkema 1998, 133–34; Maier 2008b, 146), which is how the Peshitta's *ndt'* understands it.

The narrator who speaks this incipient collective trauma is sometimes called "objective" and seen as a dispassionate voice that lays out the facts for Zion and for readers (e.g., Lanahan 1974, 41; Johnson 1985, 63–64; Conway 2012, 113). Other scholars see emotional involvement in Zion's plight on the part of the narrator here (e.g., Salters 2000, 300–301; Miller 2001, 393–95), but he does not yet express obvious signs of emotional response to Zion's suffering as he does in 2:11, where he refers to his weeping and physiological distress in the context of witnessing her pain. The "facts" in this first part of his speech would not appear out of place in Dtr, although there is more concentrated focus on suffering here and throughout Lamentations than there is anywhere in Dtr, except in the collective trauma the Deuteronomist creates in Deut 28, a chapter that agrees with the narrator here insofar as it blames the people for any mass suffering they experience.[15] Without any overt expressions of sympathy for Zion in Lam 1:1–9, one can see why readers might experience the narrator as a dispassionate voice, laying out the facts of history and collective trauma, even while acknowledging Zion's great suffering. Facts, as discussed in chapter 2, are facts because they are widely accepted as true, and in Zion's own speech in Lam 1 she parrots the narrator's explanation, as we discuss below. This imitation and acceptance of the narrator's development of collective trauma suggests that Zion sees the narrator as an authoritative voice, advancing a truth with facts that she should also believe. Zion speaks one line in 1:9c, where she asks God to see her "affliction," apparently a search for a "comforter." This can be taken as a response to the narrator, who says in 1:9b that Zion has no comforter to respond to her suffering, a reiteration of the same point he made in 1:2, where he said no comforter was to be found among her old allies since they had become her enemies.

Yet even while the narrator makes a start at creating this history for Zion, he seems fixated on her suffering and interrupts her speech of 1:9c as he speaks again in 1:10a–11b, repeating aspects of her suffering that he has already mentioned. Like Zion in 1:9c he also addresses YHWH, suggesting

---

15. In fact, Lam 1:3, 5 even share language with Deut 28 (Albrektson 1963, 231–32; Parry 2007, 142). Lam 1:3 refers to Judah dwelling "among the nations," where "she has not found rest," and Deut 28:65 says Israel's foot will not have "rest" when they are exiled "among the nations." Lam 1:5 refers to Zion's adversaries as becoming "head," the position Deut 28:44 says Israel's invaders will have. These similarities are perhaps not enough to posit dependence of one text on the other, though.

he has been influenced by her direct appeal to God (Miller 2001, 397). He uses language here that suggests Zion's rape, as he did in 1:8,[16] and returns to the matter of the "precious things" he first mentioned in 1:7, which he now says are gone because the adversary has taken them and because the people have had to sell them to avoid starvation. The narrator seems to feel that this repetition of Zion's suffering rather than an explanation of its justice is what deserves emphasis. He has begun to assemble core aspects of collective trauma, identifying perpetrators—Zion, primarily, but also the adversaries who have acted treacherously (1:2), laughed at Zion (1:7), and entered the sanctuary contrary to divine command (1:10)—as well as victims, and assigning guilt and responsibility. The narrator sounds at this point rather like someone who accepts the basic beliefs of a worldview that seems at least to some degree like that which structured the Deuteronomist's thought, albeit one with far more concern for the people's suffering, and as Zion begins to speak for the second time in 1:11c she repeats the narrator's observations and analysis of her situation.

Zion's dialogue with the narrator is implicit in Lam 1; neither voice directly addresses the other, but they appear to be affected by what the other says (Miller 2001, 393–95; Lee 2002, 160; Harris and Mandolfo 2013, 134–35). This seems to be true when the narrator interrupts Zion in 1:10a–11b and addresses God just as she does in 1:9c, but it is even more obvious in Zion's speech that takes up the rest of the poem of Lam 1 (except for another interruption by the narrator in 1:17). She repeats some of the narrator's assertions: she uses the verb יגה just as he does in repeating his claim that YHWH has made her suffer (see 1:12 and 5); she is שממה, "desolate," as the narrator had said (1:13 and 4); the enemy's hands are on her, just as he also has asserted (1:13 and 4); her people are starving and in search of food to "restore their lives" (1:19 and 11); she does indeed weep, just as the narrator has claimed (1:16 and 2); and she is in fact without a comforter (1:16, 21 and 2, 9). And although she begins her speech anew in 1:11c by asking YHWH to "see," as she did in 1:9c, and to "give heed," she immediately turns her address in 1:12a to "all who cross along the way," not to God. She certainly speaks as if she is convinced by

---

16. For the use of מחמד, בוא, מקדש, and פרש in 1:10 as suggesting Zion's rape by the nations, see Dobbs-Allsopp and Linafelt 2001 as well as Guest 1999, 416; Stiebert 2003, 200; Maier 2008a, 129; Trudinger 2008, 46; Bosworth 2013, 227. As most of these scholars point out, the narrator has also used the expression ראה ערוה in 1:8, which also suggests the rape of Zion by the enemy.

the narrator's assertion that God is responsible for her suffering (1:12–15, 21–22), and that assertion is perhaps enough to convince her that YHWH is unlikely to act as her comforter. She does not bother to appeal to her "lovers" and "friends," accepting the narrator's claim that "they have acted treacherously" (1:2)—"my lovers," Zion says in 1:19, "have deceived me"— so no one appears to be left to address except those who happen to pass by and see her devastation.

Just as Zion seems to believe that the narrator has gotten so much right about her current situation, she also agrees with him in his explanation of it. Like him, Zion refers to her פשע, "iniquity" (see 1:14, 22 and 5), and says that YHWH has acted against her because of it (1:22 and 5); she says, in fact, that she has rebelled against God's command (1:18).[17] She is even more insistent than the narrator that YHWH is responsible for her suffering, for he refers to YHWH's involvement in it only once (1:5),[18] and in 1:12 Zion not only repeats his claim that YHWH made her suffer but refers to the ways in which YHWH did this in each verse from 1:12 to 1:15 (Mintz 1982, 5; Miller 2001, 402–6), and she insists in the context of discussing her rebellion in 1:18 that YHWH is צדיק, "righteous." So not only does Zion seem to accept the narrative of explanation the narrator advances in 1:1–9, but she seems to accept it more wholeheartedly, or at least focuses on it more, than he does. Like him, she says more about her suffering than her guilt for it, but in the conclusion of the poem (1:20–22, or verses *resh*, *shin*, and *tav*) she even goes one step beyond the narrator in regard to the collective trauma that he began to create. While he spoke of a beginning and middle to such a trauma—Zion's original glorious state, followed by the sin that led to the suffering of her punishment—Zion now creates an end to this story, by calling on YHWH once more to look on her distress, not so YHWH will act as comforter—"I have no comforter," she admits for the second time in 1:21—but to punish her enemies for

---

17. Zion says in 1:18 that פיה מריתי, and the word מריתי comes from the root מרה, "to rebel." In the MT of 1:20, we find מרו מריתי, where both words are also from the root מרה, but there the LXX's παραπικραίνουσα παρεπικράνα and Peshitta's *mmrmrw mrmrt* reflect the Hebrew מר(ו)ר מר(ו)תי, "I am very bitter," rather than the MT's "I have surely rebelled" (see Seow 1985). However, if the MT has the original text in 1:20 (so, e.g., Renkema 1998, 189–90; Parry 2010, 63–64), then that is another place where Zion admits to rebellion against YHWH.

18. The only other verb besides יגה in 1:5 of which God is the subject in the narrator's speech of 1:1–9b, 10a–11b is צוה in 1:10, but this appears in the narrator's claim that God "commanded" the adversary not to enter the temple.

their evil, just as she has been punished for her iniquity (1:22). If the traditional role of the comforter in ancient Judah and Israel was to identify with the mourner and give advice as to how to overcome pain (Pham 1999, 27–28), YHWH will not suffice, but Zion does believe God is just and can deliver some sort of closure to her suffering by making her enemies suffer as she does.

Supposing Lamentations contained this poem alone, then the collective trauma begun by the narrator that Zion not only accepts but completes might seem fairly well established, especially with its acrostic structure, which could be seen as pointing to a totalizing explanation: Zion sinned, she now suffers from divine punishment, but even if she has no comforter she hopes divine justice will be exercised against those evildoers who deceived her (1:19) and now rejoice (1:22) and laugh (1:7) at her desolation. Traumatic events, perpetrators, victim, and target of retribution have been identified by these juxtaposed voices, but the next acrostic poem does not go on to provide Zion with the closure for which she has asked, nor to provide her with a comforter to ease her pain, nor even to reinforce the narrative of collective trauma of Lam 1. The end to the story that Zion desires, an end that she assumedly hopes will close off her mourning, is what she calls "the day you have announced" (1:21), the day of YHWH that would bring Zion the closure she wants, the punishment of her enemies. But as the narrator begins to speak again in 2:1, he refers to "the day of his [God's] anger" not as the time of the destruction of Zion's enemies but of YHWH's punishment of Zion, something that has already happened and been described in the previous poem but from which Zion obviously continues to suffer. This destruction of Zion and her suffering is "the day" for which her enemies say they have waited (2:16). The opening of Lam 2, that is, denies the fetishistic closure to which the end of the previous poem pointed. The *aleph* of 2:1 does not continue or more fully flesh out the earlier story and explanation created by the narrator and Zion, and it does not narrate the closure Zion says she wants at the end of that poem; it only returns readers to Zion's suffering at YHWH's hand, and this is what dominates the speech of the narrator and Zion in Lam 2. The repetition of the suffering and the abandonment of the narrative of collective trauma here throw that earlier narrative construction into unresolved doubt. Have the narrator and Zion rejected their belief in it? If not, why do they not repeat any aspect of its explanation of things as they continue speaking of Zion's suffering in the second poem? Why has the future day of the punishment of Zion's enemies been converted into the repetition of the day of her own suffering? Neither Zion nor her enemies are portrayed as perpetrators in Lam 2,[19] and the poem does not move toward closure. The collective trauma of Lam 1 now appears overwhelmed by the suffering from that chapter that repeats in this one from beginning (*aleph*) to end (*tav*), that is obviously still as real as the time it was inflicted, and that repeats again as soon as Lam 3 begins. The dialogue of Lam 1–2 is not a triumph of the establishment of collective trauma, for what narrative explanation we do see in the first chapter does not repress the unexplainable testimonies of psychological trauma but is instead abandoned in Lam 2, overwhelmed by suffering's repetition in this new poem.

The narrator speaks throughout almost the entire chapter, and he has obviously been moved by Zion's pain. He now weeps as she does (see 2:11; 1:16) and feels precisely the same physiological distress: חמרמרו מעי, "my stomach churns" (2:11; 1:20). He has clearly been shaken from his earlier attempt to lay out the facts and story of collective trauma.[20] He says in 2:13 that Zion's pain is so vast there is nothing to compare it to, and this begins to sound much like the psychological trauma chapter 4 discusses, a suffering that words literally cannot express. The weeping narrator goes on to say in the verse, "To what will I liken you, how will I comfort you [ואנחמך]?"[21] The repetitive search for a מנחם, "comforter," in Lam 1 is revealed to be hopeless here because Zion's pain is on such an unimaginable scale that not even the now-sympathetic narrator knows how to provide comfort. With this verse, nonetheless, he addresses Zion directly for the first time and continues to do so until her speech begins. Perhaps the narrator has been shocked by the pain he has witnessed and that Zion has voiced in Lam 1, and he appears fixated to Zion's trauma, repeating aspects of it mentioned in the previous poem. He again refers to the "precious things" of Zion (see 2:4; 1:7–8, 10), although he now uses the term to refer

---

19. Even though the narrator describes the enemies as rejoicing in 2:16–17, this is merely part of the larger devastation of Zion wrought by YHWH.

20. For the narrator's move to a more sympathetic position in regard to Zion's suffering, see Lanahan 1974, 43; O'Connor, 2002, 35; Parry 2007, 151–52; Conway 2012, 117.

21. The LXX of 2:13 reads τίς σώσει σε καὶ παρακαλέσει σε, "Who will save you and comfort you?" The translator may have misread Hebrew שוה as ישע, but it is possible that the corruption occurred following the translation into Greek and that the OG actually read the text Symmachus did in translating τι ισωσω σοι ινα παρακαλεσω σε, "Whom may I liken to you so that I may comfort you?" In that case, the OG's Hebrew text is virtually identical to that of the MT (Albrektson 1963, 108–9).

to people whom he says YHWH is responsible for killing; he says YHWH has burned in Zion like a fire (2:4; see also 2:3), reflecting Zion's claim in 1:13; the festivals are no longer celebrated in the city, a point the narrator made in the previous poem (1:4), although he now says that this is due to YHWH's actions (2:6); God has abandoned the sanctuary to the enemy (2:6–7; see also 2:1),[22] an apparent revision of or addendum to his earlier claim that the enemy's entry into the sanctuary violated divine command (1:10); Zion's princes have gone into exile (2:9; 1:6); and the rejoicing of the enemy is as problematic for the narrator (2:15–17) as it is for Zion (1:20–22). His references to the famine ravaging Jerusalem's population are even more graphic than those in the previous poem (1:11, 19), and he now describes children starving to death in the streets (2:11–12, 19). New aspects are added to the suffering of Zion the speakers covered in the previous chapter, but it is basically a repetition of it, as present in this poem as it was in the last.

The case is not merely that the narrator repeats language and ideas associated with Zion's suffering in the first poem, for he also adopts her view that God is largely responsible for it. In 2:1–9 alone YHWH is the subject of twenty-nine verbs (Dobbs-Allsopp 2004, 34), and the narrator refers to YHWH's anger six times (Boase 2008a, 35). In 1:1–11, the narrator had been much more interested in describing the change in Zion's fortunes and what the adversaries had done, and there YHWH was the subject of only two verbs, only one of which affected Zion's suffering ("YHWH made her suffer [הוגה]" in 1:5). In Lam 2, though, the narrator adopts Zion's focus in 1:12–15, in which she describes YHWH as primarily responsible for her suffering, and in those four verses Zion makes God the subject of ten verbs. Now, the narrator says, the nations are not the perpetrators of this violence, as he had claimed in 1:2 and 10, and their insistence that they have destroyed the city (2:16) simply is not true, as he makes repetitively clear throughout the chapter. He says in 2:17 that "YHWH did what he devised, he completed his word," and claims in 2:15–17 that God is responsible for the nations' joy at the destruction of the city. YHWH "has bent his bow like an enemy," the narrator says now, "he has

---

22. The use of הדם, "footstool," in 2:1 and ג, "garden" (not to mention מועד, "tabernacle"), in 2:6 can be seen as references to the temple that God has forgotten, broken down, and ruined (Dobbs-Allsopp 1993, 69–70; Renkema 1998, 240–41). For the textual critical issues in 2:6—where, among other things, the LXX reflects Hebrew גפן, "vine," rather than the MT's ג, "garden," see Provan 1990a.

established his right hand like an adversary" (2:4); "the lord was like an enemy" (2:5). Even the basic structure of the narrator's speech in 2:1–17 follows the pattern set by Zion in 1:12–16, 18–22, focusing first on what God has done and then on the joy of the enemies that resulted from it. As the narrator becomes fixated to Zion's description of the awful results of YHWH's anger, he abandons the collective trauma he had begun to articulate in the previous poem.

So if the narrator seems the more authoritative voice in Lam 1, the one producing observations that Zion echoes, the situation seems reversed as their speech continues in Lam 2, and the observations that are repeated are those concerning the suffering that continues as a result of the day of YHWH's anger. What the narrator does not repeat of Zion's earlier speech, however, are her claims concerning her guilt and God's righteousness. Lamentations 2:14 might seem like an exception to this, for here the narrator refers to the prophets' failure to tell Zion of her "guilt" (עָוֹן), something that would have prevented her captivity, but in the larger context of his focus on YHWH's adversarial stance against Zion, it is no wonder that "her prophets did not find any vision from YHWH," as the narrator says in 2:9, or, in a potentially contradictory explanation in 2:14, that "your prophets saw for you what was false and deceptive." The divine world, after all, is responsible for what visions prophets actually see, and if the prophets were sent no visions, or only ones that were "false and deceptive," that was apparently so that they could not speak the truth to Zion of her guilt and make her change her ways to avoid the suffering that has befallen her. The whole point of YHWH's day of anger is to make Zion suffer, and if the prophets could have helped her avoid that then, as the narrator sees it here, they needed to be denied their visions or sent false ones. The point of 2:14 is not to focus on Zion's guilt but on the false visions sent to the prophets so that they would fail to warn her of it and prevent the punishment.

As the narrator now articulates and identifies with Zion's suffering, this identification becomes so close that it is difficult to say which of the two voices speaks in 2:20. In 2:18–19 the narrator, who himself is weeping (2:11), urges Zion to weep and appeal to YHWH for the lives of her starving children, and in 2:20 either he or Zion reuses her language of 1:11 ("See, O YHWH, and give heed") in order to plead for the fate of these offspring. The address to YHWH continues in 2:21–22 and concludes the poem, and in these final two verses Zion is clearly speaking—here she refers to "my young women and my young men" and "my enemies"—and while it is possible that she opens the address in 2:20, it is just as possible that the narrator now so deeply empathizes with her that he begins the appeal to God there, adopting her language from 1:11 as he has adopted her outlook on the disaster throughout the second poem.[23] Zion does not directly address the narrator in this poem as he does her, but she does adopt some of his language from the chapter, agreeing that "the day of YHWH's anger" has been the violence directed against her and from which she still suffers (see 2:22 and 1), and like the narrator she does not refer to the future punishment of her enemies of which she had spoken in 1:21–22.[24] She accepts the narrator's counsel that she petition YHWH—or perhaps she continues the petition he begins, depending on who speaks in 2:20—and agrees that YHWH has not "spared/shown mercy" (we see the verb חמל in 2:2, 17, and 21), and she, too, now refers to bodies that litter the streets (2:21 and 19) and claims that YHWH "killed" her citizens (2:21 and 4).

As the positions of the narrator and Zion merge in this poem, the fetishism and narrative of the collective trauma of Lam 1 are abandoned. There is no end to Zion's suffering in Lam 2, nor any explanation for it beyond unexplained divine anger. YHWH is not righteous in this second poem, merely the one who acts as enemy and refuses to spare or show mercy. Whatever potentially comforting closure to which 1:21–22 pointed in a day of punishment of Zion's enemies has been dashed here, for the only day of YHWH in Lam 2 is the suffering inflicted on Zion, the suffering already described in Lam 1 that now repeats in this poem, the suffering that Zion relives. The narrator, who advanced the collective trauma in Lam 1, and Zion, who accepted and completed it, speak almost as one in Lam 2 about the suffering of YHWH's day that is the same day over and over, the uncanny repetition of trauma. The poem envisions no closure that one could associate with fetishistic narrative; even though Zion follows the narrator's advice, or even his lead, and appeals to YHWH at the end of the poem, the sole content of the plea is merely that God observe her suffering. Neither character, apparently, can now believe that YHWH would act to end the horrific pain for which YHWH alone appears to be responsible, or at least cannot believe it enough to articulate the possibility. If closure, an end to the story, seemed like a real possibility at the end of the collective

---

23. Scholarship tends to attribute 2:20 to Zion because it repeats her appeal in 1:11, but see Parry 2007, 152.

24. For reflections of day of YHWH imagery that Lam 2 describes as directed against Jerusalem, see Dobbs-Allsopp 2004, 28–36.

trauma of Lam 1, it has been swallowed up by the psychological trauma of Lam 2, which can only repeat.

5.3. The Irresolvablility of Collective Trauma in Lamentations 3

Lamentations 3 opens with a new speaker, someone who refers to himself simply as הגבר, "the man" (3:1). While some argue that the man represents the continuation of Zion's speech from Lam 1–2 (e.g., Gottwald 1954, 39–41; Berges 2004), we clearly encounter a different speaker here, and as we move from Zion as a female voice in the first two chapters to the male speaker in Lam 3, it seems unlikely that most readers would see the same character behind each speaker (see Boase 2006, 222–23, and the works cited there). Some claim that the man represents a specific Judean royal figure (e.g., Porteous 1961, 244–45; Gottlieb 1987, 125–26; Saebø 1993, 302–4), but the poem steadfastly avoids any attempt to identify him in any way and gives no sense that he once ruled as a king. The noun גבר has martial overtones, so others see the character as a member of Judah's defeated army (e.g., Lanahan 1974, 45; Owens 1990, 83), but the word is sometimes used to refer simply to adult males (e.g., Exod 10:11; Num 24:3, 15; Deut 22:5; Josh 7:14, 17), so it is not necessary to see him as an ex-soldier. Some readers identify multiple voices in the chapter, seeing shifts of speaker where the voice changes from first-person singular to first-person plural or where they see conflicting perspectives in the response to the sixth-century disaster, although there is no agreement in regard to how many different voices are supposedly present, their identity, or even where one voice should be understood as succeeding another.[25] That there are conflicting responses to the annihilation of Judah and Jerusalem in this chapter is beyond any doubt, but we have just seen conflicting reactions expressed by both the narrator and Zion in Lam 1–2, so there is no particular reason why this acrostic poem should not portray yet another figure who cannot settle on a single response and who engages in an internal dialogue (so also Bier 2014, 150–54), speaking at times in a first-person plural voice in order to identify with his community and urge them to look at the matter in a particular light. This dialogue, as we see, is one in which a struggle around collective trauma emerges, as was the case in the first two chapters.

---

25. See the varying opinions in these regards in, e.g., Heim 1999, 160–61; Lee 2002, 168; Boase 2006, 223; Mandolfo 2007, 71–72.

As his speech opens in 3:1–20, the man sounds rather like the voice of Zion in the previous two poems, insofar as he focuses on the pain he has suffered, although unlike Zion, who talks about the suffering of her children, young women and men, and elders, the man refers here only to his own pain (O'Connor 2002, 44; Kalmonofsky 2007, 61–62), for he does not represent an entire city, as she does. But he does continue Zion's and the narrator's focus in Lam 2 on the suffering imposed by YHWH. So closely is his speech of 3:1–20 bound to that which has immediately preceded that he does not even mention that YHWH is the cause of his suffering, and YHWH's name does not appear until 3:18. Nonetheless, in 3:1–17 he uses twenty-four verbs with an unnamed subject who has imposed suffering on him, and since his speech follows Lam 2's focus on the suffering YHWH has inflicted, it is not a mystery as to who this subject is. The man's description of what God has done to him shares some of the language and imagery of the preceding two poems: God "bent his arrow" against him, precisely the language the narrator used to refer to God's attack on Zion (see 3:12; 2:4); God has made the man שׁמם, "desolate," just what Zion has said YHWH has done to her (3:11; 1:13; and see 1:4, 16); he is beset by עני, "affliction," just like Zion (3:1, 19; 1:3), the result of God's עברה, "fury" (3:1; 2:2). Largely, however, the man's description of his suffering remains in the realm of the metaphorical in 3:1–20: God has brought him into darkness (3:2), made him like "the eternal dead" (3:6), set a wall around him (3:7), and so on. The return of a progression from *aleph* in yet another alphabetic acrostic serves merely as a way for suffering to repeat in another example of the uncanny return of trauma in Lamentations. If one could envision any sort of closure and relief to suffering at the end of Lam 2, it would be in Zion's appeal to YHWH, the appeal urged by the narrator in 2:18–19. Even if neither narrator nor Zion articulates the possibility of YHWH ending the suffering there, perhaps readers might understand that to be the implicit goal of the address to the deity, yet that has not happened, for in the opening of Lam 3 readers encounter only a repetition of the suffering to which they have already been exposed.

Yet the construction of collective trauma and the possibility of closure in a fetishistic narrative is not absent in Lam 3 any more than it is in Lam 1. The man's speech of 3:18–20 effectively functions as a bridge to 3:21–41, the next main section of the poem, one in which the man offers a hopeful response to the suffering at YHWH's hands of which he has just spoken. In 3:19 he calls on YHWH to "remember" his affliction, as Zion had called on God to see hers, but since YHWH provides no answers in Lamentations the man must give himself hope, and in 3:21–41 he provides a general statement about divine mercy, human sin, and the justness of divine punishment. The man is clearly looking forward to an end to his suffering and uses the root יחל, "to hope, wait," in 3:21, 24, and 26, having said initially in 3:18 that his תוחלת, "hope," had already perished. He now has hope, he says in 3:21, and it is specifically hope in YHWH's future action to end suffering (3:24, 26). One must wait (קוה) for God to act, he says in 3:25, and he reuses the same root in 3:29 when he says, with somewhat less confidence, "perhaps there is hope [תקוה]." The man is waiting in hope for YHWH's steadfast love, mercy, and salvation to manifest themselves (3:22, 26, 32);[26] he admits in 3:32 that YHWH has caused the suffering and uses the verb יגה to express this, as the narrator and Zion did in 1:5 and 12, but the man goes on to say in the next verse that God does not willingly impose the sort of affliction that defines his suffering.[27] Nevertheless, God apparently must respond to the sort of evil the man describes in 3:34–36, where prisoners are crushed, justice is not done, and lawsuits are perverted, a corporate evil of which he apparently sees Judah and Jerusalem as guilty, since he goes on in 3:40–41 to urge "us" to search out (נחפשה) and examine (נחקרה) "our" ways and repent (נשובה).

The verbs חפש and חקר appear in wisdom literature, and aspects of the man's abstract reflection about sin, divine punishment, and the appropriate human response to it in 3:21–41 in general are reminiscent of the wisdom tradition (Brandscheidt 1983, 222–23; Berges 2002, 182–83; Boase 2008b, 463–64; Thomas 2011, 215; Bier 2014, 161–62). This reflection seems to have little to do with his own pain and appears dependent on existing cultural narratives and traditions, so that it remains on a general

---

26. The man opens 3:22 by saying חסדי יהוה כי לא תמנו, "the steadfast love of YHWH we have not exhausted," but the Targums and Peshitta reflect Hebrew תמו, so they read "the steadfast love of YHWH is not exhausted." For a discussion of the text-critical issue, see Greer 2009.

27. In 3:33 the man says לא ענה מלבו, and the use of לב here points to divine choice. God does not choose to cause affliction, but apparently must do so in response to the sin the man is about to discuss. We see לב(ב) used in the same way when, for example, Samuel tells Saul that בקש יהוה לו איש כלבבו, "YHWH has sought out for himself a man of his own choosing" (1 Sam 13:14) who will replace Saul as king. The author of one of the Neo-Babylonian chronicles uses a similar expression when referring to Nebuchadnezzar replacing one unnamed king in Jerusalem with another, who is described simply as *šarra ša libbišu*, "a king of his own choosing" (*ABC* chronicle 5, reverse, 13).

and abstract level, providing no evidence for the hope of which he speaks (Mintz 1982, 11–12). The man "interacts with authoritative discourses from earlier traditions," as Miriam Bier puts it (2014, 154); he adopts a collective trauma, to put this another way, or creates one based on preexisting cultural notions, some of which are based in wisdom traditions. The collective trauma he articulates is roughly the same as that which the narrator and Zion create in Lam 1, in which the people have sinned and the suffering they experience is the result of divine punishment. In 3:21–41, however, the man advances further than they to fetishistic closure, since, he claims, "the lord will not reject forever; although he caused suffering he will have mercy according to his steadfast love" (3:31–32). The conclusion of his collective trauma, in short, is one where the suffering YHWH has reluctantly caused comes to an end through divine mercy and steadfast love and a response to repentance, an end for which even Zion did not dare hope in Lam 1–2.

One might see in Lam 3 a reversal of the pattern in the dialogue of the first two poems, where collective trauma was created but then abandoned in a cascade of references to Zion's ongoing suffering, for here in Lam 3 the focus on pain is followed by explanation for it and hope for an end to suffering. We could see 3:42–43 as a continuation of the collective trauma the man has created, for, following the references to the corporate sin described in 3:34–36 and the plea for corporate repentance in 3:40–41, the man goes on to say that "we have transgressed [פשענו] and rebelled [מרינו]," reflecting language used for Zion's guilt in 1:5, 18, and 22. However, the man immediately adds that "you have not forgiven," and in 3:42–51 he returns to a focus on the suffering to which he was fixated in 3:1–20, an apparent rejection of the collective trauma he accepted or created in 3:21–41. He maintained earlier that the community should repent and depend on divine mercy; now he says that not only has God not forgiven but that the divine presence is so thoroughly cut off from the community that "no prayer can pass through" (3:44). YHWH is hidden בענן, "in the cloud," an assertion that reflects not just language used in describing divine anger directed against Zion in 2:1, where the narrator says in reference to God that יעיב, "he beclouded himself," but language associated with the divine warrior, who is fighting against the man and his community in Lam 3, just as the narrator describes YHWH as fighting against Zion in Lam 2 on the repetitive "day" of Zion's suffering (see Dobbs-Allsopp 2004, 35–39). Repentance is clearly of no use if YHWH is not willing to hear or accept it, and it would appear that God, hidden in the clouds, does not see, despite the man's earlier suggestion to the contrary in 3:36.

In Lam 3:42–51 the man has effectively returned to his earlier and hope-less position in 3:1–20, where he says that "I call and cry out; he shuts out my prayer" (3:8).[28] Other specific examples of the language of Zion's suffering in Lam 2 appear once again in the man's speech: YHWH has "killed" (see 3:43; 2:21) and not spared (3:43; 2:2, 17, 21); the man's eyes pour out water, just as the narrator's do (3:48; 2:11; and see 1:16, where Zion's eyes do likewise), out of a concern for "the destruction of the daughter of my people" (3:48 and 2:11). His eyes flow without ceasing (ולא תדמה) in 3:49, as if he is following the advice the narrator gives to Zion in 2:18 to let her tears flow rather than to be silent (אל־תדם), so the man contradicts his own conclusions in 3:26 and 28 that those receiving divine punishment should remain silent. Whatever hope the man was able to conjure through his abstract reflections on God, sin, punishment, and mercy has vanished here. God does not hear the corporate repentance he urged, and the man's voice now sounds like those of the narrator and Zion in Lam 2, as it did in the opening of Lam 3. Zion's suffering, or at least his part of it, repeats yet again. Commentators sometimes understand this poem, and particularly 3:21–41, as the theological center or key to Lamentations as a whole (see Linafelt 2000, 2–13), describing it as a "rebuttal" to the speech of Lam 2 (Middlemas 2006a, 515) or as the "theological answer" to the suffering portrayed elsewhere in the book (Johnson 1985, 65–67), pointing to the restoration that the man expects to follow the just punishment for Judah's sin (Labahn 2002) and providing readers with a "call to conversion" (Krašovec 1992, 232). The fact is, however, that having created or accepted collective trauma in 3:21–41, the man then withdraws his acceptance, and the hope he derived from other traditions and expressed in impersonal terms simply cannot seem to withstand or explain his trauma.

Yet in 3:52–66, the final part of the poem, the man turns once more to hope. In reference to some event from his past, he talks about "my enemies" who hunted him חנם, "for no reason" (3:52). At that time of great distress, when he was near death (3:53–54), God responded to his call for help and saved him (3:55–58). Unlike the case of 3:21–41, the man refers

---

28. So the case may be, then, that the metaphors of encircling and blockage in 3:1–9 refer to the failure of communication with the divine (Eidevall 2005).

here not to abstract musings about God and sin but to his own experience, citing God's act of redemption in his own past (note "you redeemed my life" in 3:58) in order to provide a sense of hope for the future. In the concluding eight verses of the poem, then, when the man asks that God thwart his enemies, since they are apparently still rising against him, he might seem to have some basis of confidence that God will fulfill his request and punish their evil and destroy them, since he has experienced divine salvation from them in the past.

In short, Lam 3:52–66 would appear to return readers to the man's more hopeful position of 3:21–41, for in the poem's conclusion God acts on behalf of the innocent, rightly judging their case and punishing those who would rise against them and pervert justice "for no reason." But even though the end of the poem sounds rather like Zion's plea in 1:21–22 that God punish her enemies' evil, this is not really a return of the same collective trauma of Lam 1 or even that of 3:21–41. In the collective trauma the man created earlier in the chapter neither he nor his community was innocent, just as Zion was not in the narrative explanation that appears in Lam 1, whereas in the event in his past that he describes in 3:52–58 he clearly was; his enemies hunted him "for no reason" and he needed a divine ally to save him (O'Connor 2002, 56), just as 3:59–66 says he needs one now. Yet in 3:35–36 the man states that his community is guilty of the same perversion of justice to which his enemies now subject him: both 3:35–36 and 3:59–60 refer to a lack of מִשְׁפָּט, "justice"; both use the root עות to refer to the perversion of justice; and both point to a failure to properly adjudicate the רִיב, "lawsuit." It is difficult to see, then, how the past divine intervention to which he refers in 3:52–58 provides any hope for the current situation of the sinful community he describes in 3:21–41. If the man and his community are now guilty, as he says they are in 3:34–36, 40–42, then reference to a past case of God redeeming the innocent does not apply to their situation, since the man has explained that God does not willingly make people suffer but does so only in response to their sin. Thus, as a guilty people, the community should expect God to treat them differently than the man was treated by God in the past when he was innocent. The man asks God in 3:59–66 to intervene in at least his personal experience of ongoing suffering, but this occurs in the larger context of 3:53–66, in which the man claims innocence of any wrongdoing, a different situation from the communal guilt of 3:21–41. Perhaps the man assumes that the corporate repentance he urges in 3:40–42 would signal to God the people's shift from guilt to innocence, yet the man says in 3:44 that no prayer can reach God, so God is not able to recognize any such change on their part. But if the man and his community are currently innocent, as the man says he was in the case of the past event of divine salvation, then God is not just, for he is the one who is responsible for their ongoing suffering, so God is like the enemy in the man's past who hunted him "for no reason," not the just judge the man describes in 3:21–41.[29]

In Lam 3 as in Lam 1–2, collective trauma is proposed and then rejected, although the rejection is of a somewhat different sort in chapter 3. This chapter suggests that, in the end, there is no collective trauma and no totalizing history of the sixth-century disaster with a comforting fetishistic narrative that is adequate. In the collective trauma of 3:21–41, God is said to respond in mercy to corporate repentance, only for the man to immediately claim in 3:42–44 that God does not do this. In the poem's conclusion the man says that, in his experience, God saves the innocent, but this hardly applies in a case where he has said his community is guilty. The two different closures to trauma that the man attempts to impose in 3:21–41 and 3:52–66 cannot both be accepted by the same logical person as applying to the same situation, and the fact that the same individual articulates both narratives points to a swirling and unresolved debate among competing and contradictory histories. In one hopeful story the man tells to explain suffering completely, it is the result of sin and can be brought to an end with repentance, although he immediately rejects this hopeful conclusion. In another, it is the result of a perversion of justice inflicted on the sinless that he expects God to address. This alphabetic acrostic does not function to move readers from suffering at *aleph* to resolution and closure at *tav*, for we see only the basis of an endless debate: perhaps Zion is not guilty, and God will intervene to correct an injustice; or perhaps Zion is guilty, but repentance will end the suffering; or perhaps Zion is guilty but God will not listen to repentance; or perhaps Zion is not guilty and God is the enemy, responsible for

---

29. It makes no difference whether we decide to read the string of verbs in the perfect in 3:55–61 as precative perfects, which would mean that the man refers not to a past event in which YHWH saved him but to salvation that he expects God to enact, for even in that case he would be asking God to regard him as if he were innocent when he has earlier admitted that he and his community are guilty. For bibliographic information on works that discuss the possibility of the use of the precative perfect in these verses, see the references in the notes in Gladson 2010, 325–27, and see particularly Provan 1991b; Parry 2010, 120–24.

the perversion of justice from which the community now suffers. There is no attempt in the poem to decide among the competing explanations and possible narratives that could be constructed from them, so the creation of a single authoritative collective trauma seems like an irresolvable problem. What remains constant, however, is the man's suffering, which is in part a repetition of Zion's from the first two poems, so yet again the alphabetic acrostic points to uncanny repetition rather than completion and resolution.[30]

5.4. The Failure of Collective Trauma in Lamentations 4–5

We encounter two speakers in Lam 4–5, and the voice that speaks in 4:1–16, 21–22 sounds like the narrator of Lam 1–2, discussing Zion's suffering and linking it to her sin as the narrator does in Lam 1, even addressing her directly like the narrator in Lam 2. The speaker of 4:17–20, whose speech also includes all of Lam 5, is a collective voice that seems to emerge from and speak for the community of sufferers. While Lam 4 is clearly marked off as a separate poem from the following chapter by its alphabetic acrostic, the continuation of the communal voice of 4:17–20 in Lam 5 suggests that it is reasonable to examine these final two poems as a group, one in which a community of speakers fails to adopt the more hopeful attempts of a narrator to impose a collective trauma. It is always possible that the communal voice is a union of the narrator and Zion (so Kang and Ventner 2009, 260), whose speech and viewpoints merged toward the end of Lam 1–2, yet the communal voice's failure in 4:17–20 to adopt the perspective and language of the narrator of 4:1–16, and the narrator's overwhelming surety of a positive future for Zion in 4:21–22, which seems to ignore or at least react strongly against the speech of the community in 4:17–20, makes it unlikely that we should see the narrator as part of that plural voice. The latter is assumedly that of the survivors in Zion (e.g., Provan 1991a, 33–34; Lee 2002, 182; Boase 2006, 232), who do not articulate a collective trauma but instead focus on suffering, a suffering that they see as leading to their extinction. The narrator, on the other hand, concludes Lam 4 on an aggressively positive note and points in 4:21–22 not only to

---

30. Because Lam 3 does not provide some sort of clear resolution and hope, it has much in common with the other poems of the book, and there is no need to see it (or parts of it) as the product of a different and later author, contra, e.g., Brandscheidt 1983, 344–52; Westermann 1994b, 72; Middlemas 2006b, 183–84.

the resolution Zion desired in 1:21–22, the punishment of her enemies, but also to an end to the community's suffering. The final acrostic *tav* of the book has been reached there, since Lam 5 is not structured by an alphabetic acrostic, yet this hopeful and fetishistic ending in Lam 4 simply collapses beneath the weight of the inchoate pain that the suffering community repeats yet again in the final poem. In that chapter, where there is no movement from *aleph* to *tav*, from beginning to end, there is only suffering that has no end. Collective trauma in Lamentations is unable to silence the many who speak of a suffering that repetitively returns, and it is unable to repress the testimonies of psychological trauma of Jerusalem's survivors, who cannot provide or accept a single narrative to explain their suffering and create closure for it.

The narrator of Lam 4 repeats themes and language from the speech of the narrator of the first two poems as he addresses the community.[31] The narrator here, as in Lam 1, focuses to some degree on the reversal of Zion's fortunes (Reimer 2002, 552–53), just as is the case in 1:1–9, and says here that those who were wealthy now have absolutely nothing (4:5) and that the once-beautiful Nazirites are now unrecognizable as "their skin has shriveled on their bones" (4:7–8). The narrator here is as fixated to the horror of starvation in Zion as the first narrator, and the opening of his speech in this poem focuses on the terrible change in the way the children of Zion are now treated: once valued as "gold" and "jewels,"[32] they are now seen as worth no more than clay pots, abandoned by their mothers and without food or even any water to drink (4:1–4; see also 2:11–12, 19); as jewels that no one values, they are being poured out (תשתפכנה) into the streets (4:1), just what the narrator of Lam 1–2 says in 2:12 is happening to the lives of the starving children (Mitchell 2008, 79–80). The starvation is so terrible, our narrator says here, that even "compassionate women" eat their own children (4:10), repeating the horrifying observation that either the narrator or Zion makes in 2:20.

Just like the narrator in Lam 1, the narrator here does provide some sort of link between Zion's sin and the portrayals of suffering that domi-

---

31. For links between Lam 4 and Lam 1–2, see also Lanahan 1974, 47–48; Johnson 1985, 68–70.

32. For the understanding of בני־קדש as "jewels," cognate with Akkadian *qudāšu*, see Emerton 1967. We could understand the phrase to refer to the stones of the temple, now destroyed (so Renkema 1998, 494–96). Adele Berlin (2002, 104–5) sees the phrase as referring to "gems" that were part of the temple apparatus.

nate the chapter, claiming in 4:6 that Zion's עָוֹן is greater than the חַטָּאת of Sodom, a city destroyed in a moment. We can understand עָוֹן to refer to "guilt, iniquity" or to the punishment that results from it, as is the case for חַטָּאת (Mitchell 2008, 80; Boase 2008b, 462); since the verse discusses Sodom's destruction, it is likely best to see the words as referring to punishment for sin, and in that case Zion's suffering is comparable to Sodom's. The word עָוֹן appears four times in this chapter and חַטָּאת three times (4:6, 13, 22), so it seems that the narrator has some interest in the link between the community's suffering and its earlier sin, and that the narrator is also interested in describing the conclusion to that suffering/punishment, since that is the focus of the narrator's speech at the end of the chapter, where he says Zion's עָוֹן has come to an end. The narrator, in short, appears to be creating a history of collective trauma here, with a beginning (sin), middle (current suffering as punishment), and end (closure in the suffering's termination). Unlike Lam 1, although like 3:34–36, the narrator provides readers with some specificity as to what led to the community's punishment, referring to the "sin" and "iniquity" of the city's prophets and priests, who spilled so much blood that the streets ran full of it and defiled the blind, who were unable to see and avoid it (4:13–15a). This is not, admittedly, among the sins the man enumerated in Lam 3, but the narrator suggests a causal link between these sins and the exile to which he immediately refers in 4:15b, and in 4:16a he seems to continue his reference to the exile when he says that YHWH "apportioned" or "divided" the people (חִלְּקָם), assumedly among the nations. He goes on in 4:16b to provide even more explanation for Zion's suffering: "They did not honor the priests, they did not show favor to the elders." So while references to suffering certainly dominate the narrator's speech, as was also true in Lam 1, this does not stop him from searching for and trying to create some sort of explanation within the framework of collective trauma that, as a narrative and a history, has beginning, middle, and end.

However, we encounter in Lam 4 the same problem in establishing collective trauma that we do in Lam 3. If the priests were as evil as 4:13–15a claims, why would it have been wrong for the people to refuse to honor them, the sin to which the narrator refers in 4:16b? In 2:20, either the narrator or Zion attempts to appeal to divine pity by referring to the killing of the priests and prophets, but if both are responsible for shedding blood, which is what the narrator of Lam 4 claims, why would such a plea move YHWH to act? Like 4:16b, 2:20 assumes that the priests should be honored and that failure to do so is a crime, but 4:13–15 says something different.

The start to a totalizing narrative in 4:13–16 that might explain the community's suffering is really the start to two conflicting explanations, one that blames the priests and prophets for sin and another that blames the people for failing to honor the priests, even though they have just been identified as arch-sinners. It is not that there is no logical way to deal with this problem but that the narrator does not even attempt to engage the issue. So the irresolvability of collective trauma in Lam 3, which also provides two contradictory narratives, reappears in microcosm here, and like that poem Lam 4 suggests that there is no true collective trauma and no true explanation, merely an endless debate with no solution.

The survivors of Zion now begin to speak in 4:17, and they may choose precisely this moment to interrupt the narrator because of his failure to provide clear explanation. They turn away from his foray into collective trauma and in 4:17–20 focus instead on their fate at the hands of the enemy, saying, "Our end drew near, our days were fulfilled, for our end had come" (4:18). The enemy hunts them in the רחוב, "squares," of their towns, the places where the narrator of Lam 1–2 had described Zion's children as starving to death (2:11, 12), and lies in wait for them in the wilderness, having chased them outside the cities (4:19). There is now no place where life is possible for them; their king has been taken by the enemy, and they depended on his protection to survive among the nations (4:20).[33] The narrator, however, ignores this testimony to their suffering or, more charitably, decides to aggressively refute it, and concludes the poem in 4:21–22 by promising precisely the closure that Zion had requested in 1:21–22: Zion's enemies—or at least Edom—will be punished. The narrator goes even further here, saying as well that Zion's עון, "punishment (for iniquity)," is complete (תם)[34] and that her exile will not continue, while God will instead punish Edom's עון and חטאת. Zion's end most emphatically has not come, says the narrator, speaking over

---

33. Specifically, the community says that they depended on צלו, "his shade, shadow," to live among the nations. Both Akkadian and Egyptian literature use the expression "the shade/shadow of the king" to refer to the protection and benefits provided by the monarch (Oppenheimer 1947). Passages such as Hos 14:8 [7] and Pss 91:1; 121:5 use צל to refer to divine protection, but Lam 4:20 is the only biblical passage to use the noun in reference to the king. God, as far as the survivors of Zion are concerned here, does not provide protection.

34. Because it is followed by a verb in the imperfect (יוסיף), תם could be understood as having future sense: "Your punishment will be completed" (Middlemas 2006b, 205–6).

and rewriting the survivors' testimony of 4:18, and instead it is her punishment that is coming to a conclusion. So if readers decide to overlook the unresolved and contradictory explanations for suffering the narrator offers in 4:13–16, then they might reach the end of this acrostic feeling as if they have found some sort of closure and resolution, where an end to mourning is in sight.

Of course, given the contradiction of 4:13–16, readers might be skeptical of the closure the narrator offers upon interrupting the community's own witness to their pain; the community certainly seems skeptical, for Lamentations closes in its final chapter with their voice alone, and they virtually ignore all aspects of the narrator's speech of Lam 4 except his focus on their pain. They most certainly do not repeat the narrator's hope-filled conclusion of 4:21–22, and Lam 5, the only poem of the book not structured by an alphabetic acrostic, does not suggest that there is any movement from *aleph* to *tav*, from one point to another, whether from suffering to explanation or from despair to hope. The community's suffering repeats yet again in this chapter, and there is no *tav*, no resolution or closure to it, simply the uncanny appearance of trauma that readers encounter elsewhere in Lamentations: their possessions have been taken (see 5:2; 1:10); they do not have enough food and struggle to survive the famine (5:4, 6, 9, 10; 1:11, 19; 2:11–12, 19–20; 4:3–4, 10); women in Zion are raped (5:11; 1:8, 10);[35] the people have become forced labor (5:5, 13; 1:1); and princes have been removed from power and the elders are not honored (5:12; 1:6; 2:2; 4:16). So Zion's sovereignty is gone (5:8, 16; 1:1), her heart is—or here, the hearts of the survivors are—"faint" (5:17; 1:22), and Zion is "desolate" (5:18; 1:4, 13, 16; 3:11; 4:5). There is no change in Zion's condition from that described in the previous poems and no alleviation of their suffering, despite the narrator's promise in 4:21–22 to the contrary, only the same pain over and over. Without the alphabetic acrostic, there is not even some sort of formal indication that the suffering has come to an end, merely the potential for it to go on forever.

The entirety of the communal speech in this final poem is directed to God, and the community asks YHWH in 5:1 to "remember," "give heed," and "see" the suffering they describe throughout the chapter. In 5:21, the book's penultimate verse, they ask God to הֲשִׁיבֵנוּ, "return/restore us," and חַדֵּשׁ יָמֵינוּ, "renew our days." This concluding plea might appear

---

35. The use of עָנָה in the *piel* in 5:11 indicates rape (Helberg 2004).

to point to an end to the community's suffering, yet they seem to have little confidence that God will actually act to restore and renew. YHWH, they say in 5:19–20, is enthroned לְעוֹלָם, "forever," but has "forgotten us" and "abandoned us forever [אֹרֶךְ יָמִים]."[36] Moreover, following the request for YHWH's intervention in 5:21, the book's final verse largely seems to despair of divine action that will end their suffering. The meaning of כִּי אִם, the words that open 5:22 and connect it to 5:21, is not precisely clear. Of the most likely possibilities for the basic sense of the phrase, one is to read it in the sense of "even if, although," and in that case, we would translate the verse as the continuation of the request in 5:21 that God restore them, "although you have utterly rejected us, are extremely angry with us" (Gordis 1974). We could translate כִּי אִם as "if," and in that case Lamentations trails off in ellipsis without any resolution to the plea of 5:21: "If you have utterly rejected us, are extremely angry with us…" (Linafelt 2001). One other possibility would be to translate it as "but rather, instead": "instead [of restoring us, as we have just asked,] you have utterly rejected us, are extremely angry with us" (Williamson 2008, 73–74). Translating the phrase as "unless, except" does not appear to be a viable option here, since the phrase has this sense only when it follows some sort of negative statement or oath, which the clause to which כִּי אִם is attached acts to limit (Linafelt 2001, 340–42). So even the most hopeful of these translations admits of only the possibility that God might act positively for the survivors, but given the verse's emphasis on divine rejection and anger, the community even in this understanding does not seem confident that this will happen. Of course, readers might also have understood the conclusion as the survivors' denial that God would act, or have seen their speech as simply trailing away into the absence of ellipsis, as if the survivors are unable to contemplate a life forever defined by a continual repetition of the trauma that readers have witnessed in every chapter of the book. The conclusion of Lamentations offers no finality and no clear hope that the community's suffering, which has repeated over and over in the poems, will ever come to an end. There is no fetishistic narrative that concludes

---

36. The phrase אֹרֶךְ יָמִים need not necessarily be translated as "forever," although that is its sense in a passage such as Ps 93:5. More frequently it refers to a long life (e.g., Josh 12:12; Prov 3:2, 16), and Berlin translates the phrase here as "our whole life long" (2002, 115). The survivors may well be saying here that they think God has abandoned the community for at least as long as its current members will live, which means that, as far as they are concerned, God has abandoned them forever.

with mourning being overcome and no totalizing collective trauma in which everything is explained.

The survivors' speech in this final poem may be without collective trauma, but it is not without aspects of it. "Our ancestors have sinned," the community says in 5:7; "we bear their punishment [עונתיהם]." Yet the survivors also say in 5:16 that "we have sinned," and these somewhat conflicting explanations are the sum of their attempts to locate a perpetrator for their current suffering in the poem. There is just enough conflicting information here to remind readers of the fuller yet also contradictory attempts to locate collective trauma in Lam 3 and 4, contradictions that make the enterprise seem a futile and unending one to which there is no resolution. Attempts to create totalizing narratives that firmly establish guilt and that might point to a future when suffering will be overcome, thus minimizing the psychological trauma the survivors continue to undergo, always fail in Lamentations. The narrator begins to create one in Lam 1 that Zion then accepts and develops, and yet, as their speech continues in Lam 2, this narrative collapses beneath the weight of Zion's suffering that repeats in the chapter and for which YHWH bears sole responsibility. The man's attempt in Lam 3 to give himself hope in the depths of his suffering through collective trauma fails when he himself is unable to accept it; when he goes on to create yet another explanation, it is one that contradicts his earlier creation of collective trauma. This problem appears again in Lam 4, as we demonstrate in our recent discussions, and the community nods at the impossibility of establishing a true history of trauma in Lam 5.

What we do not find in Lamentations, however, is the repression and silencing of testimony to trauma. We see an attempt to do so in 4:21–22 as the narrator ignores the community's testimony to their suffering, but what dominates these poems is pain, and often fairly similar expressions of it. The survivors' suffering repeats over and over, even as attempts to blame them for it and to point to some sort of end to it fail in the face of the continual repetition of psychological trauma. Lamentations bears witness to the desire to create totalizing narratives to explain great suffering, even to the need of trauma victims to accept such narratives, but these are never able to silence the psychological trauma of sufferers that uncannily repeats throughout the work. The intrusion of trauma sometimes silences history, in fact, as is the case in Lam 2, where the explanation of Lam 1 is forgotten, and where even the narrator is overwhelmed by Zion's suffering. At other points such as Lam 3, we could refer to trauma as confounding or problematizing explanations to the point that the creation of a history seems a futile endeavor, a never-ending process of an inability to settle on true causation that would explain the past. In the end, there is no narrative in Lamentations that does not collapse beneath the weight of the suffering of trauma's uncanny return or stand in contradiction with another explanation, there is no salvation, and there is no divine response. History and collective trauma fail in Lamentations as trauma rejects them.

6

Trauma and History: Intertextual Readings

As we discuss in chapter 4, psychological trauma cannot be narrativized, so it cannot form part of the histories that create the past, since narrative is a necessary part of history. In chapter 5 we learn that Lamentations witnesses to a struggle between collective and psychological trauma, and in the end the history of collective trauma fails to repress and overwrite the psychological trauma there, no matter how much some of the speakers may want to accept the explanations on offer. The failure of attempts to formulate a single collective trauma and have it accepted in Lamentations is an important warning lest we believe that a history that claims that victims were to blame for their suffering in national disaster, a not-uncommon assertion of Judean and Israelite literature, not to mention the position of the Deuteronomist, would always be accepted by trauma victims. Some sixth-century BCE Judean trauma survivors surely did publicly assent to the validity of narratives such as the one composed by the Deuteronomist, as it might have seemed like the sort of thing one should believe, and this would have bound them more closely to the groups who created collective traumas, since such assent validated the group's worldview and morality. Yet it would not have helped them assimilate and make sense of their trauma—it would not have provided them with therapy in the modern understanding of the term, in other words—since the kind of therapy necessary for trauma victims to know their trauma involves the use of their own voices to speak their not-stories to empathetic listeners (see Laub 1992a; 1992b), something quite different from a passive acceptance of a narrative that explains what the trauma was and how they are to make sense of it. Bessel van der Kolk writes that social support is absolutely necessary if victims hope to assimilate their trauma into the self, and he defines this as reciprocity, "being truly heard and seen by the people around us" (2014, 79). This is possible when one has an empathetic listener who suspends disbelief in hearing a story even the victim cannot fully believe (Hartman 1995, 541–42), but that is a different process altogether from a social imposition of narrative. Creating explanatory narratives in line with existing worldviews, or perhaps as reformations of them, may have helped maintain social cohesion among different groups of Judeans after the sixth-century disaster by drawing their public assent to a particular worldview and its concomitant moral system, as chapter 4 explores, but we should not confuse that with the process of therapy for victims that would allow them to assimilate and know their trauma. The trauma victims of Lamentations, as chapter 5 shows, cannot accept the attempts to provide them with meaning, even though some of them try to do so, and in the end narratives of collective trauma fail to repress their testimonies of a suffering that uncannily repeats.

But having considered how trauma victims respond to and ultimately reject historical explanations of suffering in Lamentations, it is worthwhile pursuing the question as to why historians, ancient or modern, would bother to concern themselves with the not-story and antinarrative that is psychological trauma. Historians, after all, are in the business of narrative, a basic point of the theoretical discussion of chapter 2 and our reading of Kings and the Deuteronomistic History in chapter 3, and it seems natural that they might simply ignore the testimonies of trauma victims that challenge and reject their narratives, as chapter 4 demonstrates. One could even conceive of Lamentations as the result of empathetic historians engaging in dialogue with trauma victims—or, in Lam 3, a historian in dialogue with himself—and becoming overwhelmed by the continual repetition of traumatic suffering, thus failing to produce a history at all. For historians to continue to be historians, it might make more sense for them to ignore the horrifying repetition of trauma, so that they themselves do not suffer from secondary trauma (see LaCapra 2001, 41–42) and can get on with the job of creating the past in believable ways, explaining what really happened. For the trauma victims there was no sixth-century disaster and no history of it, only the trauma that resulted from its nonexperience, something that for them was an eternally recurring now rather than a past. This is why Dori Laub (1992b, 83), a Holocaust survivor and psychologist who has worked with survivors, can say that the Holocaust "had no witness to its truth" and so "essentially did not exist." Laub does not mean that the events that traumatized his patients did not occur but that this trauma "was beyond the limits of human ability (and willingness) to grasp, to transmit, or to imagine," even the ability of the victims themselves (1992b, 84).

This sort of description of trauma, as chapter 4 explains, is neither hyperbole nor metaphorical but literally true. For a history to be a history, readers must believe it to be true, but trauma victims cannot believe their trauma and so cannot make truth claims about it. Lamentations provides us with some sense as to how some traumatized survivors of the sixth-century disaster interacted with explanatory narratives such as the one Dtr offered them: some may have supported the claims of a particular history, only for that support to disappear behind the uncanny return of trauma, as we see in Lam 1–2; some may have seen explanation as an unending problem with no certain resolution, something that could never seem as certain as the repetition of trauma, as evident in Lam 3; some may have had both experiences simultaneously, as we see in Lam 4–5. In the end, for the sixth-century trauma survivors there was no past or historical reality of siege, slaughter, rape, and famine, no narrative that could create these events and give them meaning, that is, that could ever be as real as the trauma of these events that they could only relive in the present. If some decided to register their public assent to a narrative such as Dtr's, then it came at the cost of repressing their trauma. Perhaps for readers of biblical literature, as well as for modern scholars involved in the study of the history of ancient Israel and Judah, it is enough to know that psychological trauma and history are antithetical, since there is no way to reconcile or integrate them.

But in this conclusion I suggest that readers of the Bible who are interested in Judean responses to the sixth-century disaster should not confine themselves to explanations of it provided by Dtr or other writings such as Jeremiah, Second Isaiah, or Ezekiel, which create it through explanatory narrative, but should read such narratives intertextually with Lamentations. Moreover, I suggest as well that modern historians studying the disaster should create room for the nonhistory and nonnarrative of Lamentations alongside their work. To begin with the first point, that readers analyzing Judean responses to the disaster should read Lamentations intertextually with works such as Dtr, if our understanding of those responses were based only on explanations such as the one in Dtr, then we would fail to consider the trauma that resulted from the event and thus act as if there were no victims of trauma at all, erasing them from our consideration of exilic-period Judah. An intertextual reading of Dtr and Lamentations certainly creates a jarring contrast, for Lamentations is as opposed to narrative explanation as the Deuteronomist seems certain that truth resides in it, and Lamentations is as fixated to trauma as Dtr's fetishistic narrative is resolute in repressing it. This sort of intertextual reading means that the conclusions the Deuteronomist draws are questioned and its narrative disrupted, and that the closure to which it points readers in places such as Deut 30 and the final verses of 2 Kgs 25 is thrown into doubt. For the voices of Lamentations, trauma is an eternally repetitive reality, and there is no foreseeable end to it, whether or not the exiles return or a Davidide is restored as client ruler under Babylonian supervision. Since aspects of the Deuteronomistic worldview, such as the notion that national disasters are punishment for sin, were important parts of a widespread Judean worldview, Lamentations shows us trauma questioning and disrupting this belief system, precisely the system the Deuteronomist needs in order to construct the past that he or she does. This sort of intertextual reading does not incorporate trauma into history, because that is not possible, but it does avoid the repression of trauma, and it places Dtr's totalizing creation of the past on trial, even if this is a trial that renders no verdict. The verdicts of history, like the verdicts of law, may be passed only in narrative, as we discuss in chapter 3, but that is what trauma rejects.

While a reading of Lamentations alone gives us some sense as to how trauma victims might have reacted against attempts to impose historical meaning on the disaster, an intertextual reading of the book with Dtr might lead us to look for ambiguity and gaps in the writing's narrative that subvert and deconstruct it and throw its explanation into doubt. A reading of Dtr that prioritizes a search for ambiguity and gaps is one that challenges its totalizing explanation, and it potentially reflects how some trauma survivors might have encountered the attempt to create the past of the sixth-century disaster in Dtr, for it is the kind of reading that most closely approximates trauma victims' failure to incorporate the disaster as narrative and history. For example, it would seem that the first important lesson readers learn in Dtr is that God can punish disobedience of divine command with death outside the land, precisely the fate faced by its exilic readers. In Deut 1, Moses relates the story of the spy mission into Canaan undertaken by his listeners' parents after God brought them out of Egypt; the failure of the exodus generation to obey God's command to enter the land upon hearing the spies' dire report of the inhabitants' size and power leads God to condemn them to death outside it. Caleb, however, is an exception to this punishment, because his trust in YHWH's power to defeat the Canaanites does not waver, so he "completely followed YHWH" (Deut 1:36; Josh 14:8–9). Yet Moses, who exhibits the same trust in God's power that Caleb does and who urges Israel's obedience to the command to enter the land (Deut 1:29–31) is condemned to die in the Transjordan along with them (1:37; 3:27; 4:21–22). Perhaps he is punished for allowing the spying mission to proceed in the first place, but the Deuteronomist does not say this, and if that is the case then it seems odd that Joshua is not punished for authorizing an identical mission in Josh 2. The lack of explanation and ambiguity in divine rationale for punishment right at the beginning of the work subtly deconstructs a narrative that seems to have been created to explain why some Israelites must die outside the land—as, perhaps, the exiles might—so Dtr's historical project is thrown into trial at its outset (so Janzen 2012b, 79–81).

So the intertextual reading of Dtr and Lamentations may help us look at Dtr in a quite different light from that of our focus in chapter 3 on its creation of history in response to a particular worldview. By juxtaposing Lamentations' rejection of history with Dtr's creation of it, we can get a sense as to how some sixth-century trauma victims might have read and rejected its narrative. Is there truly divine justice that determines who dies outside the land, as Dtr seems to claim, or not? Or, to take another example, rather as the man of Lam 3 both affirms and rejects the efficacy of repentance that might lead to salvation, a trauma victim reading Dtr may arrive at precisely the same failure to determine the salvific value of repentance upon comparing the stories of 1 Sam 7, where national repentance in cultic reform concludes with divine protection of Israel from a Philistine invasion, and 2 Kgs 21–25, where Josiah's repentance in national cultic reform makes no difference as to how God treats the people, who are condemned to suffer the ravages of the Babylonian annihilation of Judah because of Manasseh's sin that Josiah undoes.[1] There are many other important subversions of the narrative in similar absences of explanation and ambiguity at other important junctures in the work,[2] and if Dtr is not Lamentations' obvious struggle with and rejection of explanatory history,

---

1. The concluding evaluation of Josiah says that "he repented [שב] to YHWH with all his heart, self, and might, according to all of the law of Moses" (2 Kgs 23:25), the summary of the religious reforms he enacted in Judah and the north. In 1 Sam 7:3, Samuel refers to Israel repenting (שבים) to YHWH as they undertake the kind of religious reform Josiah carries out in 2 Kgs 23. For a larger exploration of the ambiguity in stories in Dtr that seem to reflect or anticipate the work's conclusion, see Janzen 2012b, 228–36.

2. This is, in fact, the conclusion of the investigation of trauma's eruptions into Dtr's narrative in Janzen 2012b.

the failure of trauma victims in Lamentations to accept history can lead us to see how they might reject important specifics of the Deuteronomist's explanation of it once we read the works intertextually, leading, as far as the survivors are concerned, to an unraveling of Dtr's explanatory power and its creation of a true past.

A fuller understanding of Judean responses to the sixth-century disaster demands more than just comparing responses from different works; it requires juxtaposing them with Lamentations's nonresponse, and, if we want a sense as to how trauma victims might read the sort of narrative we see in Dtr—how they respond to a response, as it were—it even requires an analysis that searches such explanations for their gaps and ambiguities and allows us to read them as trauma victims might have. There were ancient Judeans who would have understood Dtr to be fiction because they simply did not share important aspects of the Deuteronomist's worldview, but for trauma victims no belief system is adequate to explain their trauma, and all narratives that attempt to provide them with explanations will be found lacking. There is no historical explanation for Nazism and the Holocaust, writes Holocaust survivor Jean Améry, nothing that can make sense of why it happened when it did: "Let no young political scientist, no matter how clever he is, tell me his conceptually untenable stories. To someone who was an eyewitness they appear utterly stupid" (1980, vii–viii). For Primo Levi as well, explanations and understanding of the great geopolitical events that resulted in his trauma are impossible because the orders and actions that made up the Holocaust are "non-human…, really counter-human," and thus beyond the reach of any human's knowledge or worldview (1996, 394–96). Any stories created to explain can thus be read by trauma victims rather as we were just reading Dtr, as a failure of explanation.

As I suggest above, even modern historians who create the sixth-century disaster for their readers would benefit from making Lamentations one of their important sources as they do so. Historians can, of course, put themselves in the position of the Deuteronomist, who repressed the trauma and forgot its victims, but even if it is impossible to remember the trauma, it is possible for historians not to forget it and its victims (see Edkins 2003, 15), for they can treat the victims with empathy and avoid sidelining them as an "abstract element" in a work of history that largely ignores the vast suffering of traumatic events, erases the existence of trauma from its narrative, and so erases trauma victims from its creation of the past. Not repressing or forgetting the trauma means to acknowledge that in history writings we are creating pasts based on our worldviews and that our histories are not "a replica of the real," as chapter 2 explores, but have created the reality of the past as far as we can know it. Trauma victims may publicly assent to histories and collective traumas but will not be able to believe them as true explanations of trauma, which is the case of the voices in Lamentations, and a juxtaposition of the story of history with the not-story of trauma reveals that history is, in fact, a narrative humans have created, the truth claims of which can be rejected. If we admit that trauma always escapes what we can create about the past then we have to admit that, while we can form true pictures of the past, they can never provide the complete truth of traumatic events, so we also have to admit that the pasts we create are not totalizing ones, at least when it comes to trauma. In the same way, when we read a work such as Dtr intertextually with Lamentations, we do not come to know the survivors' trauma, which is not possible, but we at least do not forget the trauma and its victims and erase their memory, as the Deuteronomist has done in an expression of a worldview that, like any other worldview, presents a particular kind of authority and leadership as desirable.

Some historians who deal with massive traumatic events refer to Freud's concept of "working through." As chapter 2 explains, histories might be said to mimic Freud's concept of transference, in which the relationship between child and parent is repeated in the relationship between analysand and analyst, as historians repeat their worldviews and their worldviews' concerns and interests in the pasts they create. When Freud discusses the concept of working through, he refers to the dialogue between analyst and analysand that allows patients to remember what they have repressed and so what has only existed in the unconscious, thereby escaping their compulsions to repeat their symptoms (1958, 145–56). Transference, writes Freud, is a necessary part of this process, and it is not possible—or at least not intellectually honest—for historians to create pasts that do not conform to their worldviews, but the larger point of this analogy with a psychoanalytical concept is that historians should not be content with histories that repress trauma as they reproduce their present concerns. We repress and forget trauma when we ignore trauma testimonies, the sort of material with which Lamentations provides us. Historians cannot entirely identify with trauma victims, writes Dominick LaCapra (2001, 37–42)—and were that to happen we might end up with something closer to Lamentations than to historiography—but they can write with empathy, creating an "empathetic unsettlement" that allows them to be attentive to the voices of the traumatized.

The placement of their texts and testimonies beside the histories of the sixth-century disaster that we write means being willing to allow the trauma to unsettle or question any totalizing conclusions we draw (LaCapra 2003, 223), as Lamentations would challenge those in Dtr in an intertextual reading. Working through, writes Saul Friedländer, involves avoiding simplistic conclusions in regard to suffering and closure, for it involves the interrogation of belief systems that deny the reality of trauma, and he suggests that the creation of histories that discuss massive traumatic events be accompanied by commentaries rooted in trauma testimonies that question the works' conclusions and that prevent the reality of trauma victims from being reduced to factual data (1993, 131–33). Histories that can allow the voices of trauma victims to accompany them in some way are still histories, but if their authors truly take empathetic unsettlement seriously, then they are also admitting that they cannot explain everything of importance in regard to traumatic events, because the space they have created for the voices of the traumatized will repetitively challenge and deny explanation. In empathetic unsettlement we acknowledge that our histories are not "a replica of the real," for when we refuse to repress trauma we reveal that we have created a past through a worldview that trauma places on trial in its refusal to accept explanation, just as Lamentations makes historical explanation seem a problem with no solution.

Empathetic unsettlement thus ensures the traumatic reality of victims is not repressed or forgotten, even if it inevitably questions and unsettles the truths a history presents. Primo Levi writes of those who in Auschwitz were called the *Musselmänner*, those who quickly died or were killed because they lacked the emotional or physical resources to survive for long. This group, he writes, "made up the backbone of the camp, an anonymous mass, continually renewed and always identical, of non-men who march and labour in silence.... One hesitates to call them living: one hesitates to call their death death" (Levi 1996, 96). Giorgio Agamben develops Levi's understanding of the *Musselmänner* as the "complete witnesses" to the Holocaust who were unable to bear witness; once they were murdered, they had completely experienced the Nazi project of the creation of *Musselmänner* out of human beings, and the creation of ashes out of *Musselmänner* (2002, 84–85). Yet, writes Agamben, we cannot forget them and so deny the reality of their humanity as the Nazis did, even if bearing witness for them is an impossibility (33–34, 63–64). We cannot bear witness for the victims of trauma in the sixth-century disaster either, but we can at least ensure that they are not forgotten for our present and that they are more than an abstract element in the stories we write about the past. Reading Lamentations intertextually with the sources, biblical and otherwise, that we use for our histories is one way to do this, and intertextual readings with trauma testimonies from other disasters might be another, but the point is that there are traumatic aspects of the sixth-century disaster that we cannot know or account for in our histories of the events, something Lamentations makes clear. We cannot incorporate this trauma into the stories we tell of the pasts we create, but to ignore it is to claim that all that readers could ever know about the disaster is contained in our narratives, and this closes off any reality of the trauma at all, despite the fact that this unknowable force and not historical or theological explanation was the central reality for many survivors (see Hilberg 1988, 25; Friedländer 1992).

If we as readers wish not to forget trauma victims when we search biblical material for Judean responses to the sixth-century disaster, we cannot focus solely on collective trauma, for collective trauma is simply a kind of history. Writings such as Jeremiah and Ezekiel, not to mention Dtr, may well have used historical explanation and collective trauma to restore a sense of social solidarity to a Judean community fragmented by the disaster,[3] but to acknowledge this without ever acknowledging the traumatic nonexistence of this disaster as a past event in Lamentations is to repress psychological trauma and reimpose in our own readings the totalizing and fetishistic histories of various Judean groups. Second Isaiah, for example, seems to have known Lamentations and repressed its trauma: while both the narrator and Zion say in Lam 1 that Zion has no מנחם, "comforter," Second Isaiah says that God comforts Zion (Isa 40:1; 51:3, 19; 52:9; 54:11; see Willey 1997, 130–32); the groaning (אנחה) and mourning (יגון) the narrator describes in Zion "have fled away," according to Isa 51:11 (Willey 1997, 156–57);[4] in Isa 51:22–23, Second Isaiah agrees with the narrator of Lam 4, who ignores the speech of the suffering community and who says in 4:21–22 that the כוס, "cup," of Zion's suffering will pass to her enemies (Willey 1997, 162–63); and the list of specific examples that reflect Second Isaiah's repression of Lamentations's testimony to

---

3. For such claims in the context of Jeremiah see, e.g., O'Connor 2011, 35–45, 93–102; Garber 2011, 318–20; Frechette 2015, 28–30; Stulman 2016. For Ezekiel, see, e.g., Yee 2003, 121–22; Kelle 2009; Bowen 2010, 91–93; Carr 2014, 76–77.

4. This reads with the MT (יגון) and the versions, although 1QIsaᵃ and 4QIsaᶜ read the verb as preceded by ו and thus as continuing the future sense of the preceding ישׁיגון and so as meaning "will flee away." See *IBHS* §32.2.1d.

trauma goes on and on. If we can only see explanations for suffering in the kind of narrative that Dtr offers, or only the fetishistic end of trauma and mourning on which Second Isaiah insists, and if we ourselves create histories that exclude the victims of trauma and their failure of experience of the disaster, then in our own interpretation and historiography we repress Lamentations's testimony to that trauma and to the nonexistence of the sixth-century disaster, which was not an historical event for trauma survivors who had not experienced it but who repetitively relived it in their present.

The fetishistic narrative, however, is an easy and convenient trap to fall into, because it allows us to avoid the pain of trauma, either as victims or as those who might listen to their testimonies. Narrative moves forward, and if we encounter pain in it we can always hope that its forward progress will eventually deliver us from the suffering by the time we arrive at its conclusion. The poetry of Second Isaiah does not avoid the fetishistic trap, although the poetry of Lamentations does. Even talented artists dealing with situations of trauma cannot represent it, but they can reflect its nonnarrative and nonhistorical nature as, for example, Toni Morrison does in *Beloved*, a novel that centers on the character of Sethe, a woman who escapes slavery in the American South but who cannot escape its traumatic effects. There are hints early on in the novel of what eventually becomes horrifically explicit: Sethe has killed her infant daughter rather than deliver her to men who would take her into slavery. Sethe cannot leave this or any of her other traumas behind as a past, however, for the daughter, now called Beloved, returns as a ghost. The trauma of Sethe's past literally returns to haunt her, and as the past establishes itself in the novel as something that can overpower the present, circular metaphors, imagery, and structure dominate, returning readers again and again not only to Sethe's trauma but to those of other black characters, and even to that of Africans aboard a slave ship on the Middle Passage (Page 1992). The novel refers to historical events such as the American Civil War (Morrison 1987, 28) and the Emancipation Proclamation (52), but it does so only in passing, and such things seem to have little effect on the characters' lives, unlike their trauma. The final pages of the novel repetitively state that "it was not a story to pass on," and the trauma to which the figure of Beloved alludes is not something that is or could become a history (274–75). Yet the novel's last word is "Beloved," the final sign of a ghost and a trauma that points beyond the novel's end to a not-story that continues (see Davis 1998).

The story of *Beloved* wrestles with trauma's repetitive and uncanny nature, refusing to repress it with a straightforwardly linear narrative, in a way that might remind us of Lamentations and its problematizing and refusal of history. We can see the same suspicion of history in the work of Caribbean writer Derek Walcott, notes Steed Davidson (2017, 161–63), who forcefully rejected the European understanding of history as progress that, in its construction of the past, manages to erase the trauma of the transatlantic slave trade and colonialism. As scholars construct their own pasts of ancient Israel and Judah, or deal with those constructed by biblical authors, we would do well to consider Walter Benjamin's image of the angel of history, who sees not a chain of events related to each other through explanatory narrative but "one single catastrophe which keeps piling wreckage on wreckage and hurls it in front of his feet." This, says Benjamin, is the angel's view as he faces the past, but he is being blown backward into the future by a storm we call progress (1968, 257–58). Benjamin was concerned that historians empathized with the world's victors, and he was aware that even the dead are not safe from historians who act solely as tools for rulers and their worldviews (255–56).

Such historians see not the chaos and meaninglessness of the catastrophe and the wreckage of trauma, as the angel of history does, but progress, a positive and explainable development. What the Davidides might have viewed as progress, a past disaster neatly explained that had already led to their reenthronement in Babylon, at least according to 2 Kgs 25:27–30, and that would be followed by a return to the land where Judah/Israel would forever live securely, at least according to Deut 30:1–10, was experienced differently by the trauma victims in the ruins of Judah. For them, "groaning" and "mourning" were present realities that gave no indication of fleeing away, only of repeating as they were uncannily returned to the trauma of the disaster that they did not fully experience and so could not explain. Benjamin urges historians to "brush against the grain" (1968, 257), something that might make room for victims and their testimonies to trauma next to the pasts we create, even though those histories cannot comprehend the trauma.

Shoshana Felman describes something like this happening during the trial of Adolph Eichmann in Jerusalem in 1961, at which many Holocaust survivors provided testimony. As chapter 2 notes, legal trials, like histories, assemble evidence into narratives so that they can claim that all that can be known and that is necessary to be known to pass a verdict has been accounted for, and while Hannah Arendt believed that Eichmann's actions

Appendix
The Date and Unity of the Deuteronomistic History

Chapter 3 refers to Dtr as including virtually all of the material in Deuteronomy through Kings and as produced by an author from the Judean community in Babylonia in the mid-sixth century BCE. This is hardly an undisputed understanding of the history of composition of Deuteronomy and the Former Prophets, so this appendix provides a short discussion as to why we can see Deuteronomy through Kings as a single work written to explain the exile. When discussing the formation of the Pentateuch, Joel Baden argues that no one would have turned to source criticism to explain its composition had they not encountered contradictory plot points and that variations in language, style, genre, themes, and theology are not, in and of themselves, enough to postulate the existence of different authors and redactors behind those books (2016, 243–51). There are obviously some similarities between source- and redactional-critical study, since both investigate the diachronic development of a given block of text, and in both scholars must be equally careful to avoid positing the existence of sources or redactional layers that are not actually there. Attempts to locate redactions in the Deuteronomistic History can overrread narrative subtlety and nuance with invented redactional strata, as J. P. Fokkelman points out, for scholars sometimes fail to consider the ways in which a text could have made sense to its readers in the form we now find it (1983, 417–27). Absent contradictions in plot, there is likely little reason to identify different sources or redactions in the first place.

For example, Rudolf Smend's (2000) conclusion that an original exilic Deuteronomistic History underwent somewhat later exilic redaction by an editor who wanted to emphasize the importance of law in shaping Israel's past seems an odd position to maintain when all of Moses's speeches in Deuteronomy focus on the importance of this law and its commandments (Nelson 1981a, 20–21; Römer 1994, 186), while his attempt to find textual seams that indicate redactional work simply misread subtlety in the text.[1] Since he does not actually locate contradictions in the material he examines, there is little reason to posit the presence of the redactional work he describes. Walter Dietrich's attempt to add yet another exilic redaction to the one identified by Smend, one focused on prophetic work, was not something he could establish even through style or vocabulary, as he himself admits (1972, 110), and so would appear to be an unnecessary conclusion, especially when we can simply see the stories of prophets as older narratives incorporated by the Deuteronomist (e.g., Provan 1988, 24–25; Eynikel 1996, 27).

Attempts to base redactions of Dtr on subtler criteria such as evaluation formulas for the monarchs in Kings encounter similar objections. Helga Weippert's (1972) attempt to establish redactions in Kings based on such analysis not only depends on reading the evaluations out of the order in which they appear (Nelson 2005, 323–24) but misses the fact that the differences among the formulas, as minor and inconsequential as they sometimes seem to be (Halpern and Vanderhooft 1991, 203), can be read as different theological judgments created by a single author who was directing readers' attention to subtle but important differences among the kings' cultic actions. The shifts in formulas Weippert notices are indicative of one author's attempt to point out differences in behavior among the kings, not of redaction (Cortese 1975). Attempts to use royal death and burial formulas to establish redactions in Kings (Halpern and Vanderhooft 1991) might reflect nothing more than minor differences present in Dtr's source material (Na'aman 2004).

Frank Cross (1973) based his theory of redaction on what he saw as contradictory emphases on both an eternal covenant with the Davidides and the sin of Manasseh that concluded with the Davidides' removal from the throne. But conditional formulas about Davidic rule that Cross understood as insertions of a later exilic redactor to explain the exile all occur during the narrative of Solomon's reign and are actually meant to explain the Davidides' loss of control of the Northern Kingdom upon Solomon's death due to his cultic sin narrated in 1 Kgs 11, with their rule thereafter confined only to Judah, so they do not contradict the eternal covenant with David (Nelson 1981a, 99–105; McKenzie 1991, 136–45; Halpern 1996, 157–74). Moreover, while Cross understood the original edition of

---

1. See the discussion of Smend's evidence in Janzen 2013a, 28–30.

Dtr, the one emphasizing the unconditional covenant, to have been written during the time of Josiah to promote his religious reforms, that is not a conclusion that makes much sense, as Baruch Halpern (1996, 112–14) has argued, since we would expect that an author pointing to the necessity of these reforms would hold up defeat, destruction, and dethronement as real threats were the reforms not completed; a Josianic work featuring an unconditional covenant with David would be counterproductive in the scenario Cross envisioned. Once we notice that the Davidides are punished with removal from the throne during the seven-year usurpation of Athaliah in 2 Kgs 11, following the reign of two Davidides who are said to be as evil as the rulers of the house of Ahab (2 Kgs 8:16–27), we can see that the Deuteronomist believed that the Davidides could be removed from power for periods of time, as happened in the Babylonian exile, so this latter event also does not contradict the eternal covenant with David, as Cross believed (McKenzie 2000, 139–43; Janzen 2013b, 362–63).

Arguments that concern not thoroughgoing redactions of Dtr but later insertions of blocks of material run into the same sorts of problems. One claim, for example, is that Deut 16:18–18:22, or at least the law of the king in 17:14–20, is a late addition because of its polity that seems to sharply limit the power of the monarch (e.g., Lohfink 1993; Perlitt 1994; Schäfer-Lichtenberger 1995; Mayes 2000, 467–69; Knoppers 2001; Levinson 2001), but this ignores the fact that language from the law of the king is repeated in the narrative of Josiah (McKenzie 1991, 129; Sweeney 1995, 619–20). Or, the claim that the so-called Succession Narrative, or at least the story of David and Bathsheba in 2 Sam 11–12, is a later addition from a postexilic editor suspicious of royal power, a conclusion at which some arrive because of the poor light in which this material seems to paint the house of David (Van Seters 1983, 277–91; McKenzie 2010),[2] misses the point that, as chapter 3 discusses, Dtr provides readers with a picture of a king and royal house who have an unconditional covenant that is not revoked no matter how badly they treat their subjects (Janzen 2013a, 156–89).[3] The story of Bathsheba and Uriah—2 Sam 11–20 as a whole, in fact—may not portray the house of David in the best light, but it also shows that

---

2. See also Van Seters 2009, 99–120, 163–93, where Van Seters argues that a large portion of the material about David and Saul in the so-called History of David's Rise can also be dated to the Persian period since it seems antimonarchical.

3. See also Blenkinsopp 2013; Kalimi 2016 for additional arguments as to why these sections of Samuel and Kings should be considered original parts of Dtr.

the God who made an unconditional covenant with the house in 2 Sam 7 is unlikely to revoke it no matter how unsavory their behavior has been, an important pro-Davidic message to an exilic audience who might well have been suspicious or convinced that Davidic failures of some sort were responsible for the exile and that YHWH had turned against them.

This is hardly a complete discussion of arguments concerning putative redactions of Dtr, but it demonstrates, I hope, the importance of heeding Baden's and Fokkelman's warnings concerning the need to read narrative carefully and to appeal to redaction only when we encounter contradictions in the plot. While, as chapter 3 observes, the general notions of covenant, cultic fidelity, and divine punishment of the people are features broadly shared in the literature of the Hebrew Bible, there are a number of unifying aspects of the books of Deuteronomy through Kings and indications that this material was designed as a single work. While Deuteronomy shares stories in common with the Yahwistic and Elohistic sources (Baden 2009, 99–195), its opening three chapters provide a rather lengthy summary of parts of the earlier Pentateuchal narrative, something unparalleled anywhere else in those books (Römer 2003, 246–47). Such a summary would be unnecessary were we not encountering the beginning of a work composed by an author who was aware of older traditions of an Israelite past and condensing them as a prelude to his or her own story, so it is unlikely that a pre-Priestly narrative that continues through Kings begins at any point prior to these chapters (contra Schmid 2010, 139–55). Narrative links abound in Deuteronomy through Kings, as, for example, Josiah recapitulates in 2 Kgs 23 aspects of Moses's religious reform in Deut 9:21 (Friedman 1981, 5–10), enacts the instructions for the ideal king in Deut 17 (McKenzie 1991, 129; Sweeney 1995, 619–20), and mimics the blameless leadership of Joshua (Nelson 1981b; McKenzie 1991, 130; Sweeney 1995, 619–21); in all of these cases it is not simply that we find similar images and ideas but repetition of vocabulary. The work as a whole periodizes history from Israel's entrance into the land to the exile (Knoppers 2000, 132–33), but one of its most important structural aspects is a cycle of apostasy and reform that begins with the story of the idolatrous calf in Deut 9–10 and concludes with the apostasy of Manasseh and reform of Josiah in 2 Kgs 21–23, so that Josiah becomes the model king with the model reform (Hoffmann 1980, 155–67, 192–97, 205–7). Warning references concerning the worship of אלהים אחרים, "other gods," thus become a unifying leitmotif from Deuteronomy through Kings, although elsewhere in the Bible the phrase rarely appears (Römer 2003, 247–48).

Consequently, there is no need to argue that there is no overarching theme or leitmotif in Deuteronomy through Kings (e.g., Rösel 2000; Noll 2007). Nor is there any need to argue, as Ernst Würthwein does, that Judg 2:11–12:6, where Israel is constantly punished for its repetitive worship of "other gods," most particularly the gods of Canaan, is a later addition to an earlier history because of its cyclical nature, something he believes should be understood as opposed and later added to the earlier linear narrative of Kings (Würthwein 1994, 1–11; and see Westermann 1994a, 57–74). Dtr is a story of an unfaithful people who constantly sin, as chapter 3 explores, and the cycle of apostasy and reform is an essential aspect of the work and something present in Kings. Nor need we argue, as Würthwein does, that Judges and Kings are the products of two different sets of redactors because in the former the people sin and in the latter the monarchs do for, as chapter 3 also points out, Kings does not excuse the people from participation in sin.

The books of Deuteronomy through Kings are linked by prophecies in one book that are fulfilled in another (Nelson 2005, 320–22) and by speeches of main characters that hew to the same structure and themes (Noth 1981, 5–6). Stories that begin in one book continue in another, such as the conquest commanded in Deuteronomy that is carried out in Joshua (Nelson 2005, 322–23). The books are, as Martin Noth noticed, smoothly edited together (1981, 6–9), so that the story of Joshua immediately picks up where Deuteronomy ends, and the narrative of Judges begins with the period immediately following Joshua's death,[4] while the book of Samuel begins in Shiloh, where Judges concludes, and the story of the Elides and Samuel at the beginning of the book continues the story of Israel's salvation from the Philistines begun in the narrative of Samson (see Judg 13:5 and 1 Sam 4–7). Even the book of Samuel, perhaps the book with the largest amount of preexisting material adapted by the Deuteronomist,[5] is full of stories reflected in Judges and Kings, forms a necessary narrative bridge between them, and contains important passages with Deuteronomistic theology (Nelson 2013). There is no need, then, to argue that each book

---

4. In Dtr, Judg 1:1 follows on the end of Josh 23, since Josh 24 is likely a later addition meant to create and round off a Hexateuch (see Römer 2010).

5. I qualify this statement with the word *perhaps* because Hoffmann (1980, 15–21, 316–18) and Van Seters (1983, 292–321) are correct when they argue that Dtr's source material has been so thoroughly reworked and integrated that it cannot really be recovered.

underwent independent editing (contra Westermann 1994a, 49–78). At the center of Dtr's concern, as chapter 3 points out, is the people's rebellious nature, and Dtr portrays a people constantly prone to abandoning cultic fidelity in their worship of "other gods" and the consequent necessity to find proper leadership to enforce their cultic faithfulness, a leadership the work locates in the Davidides. Dtr was attached to existing pentateuchal material, and as a result of that process we see (generally) brief appearances of those sources in Deuteronomy and Joshua,[6] but outside this all of the material from Deuteronomy through Kings was combined in a single work that appears intent on explaining through a creation of a preexilic past what kind of leadership Judah should have, an explanation centered on God's decision to choose the Davidides and uphold an eternal covenant with them.

One important theme that runs from Deuteronomy through Kings is that of exile; as Thomas Römer (2003, 247–48) points out, in the Tetrateuch only Lev 26:27–33 alludes to the exile, while Deuteronomy repetitively refers to it, and it is an important aspect of Josh 23, 1 Sam 12, 1 Kgs 8, 2 Kgs 17, and 2 Kgs 21–25. Römer's observation in this regard is an important one, and in fact there is so much focus on exile, especially at the beginning and end of Dtr, that the work seems to have been composed for the Judean community in Babylonia. The last event to which Kings refers, the decision of Evil-merodach (or Amēl-marduk) to release Jehoiachin from prison and favor him with royal rations—something corroborated by

---

6. This statement might appear inconsistent with my earlier assertion that contradiction in plot alone leads us to establish the presence of sources and redaction, but the existence of the Priestly writing and other sources is established through contradictions that appear throughout the Pentateuch. Once the existence of the sources has been so identified, we can recognize appearances of them elsewhere where we encounter their vocabulary, emphases, and writing styles.

To take just two examples of these brief insertions of pentateuchal material in Dtr, Deut 32:48–52 contains Priestly vocabulary and relates information in conformity with Priestly writing but that contradicts information from Dtr (e.g., Tigay 1996, 518), while the story of the Gideonites in Josh 9 includes material from Priestly writing as well (e.g., Sutherland 1992). There are also longer pieces of material in Joshua that are not Deuteronomistic; 22:9–34, for example, is widely recognized as pervaded by Priestly vocabulary. Some have also argued that the work of a later redactor creating a Hexateuch also appears to be visible in Joshua (e.g., Römer 2010; Albertz 2015). Baruch Schwartz (2016, 785–86 n. 11), however, maintains that a Deuteronomistic editor incorporated parts of a Priestly narrative that originally included a conquest account.

Neo-Babylonian evidence (*ANET*, 308)—suggests that Dtr may well have been written during Evil-merodach's short reign (562–560 BCE), as Serge Frolov (2007) has argued, roughly fifty years after Josiah's death and about sixty years after his reforms according to the chronology of Kings. According to 2 Kgs 25:27–30, Jehoiachin received a כסא, "throne," more exalted than that given to the other client rulers in Babylonia, and Frolov points out that it echoes the language of 2 Sam 7:16, where God promises that David's "throne" will be established forever. The story of Athaliah in 2 Kgs 11, as we have mentioned, tells readers that the Davidides' removal from power as punishment is something that is temporary, given the eternal covenant with the house, but, argues Frolov, no Judean writer would base what the author believed to be the beginning of the end of the exile on a decision made by Evil-merodach were the writer not writing while he was still in power. His reign was short, and once he was overthrown by Neriglissar, a later writer might well have no confidence that the usurper would continue his predecessor's policies. Possibly, Neriglissar did not withdraw the privileges Evil-merodach had bestowed on Jehoiachin and other client rulers kept in Babylon, even if he had no plans to return them to power as client rulers, and that the Deuteronomist was writing sometime after Neriglissar had become king, still convinced that a return to Davidic rule in Judah as clients to Babylon was imminent.

Bibliography

Agamben, Giorgio. 2002. *Remnants of Auschwitz: The Witness and the Archive*. Translated by Daniel Heller-Roazen. New York: Zone Books.

Albertz, Rainer. 2004. *Israel in Exile: The History and Literature of the Sixth Century B.C.E.* Translated by David Green. SBLStBL 3. Leiden: Brill.

———. 2005. "Why a Reform like Josiah's Must Have Happened." Pages 27–46 in *Good Kings and Bad Kings*. Edited by Lester L. Grabbe. JSOTSup 393. ESHM 5. London: T&T Clark.

———. 2015. "The Formative Impact of the Hexateuch Redaction: An Interim Result." Pages 53–74 in *The Post-Priestly Pentateuch: New Perspectives on Its Redactional Developments and Theological Profiles*. Edited by Federico Giuntoli and Konrad Schmid. FAT 101. Tübingen: Mohr Siebeck.

Albrektson, Bertil. 1963. *Studies in the Text and Theology of the Book of Lamentations with a Critical Edition of the Peshitta Text*. STL 21. Lund: Gleerup.

Alexander, Jeffrey C. 2012. *Trauma: A Social Theory*. Cambridge: Polity.

Alexander, Jeffrey C., and Elizabeth Butler Breese. 2011. "Introduction: On Social Suffering and Its Cultural Construction." Pages xi–xxxv in *Narrating Trauma: On the Impact of Collective Suffering*. Edited by Ron Eyerman, Jeffrey C. Alexander, and Elizabeth Butler Breese. YCSS. Boulder, CO: Paradigm.

Alphen, Ernst van. 1999. "Symptoms of Discursivity: Experience, Memory, and Trauma." Pages 24–38 in *Acts of Knowing: Cultural Recall in the Present*. Edited by Mieke Bal, Jonathan Crewe, and Leo Spitzer. Hanover, NH: University Press of New England.

Améry, Jean. 1980. *At the Mind's Limits: Contemplations by a Survivor on Auschwitz and Its Realities*. Translated by Sidney Rosenfeld and Stella P. Rosenfeld. Bloomington: Indiana University Press.

Amit, Yairah. 1996. *The Book of Judges: The Art of Editing*. Translated by Jonathan Chipman. BibInt 38. Leiden: Brill.

———. 1999. *History and Ideology: Introduction to Historiography in the Hebrew Bible.* Translated by Yael Lotan. Sheffield: Sheffield Academic.

Ankersmit, Frank R. 1998. "Historiography and Postmodernism." Pages 175–92 in *History and Theory: Contemporary Readings.* Edited by Brian Fay, Philip Pomper, and Richard T. Vann. Malden, MA: Blackwell.

———. 2001. *Historical Representation.* CMP. Stanford, CA: Stanford University Press.

———. 2012. *Meaning, Truth, and Reference in Historical Representation.* Ithaca, NY: Cornell University Press.

Arendt, Hannah. 1994. *Eichmann in Jerusalem: A Report on the Banality of Evil.* Rev. ed. New York: Penguin Books.

Arneth, Martin. 2001. "Die antiassyrische Reform Josias von Juda: Überlegungen zur Komposition und Intention von 2 Reg 23,4–15." *ZABR* 7:189–216.

Assis, Elie. 2005. *Self-Interest or Communal Interest: An Ideology of Leadership in the Gideon, Abimelech and Jephthah Narratives (Judg 6–12).* VTSup 106. Leiden: Brill.

———. 2007. "The Alphabetic Acrostic in the Book of Lamentations." *CBQ* 69:710–24.

Auerhahn, Nanette C., and Dori Laub. 1998. "Intergenerational Memory of the Holocaust." Pages 21–41 in *International Handbook of Multigenerational Legacies of Trauma.* Edited by Yael Danieli. New York: Plenum.

Baden, Joel S. 2009. *J, E, and the Redaction of the Pentateuch.* FAT 68. Tübingen: Mohr Siebeck.

———. 2016. "Why Is the Pentateuch Unreadable? Or, Why Are We Doing This Anyway?" Pages 243–51 in *The Formation of the Pentateuch: Bridging the Academic Cultures of Europe, Israel, and North America.* Edited by Jan C. Gertz et al. FAT 111. Tübingen: Mohr Siebeck.

Bahat, Dan. 1993. "Jerusalem." Pages 698–800 in vol. 3 of *NEAEHL.*

Balakian, Peter. 1996. *Dyer's Thistle.* Pittsburgh: Carnegie Mellon University Press.

Bann, Stephen. 1990. "Analyzing the Discourse of History." Pages 33–63 in *The Inventions of History: Essays on the Representation of the Past.* Manchester: Manchester University Press.

Barr, James. 2000. *History and Ideology in the Old Testament: Biblical Studies at the End of a Millennium.* Oxford: Oxford University Press.

Barrick, W. Boyd. 2002. *The King and the Cemeteries: Toward a New Understanding of Josiah's Reforms*. VTSup 88. Leiden: Brill.

Barstad, Hans M. 2008. *History and the Hebrew Bible: Studies in Ancient Israel and Ancient Near Eastern Historiography*. FAT 61. Tübingen: Mohr Siebeck.

Barthes, Roland. 1981. "The Discourse of History." Translated by Stephen Bann. *ComCrit* 3:7–20.

Barton, John. 2007. *The Nature of Biblical Criticism*. Louisville: Westminster John Knox.

Baudrillard, Jean. 1994. *The Illusion of the End*. Translated by Chris Turner. Cambridge: Polity.

Becker, Eve-Marie, Jan Dochhorn, and Else Kragelund Holt, eds. 2014. *Trauma and Traumatization in Individual and Collective Dimensions: Insights from Biblical Studies and Beyond*. SANt 2. Göttingen: Vandenhoeck & Ruprecht.

Ben Zvi, Ehud. 2006. "A Sense of Proportion: An Aspect of the Chronicler." Pages 160–73 in *History, Literature and Theology in the Book of Chronicles*. BibleWorld. London: Equinox.

———. 2008. "Imagining Josiah's Book and the Implications of Imagining It in Early Persian Yehud." Pages 193–212 in *Berührungspunkte: Studien zur Sozial- und Religionsgeschichte Israels und seiner Umwelt*. Edited by Ingo Kottsieper, Rüdiger Schmitt, and Jakob Wöhrle. AOAT 350. Münster: Ugarit-Verlag.

Benjamin, Walter. 1968. "Theses on the Philosophy of History." Pages 253–64 in *Illuminations*. Edited by Hannah Arendt. Translated by Harry Zohn. New York: Schocken Books.

Bennett, Tony. 1990. *Outside Literature*. London: Routledge.

Bergant, Dianne. 2013. "'ēkāh: A Gasp of Desperation." *Int* 67:144–54.

Berges, Ulrich. 2000. "'Ich bin der Mann, der Elend sah' (Klgl 3,1): Zionstheologie als Weg der Krise." *BZ* 44:1–20.

———. 2002. *Klagelieder*. HThKAT. Freiburg: Herder.

———. 2004. "Kann Zion männlich sein? Klgl 3 als 'Literarisches Drama' und 'Nachexilische Problemdichtung.'" Pages 235–46 in *Basel und Bibel: Collected Communications to the XVIIth Congress of the International Organization for the Study of the Old Testament, Basel 2001*. Edited by Matthias Augustin and Hermann Michael Niemann. BEATAJ 51. Frankfurt am Main: Lang.

Bergler, Siegfried. 1977. "Threni v – Nur ein alphabetisierendes Lied? Versuch einer Deutung." *VT* 27:304–20.

Berlin, Adele. 2002. *Lamentations: A Commentary*. OTL. Louisville: Westminster John Knox.

Bier, Miriam J. 2014. "'We Have Sinned and Rebelled; You Have Not Forgiven': The Dialogic Interaction between Authoritative and Internally Persuasive Discourse in Lamentations 3." *BibInt* 22:146–67.

———. 2015. *"Perhaps There Is Hope": Reading Lamentations as a Polyphony of Pain, Penitence, and Protest*. LHBOTS 603. London: Bloomsbury.

Blenkinsopp, Joseph. 2013. "Another Contribution to the Succession Narrative Debate (2 Samuel 11–20; 1 Kings 1–2)." *JSOT* 38:35–58.

Block, Daniel I. 2000. *The Gods of the Nations: Studies in Ancient Near Eastern National Theology*. 2nd ed. Grand Rapids: Baker Academic.

Boase, Elizabeth. 2006. *The Fulfillment of Doom? The Dialogic Interaction between the Book of Lamentations and the Pre-Exilic/Early Exilic Prophetic Literature*. LHBOTS 437. New York: Continuum.

———. 2008a. "The Characterisation of God in Lamentations." *ABR* 56:32–44.

———. 2008b. "Constructing Meaning in the Face of Suffering: Theodicy in Lamentations." *VT* 58:449–68.

———. 2016. "Fragmented Voices: Collective Identity and Traumatization in Lamentations." Pages 49–66 in *Bible through the Lens of Trauma*. Edited by Christopher G. Frechette and Elizabeth Boase. SemeiaSt 86. Atlanta: SBL Press.

Boss, Pauline. 2006. *Loss, Trauma, and Resilience: Therapeutic Work with Ambiguous Loss*. New York: Norton.

Bosworth, David A. 2013. "Daughter Zion and Weeping in Lamentations 1–2." *JSOT* 38:217–37.

Bowen, Nancy R. 2010. *Ezekiel*. AOTC. Nashville: Abingdon.

Brandscheidt, Renate. 1983. *Gotteszorn und Menschenleid: Die Gerichtsklage des leidenden Gerechten in Klgl 3*. TThSt 41. Trier: Paulinus-Verlag.

Brettler, Marc Zvi. 1989. "The Book of Judges: Literature as Politics." *JBL* 108:395–414.

———. 1991. "The Structure of 1 Kings 1–11." *JSOT* 49:87–97.

———. 1995. *The Creation of History in Ancient Israel*. London: Routledge.

———. 1999. "Predestination in Deuteronomy 30.1–10." Pages 171–88 in *Those Elusive Deuteronomists: The Phenomenon of Pan-Deuteronomism*. Edited by Linda S. Schearing and Steven L. McKenzie. JSOTSup 268. Sheffield: Sheffield Academic.

Briere, John. 2004. *Psychological Assessment of Adult Posttraumatic States: Phenomenology, Diagnosis, and Measurement.* 2nd ed. Washington: American Psychological Association.

Brown, Laura. 1995. "Not outside the Range: One Feminist Perspective on Psychic Trauma." Pages 100–112 in *Trauma: Explorations in Memory.* Edited by Cathy Caruth. Baltimore: Johns Hopkins University Press.

Campbell, Antony F. 2010. "2 Samuel 21–24: The Enigma Factor." Pages 347–58 in *For and against David: Story and History in the Books of Samuel.* Edited by A. Graeme Auld and Erik Eynikel. BETL 232. Leuven: Peeters.

Carr, David. 1991. *Time, Narrative, and History.* SPEP. Bloomington: Indiana University Press.

Carr, David M. 2011. "Reading into the Gap: Refractions of Trauma in Israelite Prophecy." Pages 295–308 in *Interpreting Exile: Displacement and Deportation in Biblical and Modern Contexts.* Edited by Brad E. Kelle, Frank Ritchel Ames, and Jacob L. Wright. AIL 9. Atlanta: Society of Biblical Literature.

———. 2014. *Holy Resilience: The Bible's Traumatic Origins.* New Haven: Yale University Press.

Carroll, Robert P. 1997. "Madonna of Silences: Clio and the Bible." Pages 84–103 in *Can a "History of Israel" Be Written?* Edited by Lester L. Grabbe. JSOTSup 245. ESHM 1. Sheffield: Sheffield Academic.

Carter, Charles E. 2003. "Ideology and Archaeology in the Neo-Babylonian Period: Excavating Text and Tell." Pages 301–22 in *Judah and the Judeans in the Neo-Babylonian Period.* Edited by Oded Lipschits and Joseph Blenkinsopp. Winona Lake, IN: Eisenbrauns.

Caruth, Cathy. 1995a. "Introduction." Pages 3–12 in *Trauma: Explorations in Memory.* Edited by Cathy Caruth. Baltimore: Johns Hopkins University Press.

———. 1995b. "Introduction." Pages 151–57 in *Trauma: Explorations in Memory.* Edited by Cathy Caruth. Baltimore: Johns Hopkins University Press.

———. 1996. *Unclaimed Experience: Trauma, Narrative, and History.* Baltimore: Johns Hopkins University Press.

Ceresko, Anthony R. 2001. "The Identity of 'the Blind and the Lame' (*ʿiwwēr ûpissēaḥ*) in 2 Samuel 5:8b." *CBQ* 63:23–30.

Certeau, Michel de. 1986. "History: Science and Fiction." Pages 199–221 in *Heterologies: Discourse on the Other.* Translated by Brian Massumi. THL 17. Minneapolis: University of Minnesota Press.

Cogan, Morton. 1974. *Imperialism and Religion: Assyria, Judah and Israel in the Eighth Century B.C.E.* SBLMS 19. Missoula, MT: Scholars Press.

Coggins, Richard. 1999. "What Does 'Deuteronomistic' Mean?" Pages 22–35 in *Those Elusive Deuteronomists: The Phenomenon of Pan-Deuteronomism.* Edited by Linda S. Schearing and Steven L. McKenzie. JSOTSup 268. Sheffield: Sheffield Academic.

Collins, John J. 2005. *The Bible after Babel: Historical Criticism in a Postmodern Age.* Grand Rapids: Eerdmans.

Connerton, Paul. 1989. *How Societies Remember.* TSS. Cambridge: Cambridge University Press.

Conway, Mary L. 2012. "Daughter Zion: Metaphor and Dialogue in the Book of Lamentations." Pages 101–26 in *Daughter Zion: Her Portrait, Her Response.* Edited by Mark J. Boda, Carol J. Dempsey, and LeAnn Snow Flesher. AIL 13. Atlanta: Society of Biblical Literature.

Cortese, Enzo. 1975. "Lo schema deuteronomistico per i re di Giuda e d'Israele." *Bib* 56:37–52.

Cousins, Mark. 1987. "The Practice of Historical Investigation." Pages 126–36 in *Post-structuralism and the Question of History.* Edited by Derek Attridge, Geoff Bennington, and Robert Young. Cambridge: Cambridge University Press.

Cross, Frank Moore. 1973. "The Themes of the Book of Kings and the Structure of the Deuteronomistic History." Pages 274–89 in *Canaanite Myth and Hebrew Epic: Essays in the History of the Religion of Israel.* Cambridge: Harvard University Press.

———. 2000. "4QLam." Pages 229–37 in *Qumran Cave 4 XI: Psalms to Chronicles.* Edited by Emanuel Tov. DJD 16. Oxford: Clarendon.

Crouch, Carly L. 2014. *Israel and the Assyrians: Deuteronomy, the Succession Treaty of Esarhaddon, and the Nature of Subversion.* ANEM 8. Atlanta: SBL Press.

Danto, Arthur C. 1965. *Analytical Philosophy of History.* Cambridge: Cambridge University Press.

Davidson, Steed. 2017. "Postcolonializing the Bible with a Little Help from Derek Walcott." Pages 156–81 in *Present and Future of Biblical Studies: Celebrating 25 Years of Brill's "Biblical Interpretation."* Edited by Tat-siong Benny Liew. BibInt 161. Leiden: Brill.

Davies, Philip R. 2008. *Memories of Ancient Israel: An Introduction to Biblical History—Ancient and Modern.* Louisville: Westminster John Knox.

———. 2010. "The Deuteronomistic History and 'Double Redaction.'" Pages 51–59 in *Raising Up a Faithful Priest: Essays in Honor of Richard*

D. Nelson. Edited by K. L. Noll and Brooks Schramm. Winona Lake, IN: Eisenbrauns.

———. 2014. *Rethinking Biblical Scholarship: Changing Perspectives 4*. CIS. Durham, NC: Acumen.

Davis, Kimberly Chabot. 1998. "'Postmodern Blackness': Toni Morrison's *Beloved* and the End of History." *Twentieth Century Literature* 44:242–60.

Delbo, Charlotte. 1995. *Auschwitz and After*. Translated by Rosette C. Lamont. New Haven: Yale University Press.

Dever, William G. 2001. *What Did the Biblical Writers Know and When Did They Know It? What Archaeology Can Tell Us about the Reality of Ancient Israel*. Grand Rapids: Eerdmans.

———. 2012. *The Lives of Ordinary People in Ancient Israel: Where Archaeology and the Bible Intersect*. Grand Rapids: Eerdmans.

Dietrich, Walter. 1972. *Prophetie und Geschichte: Eine redaktionsgeschichtliche Untersuchung zum deuteronomistischen Geschichtswerk*. FRLANT 108. Göttingen: Vandenhoeck & Ruprecht.

Dobbs-Allsopp, F. W. 1993. *Weep, O Daughter Zion: A Study of the City-Lament Genre in the Hebrew Bible*. BibOr 44. Rome: Editrice Pontificio Istituto Biblico.

———. 1995. "The Syntagma of *bat* Followed by a Geographical Name in the Hebrew Bible: A Reconsideration of Its Meaning and Grammar." *CBQ* 57:451–70.

———. 1998. "Linguistic Evidence for the Dating of Lamentations." *JANES* 26:1–36.

———. 2004. "R(az/ais)ing Zion in Lamentations 2." Pages 21–68 in *David and Zion: Biblical Studies in Honor of J. J. M. Roberts*. Edited by Bernard F. Batto and Kathryn L. Roberts. Winona Lake, IN: Eisenbrauns.

Dobbs-Allsopp, F. W., and Tod Linafelt. 2001. "The Rape of Zion in Thr 1,10." *ZAW* 113:77–81.

Dumbrell, W. J. 1983. "'In Those Days There Were No Kings in Israel; Every Man Did What Was Right in His Own Eyes': The Purpose of the Book of Judges Reconsidered." *JSOT* 25:23–33.

Eaglestone, Robert. 2004. *The Holocaust and the Postmodern*. Oxford: Oxford University Press.

Edelman, Diana. 1996. "Saul ben Kish in History and Tradition." Pages 142–59 in *The Origins of the Ancient Israelite States*. Edited by Volkman Fritz and Philip R. Davies. JSOTSup 228. Sheffield: Sheffield Academic.

Edkins, Jenny. 2003. *Trauma and the Memory of Politics*. Cambridge: Cambridge University Press.

Eidevall, Göran. 2005. "Spatial Metaphors in Lamentations 3,1–9." Pages 133–37 in *Metaphor in the Hebrew Bible*. Edited by P. Van Hecke. BETL 187. Leuven: Leuven University Press.

Emerton, J. A. 1967. "The Meaning of אַבְנֵי־קֹדֶשׁ in Lamentations 4." *ZAW* 79:233–36.

Erikson, Kai. 1995. "Notes on Trauma and Community." Pages 183–99 in *Trauma: Explorations in Memory*. Edited by Cathy Caruth. Baltimore: Johns Hopkins University Press.

Eyerman, Ron. 2001. *Cultural Trauma: Slavery and the Formation of African American Identity*. CSS. Cambridge: Cambridge University Press.

Eynikel, Erik. 1996. *The Reform of King Josiah and the Composition of the Deuteronomistic History*. OtSt 33. Leiden: Brill.

Faust, Avraham. 2003. "Judah in the Sixth Century B.C.E.: A Rural Perspective." *PEQ* 135:37–53.

———. 2004. "Social and Cultural Changes in Judah during the 6th Century BCE and Their Implications for Our Understanding of the Nature of the Neo-Babylonian Period." *UF* 36:157–76.

———. 2011. "Deportation and Demography in Sixth-Century B.C.E. Judah." Pages 91–103 in *Interpreting Exile: Displacement and Deportation in Biblical and Modern Contexts*. Edited by Brad E. Kelle, Frank Ritchel Ames, and Jacob L. Wright. AIL 10. Atlanta: Society of Biblical Literature.

———. 2012a. *Judah in the Neo-Babylonian Period: The Archaeology of Destruction*. ABS 18. Atlanta: Society of Biblical Literature, 2012.

———. 2012b. "Social, Cultural and Demographic Changes in Judah during the Transition from the Iron Age to the Persian Period and the Nature of the Society during the Persian Period." Pages 106–32 in *From Judah to Judaea: Socio-economic Structures and Processes in the Persian Period*. Edited by Johannes Unsok Ro. HBM 43. Sheffield: Sheffield Phoenix.

Felman, Shoshana. 1992. "Education and Crisis, or the Vicissitudes of Teaching." Pages 1–56 in *Testimony: Crises of Witnessing in Literature, Psychoanalysis, and History*. Edited by Shoshana Felman and Dori Laub. New York: Routledge.

———. 2002. *The Judicial Unconscious: Trials and Traumas in the Twentieth Century*. Cambridge: Harvard University Press.

Feyerabend, Paul. 1975. *Against Method: Outline of an Anarchistic Theory of Knowledge*. London: NLB.

Finkelstein, Israel, and Neil Asher Silberman. 2001. *The Bible Unearthed: Archaeology's New Vision of Ancient Israel and the Origin of Its Sacred Texts*. New York: Free Press.

Fish, Stanley. 1980. *Is There a Text in This Class? The Authority of Interpretive Communities*. Cambridge: Harvard University Press.

———. 1989. *Doing What Comes Naturally: Change, Rhetoric, and the Practice of Theory in Literary and Legal Studies*. PCI. Durham, NC: Duke University Press.

Flanagan, Joseph. 2002. "The Seduction of History: Trauma, Re-Memory, and the Ethics of the Real." *Clio* 31:387–402.

Fokkelman, J. P. 1983. *Narrative Art and Poetry in the Books of Samuel: A Full Interpretation Based on Stylistic and Structural Analyses*. Vol 1. SSN 20. Assen: Van Gorcum.

Forster, E. M. 1927. *Aspects of the Novel*. San Diego: Harcourt.

Foucault, Michel. 1971. "The Discourse on Language." Translated by Rupert Swyer. Pages 215–37 in *The Archaeology of Knowledge and the Discourse on Language*. New York: Pantheon.

Frechette, Christopher G. 2014. "Destroying the Internalized Perpetrator: A Healing Function of the Violent Language against Enemies in the Psalms." Pages 71–84 in *Trauma and Traumatization in Individual and Collective Dimensions: Insights from Biblical Studies and Beyond*. Edited by Eve-Marie Becker, Jan Dochhorn, and Else Kragelund Holt. SANt 2. Göttingen: Vandenhoeck & Ruprecht.

———. 2015. "The Old Testament as Controlled Substance: How Insights from Trauma Studies Reveal Healing Capacities in Potentially Harmful Texts." *Int* 69:20–34.

———. 2016. "Daughter Babylon Raped and Bereaved (Isaiah 47): Symbolic Violence and Meaning-Making in Recovery from Trauma." Pages 67–83 in *Bible through the Lens of Trauma*. Edited by Christopher G. Frechette and Elizabeth Boase. SemeiaSt 86. Atlanta: SBL Press.

Frechette, Christopher G., and Elizabeth Boase, eds. 2016. *Bible through the Lens of Trauma*. SemeiaSt 86. Atlanta: SBL Press.

Freud, Sigmund. 1955a. *Beyond the Pleasure Principle*. Pages 7–64 in *Beyond the Pleasure Principle, Group Psychology and Other Works*. Vol. 18 of *The Standard Edition of the Complete Psychological Works of Sigmund Freud*. Edited by James Strachey. London: Hogarth.

———. 1955b. "Introduction to *Psycho-Analysis and the War Neuroses.*" Pages 207–10 in *An Infantile Neurosis and Other Works.* Vol. 17 of *The Standard Edition of the Complete Psychological Works of Sigmund Freud.* Edited by James Strachey. London: Hogarth.

———. 1955c. "The Uncanny." Pages 219–52 in *An Infantile Neurosis and Other Works.* Vol. 17 of *The Standard Edition of the Complete Psychological Works of Sigmund Freud.* Edited by James Strachey. London: Hogarth.

———. 1958. "'Remembering,' 'Repeating' and 'Working-Through' (Further Recommendations on the Technique of Psycho-Analysis II)." Pages 145–56 in *The Case of Schreber, Papers on Technique and Other Works.* Vol. 12 of *The Standard Edition of the Complete Psychological Works of Sigmund Freud.* Edited by James Strachey. London: Hogarth.

Fridman, Lea Wernick. 2000. *Words and Witness: Narrative and Aesthetic Strategies in the Representation of the Holocaust.* Albany: State University of New York Press.

Fried, Lisbeth S. 2002. "The High Places (*bāmôt*) and the Reforms of Hezekiah and Josiah: An Archaeological Investigation." *JAOS* 122:437–65.

Friedländer, Saul. 1992. "Trauma, Transference and 'Working Through' in Writing the History of the *Shoah.*" *History and Memory* 4:39–59.

———. 1993. *Memory, History, and the Extermination of the Jews of Europe.* Bloomington: Indiana University Press.

———. 1997. *Nazi Germany and the Jews.* Vol. 1. London: Weidenfeld & Nicolson.

Friedman, Richard Elliott. 1981. *The Exile and Biblical Narrative: The Formation of the Deuteronomistic and Priestly Works.* HSM 22. Chico, CA: Scholars Press.

Frolov, Serge. 2007. "Evil-Merodach and the Deuteronomist: The Sociohistorical Setting of Dtr in the Light of 2 Kgs 25,27–30." *Bib* 88:174–90.

Galil, G. 2010. "'The Secret Things Belong to the Lord Our God' (*Deut* 29:29): Retribution in the Persian Period." *Transeu* 39:91–96.

Gana, Nouri. 2014. "Trauma Ties: Chiasmus and Community in Lebanese Civil War Literature." Pages 77–90 in *The Future of Trauma Theory: Contemporary Literary and Cultural Criticism.* Edited by Gert Buelens, Sam Durrant and Robert Eaglestone. London: Routledge.

Garber, David G., Jr. 2011. "A Vocabulary of Trauma in the Exilic Writings." Pages 309–22 in *Interpreting Exile: Displacement and Deportation in Biblical and Modern Contexts.* Edited by Brad E. Kelle, Frank

Ritchel Ames, and Jacob L. Wright. AIL 9. Atlanta: Society of Biblical Literature.

Garbini, Giovanni. 1988. *History and Ideology in Ancient Israel*. Translated by John Bowden. London: SCM Press.

George, Mark K. 2009. "Postmodern Literary Criticism: The Impossibility of Method." Pages 459–77 in *Method Matters: Essays on the Interpretation of the Hebrew Bible in Honor of David L. Petersen*. Edited by Joel M. LeMon and Kent Harold Richards. RBS 56. Atlanta: Society of Biblical Literature.

Giffone, Benjamin D. 2010. "A 'Perfect' Poem: The Use of the Qatal Verbal Form in the Biblical Acrostics." *HS* 51:49–72.

Gil, Thomas. 2011. "Leopold Ranke." Pages 383–92 in *A Companion to the Philosophy of History and Historiography*. Edited by Aviezer Tucker. BCP 41. Malden, MA: Wiley-Blackwell.

Gilmour, Rachelle. 2011. *Representing the Past: A Literary Analysis of Narrative Historiography in the Book of Samuel*. VTSup 143. Leiden: Brill.

Gladson, Jerry A. 2010. "Postmodernism and the *Deus absconditus* in Lamentations 3." *Bib* 91:321–34.

Goitein, S. D. 1988. "Women as Creators of Biblical Genres." *Proof* 8:1–33.

Gordis, Robert. 1974. "The Conclusion of the Book of Lamentations (5:22)." *JBL* 93:289–93.

Gottlieb, Hans. 1987. "Die kultische Leiden des Königs: Zu den Klageliedern 3:1." *SJOT* 1:121–26.

Gottwald, Norman. 1954. *Studies in the Book of Lamentations*. SBT. London: SCM Press.

Grabbe, Lester L. 1997. "Are Historians of Ancient Palestine Fellow Creatures—or Different Animals?" Pages 19–36 in *Can a "History of Israel" Be Written?* Edited by Lester L. Grabbe. JSOTSup 245. ESHM 1. Sheffield: Sheffield Academic.

———. 2001. "Who Were the First Real Historians? On the Origins of Critical Historiography." Pages 156–81 in *Did Moses Speak Attic? Jewish Historiography and Scripture in the Hellenistic Period*. Edited by Lester L. Grabbe. JSOTSup 317. ESHM 3. Sheffield: Sheffield Academic.

———. 2011. "The Big Max: Review of *A Biblical History of Israel*, by Iain Provan, V. Philips Long, and Tremper Longman, III." Pages 215–34 in *Enquire of the Former Age: Ancient Historiography and Writing the History of Israel*. Edited by Lester L. Grabbe. LHBOTS 554. ESHM 9. New York: Bloomsbury.

———. 2017. *Ancient Israel: What Do We Know and How Do We Know It?* Rev. ed. London: Bloomsbury.

Granowski, Jan Jaynes. 1992. "Jehoiachin at the King's Table: A Reading of the Ending of the Second Book of Kings." Pages 173–88 in *Reading between Texts: Intertextuality and the Bible.* Edited by Danna Nolan Fewell. LCBI. Louisville: Westminster John Knox.

Greenspan, Henry. 2010. *On Listening to Holocaust Survivors: Beyond Testimony.* 2nd ed. St. Paul, MN: Paragon House.

Greer, Jonathan. 2009. "A Chiastic Key to a Text-Critical Crux in Lamentations 3.22." *BT* 60:184–86.

Guest, Deryn. 1999. "Hiding behind the Naked Woman in Lamentations: A Recriminative Response." *BibInt* 7:413–48.

Guillaume, Phillipe. 2009. "Lamentations 5: The Seventh Acrostic." *JHebS* 9: article 16.

Gunn, David M. 1980. *The Fate of King Saul: An Interpretation of a Biblical Story.* JSOTSup 14. Sheffield: JSOT Press.

Gwaltney, W. C., Jr. 1983. "The Biblical Book of Lamentations in the Context of Near Eastern Lament Literature." Pages 191–211 in *Scripture in Context II: More Essays on the Comparative Method.* Edited by William W. Hallo, James C. Moyer, and Leo G. Perdue. Winona Lake, IN: Eisenbrauns.

Halpern, Baruch. 1996. *The First Historians: The Hebrew Bible and History.* University Park: Pennsylvania State University Press.

———. 1998. "Why Mannaseh Is Blamed for the Babylonian Exile: The Evolution of a Biblical Tradition." *VT* 48:473–514.

———. 1999. "Erasing History: The Minimalist Assault on Ancient Israel." Pages 415–26 in *Israel's Past in Present Research: Essays on Ancient Israelite Historiography.* Edited by V. Philips Long. SBTS 7. Winona Lake, IN: Eisenbrauns.

Halpern, Baruch, and David Vanderhooft. 1991. "The Editions of Kings in the 7th–6th Centuries B.C.E." *HUCA* 62:179–244.

Handy, Lowell K. 2007. "Josiah in a New Light: Assyriology Touches the Reforming King." Pages 415–31 in *Orientalism, Assyriology and the Bible.* Edited by Steven W. Holloway. HBM 10. Sheffield: Sheffield Phoenix.

Harris, Beau, and Carleen Mandolfo. 2013. "The Silent God in Lamentations." *Int* 67:133–43.

Hartman, Geoffrey H. 1991. *Minor Prophecies: The Literary Essay in the Culture Wars.* Cambridge: Harvard University Press.

———. 1995. "On Traumatic Knowledge and Literary Studies." *NLH* 26:537–63.

Haskell, Thomas. 1998. "Objectivity Is Not Neutrality: Rhetoric versus Practice in Peter Novick's *That Noble Dream.*" Pages 299–319 in *History and Theory: Contemporary Readings.* Edited by Brian Fay, Philip Pomper, and Richard T. Vann. Malden, MA: Blackwell.

Heim, Knut M. 1999. "The Personification of Jerusalem and the Drama of Her Bereavement in Lamentations." Pages 129–69 in *Zion, City of Our God.* Edited by Richard S. Hess and Gordon J. Wenham. Grand Rapids: Eerdmans.

Heins, Volker and Andreas Langenohl. 2011. "A Fire That Doesn't Burn? The Allied Bombing of Germany and the Cultural Politics of Trauma." Pages 3–26 in *Narrating Trauma: On the Impact of Collective Suffering.* Edited by Ron Eyerman, Jeffrey C. Alexander, and Elizabeth Butler Breese. YCSS. Boulder, CO: Paradigm.

Helberg, J. L. 2004. "Reading 'Rape' in the Hebrew Bible: A Consideration of Language." *JSOT* 28:279–99.

Heller, Roy L. 2006. *Power, Politics, and Prophecy: The Character of Samuel and the Deuteronomistic Evaluation of Prophecy.* LHBOTS 440. New York: T&T Clark.

Herman, Judith. 1992. *Trauma and Recovery.* New York: Basic Books.

Hilberg, Raul. 1988. "I Was Not There." Pages 17–25 in *Writing and the Holocaust.* Edited by Berel Lang. New York: Holmes & Meier.

Hirsch, E. D., Jr. 1984. "Meaning and Significance Reinterpreted." *CriInq* 11:202–25.

Hoffmann, Hans Detlef. 1980. *Reform und Reformen: Unters. zu e. Grundthema d. deuteronomist. Geschichtsschreibung.* ATANT 66. Zurich: Theologischer Verlag.

Holloway, Steven W. 2002. *Aššur Is King! Aššur Is King! Religion in the Exercise of Power in the Neo-Assyrian Empire.* CHANE 10. Leiden: Brill.

House, Paul R. 2011. "Outrageous Demonstrations of Grace: The Theology of Lamentations." Pages 26–52 in *Great Is Thy Faithfulness? Reading Lamentations as Sacred Scripture.* Edited by Robin A. Parry and Heath Thomas. Eugene, OR: Pickwick.

James, William. 1910. *Pragmatism: A New Name for Some Old Ways of Thinking.* London: Longmans, Green.

Janet, Pierre. 1925. *Psychological Healing: A Historical and Clinical Study.* 2 vols. Translated by Eden Paul and Cedar Paul. London: Allen & Unwin.

Janzen, David. 2005. "Why the Deuteronomist Told about the Sacrifice of Jephthah's Daughter." *JSOT* 29:339–57.

———. 2008. "An Ambiguous Ending: Dynastic Punishment in Kings and the Fate of the Davidides in 2 Kings 25.27–30." *JSOT* 33:39–58.

———. 2012a. "The Condemnation of David's 'Taking' in 2 Samuel 12:1–14." *JBL* 131:209–20.

———. 2012b. *The Violent Gift: Trauma's Subversion of the Deuteronomistic History's Narrative.* LHBOTS 561. New York: T&T Clark.

———. 2013a. *The Necessary King: A Postcolonial Reading of the Deuteronomistic Portrait of the Monarchy.* HBM 57. Sheffield: Sheffield Phoenix.

———. 2013b. "The Sins of Josiah and Hezekiah: A Synchronic Reading of the Final Chapters of Kings." *JSOT* 37:349–70.

———. 2017. *Chronicles and the Politics of Davidic Restoration: A Quiet Revolution.* LHBOTS 657. London: Bloomsbury.

Japhet, Sara. 2006. "Theodicy in Ezra-Nehemiah and Chronicles." Pages 367–98 in *From the Rivers of Babylon to the Highlands of Judah: Collected Studies on the Restoration Period.* Winona Lake, IN: Eisenbrauns.

Jenkins, Keith. 1999. *Why History? Ethics and Postmodernity.* London: Routledge.

Joannès, F., and A. Lemaire. 1999. "Trois tablettes cunéiformes à onomastique ouest-sémitique." *Transeu* 17:17–34.

Johnson, Bo. 1985. "Form and Message in Lamentations." *ZAW* 97:58–73.

Joyce, Paul M. 1999. "Sitting Loose to History: Reading the Book of Lamentations without Primary Reference to Its Original Historical Setting." Pages 246–62 in *In Search of Wisdom: Essays in Old Testament Interpretation in Honour of Ronald E. Clements.* Edited by Edward Ball. JSOTSup 300. Sheffield: Sheffield Academic.

Kaiser, Otto. 1993. *Der Gott des Alten Testaments.* Göttingen: Vandenhoeck & Ruprecht.

Kalaidjian, Walter. 2006. *The Edge of Modernism: American Poetry and the Traumatic Past.* Baltimore: Johns Hopkins University Press.

Kalimi, Isaac. 2016. "Reexamining 2 Samuel 10–12: Redaction History versus Compositional Unity." *CBQ* 78:24–46.

Kalmanofsky, Amy. 2007. "Their Heart Cried Out to God: Gender and Prayer in the Book of Lamentations." Pages 53–65 in *A Question of Sex? Gender and Difference in the Hebrew Bible and Beyond.* Edited by Deborah W. Rooke. HBM 14. Sheffield: Sheffield Phoenix.

Kang, Shinman, and Pieter M. Ventner. 2009. "A Canonical-Literary Reading of Lamentations 5." *HvTSt* 65:257–63.

Kelle, Brad E. 2009. "Dealing with the Trauma of Defeat: The Rhetoric of the Devastation and Rejuvenation of Nature in Ezekiel." *JBL* 128:469–90.

Kelle, Brad E., Frank Ritchel Ames, and Jacob L. Wright, eds. 2011. *Interpreting Exile: Displacement and Deportation in Biblical and Modern Contexts*. AIL 9. Atlanta: Society of Biblical Literature.

Kelly, Brian E. 2003. " 'Retribution' Revisited: Covenant, Grace and Restoration." Pages 206–27 in *The Chronicler as Theologian: Essays in Honor of Ralph W. Klein*. Edited by M. Patrick Graham, Steven L. McKenzie, and Gary N. Knoppers. JSOTSup 371. London: T&T Clark.

Kessler, John. 2000. "Sexuality and Politics: The Motif of the Displaced Husband in the Books of Samuel." *CBQ* 62:409–23.

Kitchen, K. A. 2003. *On the Reliability of the Old Testament*. Grand Rapids: Eerdmans.

Knauf, Ernst Axel. 1991. "From History to Interpretation." Pages 26–64 in *The Fabric of History: Text, Artifact and Israel's Past*. Edited by Diana Vikander Edelman. JSOTSup 127. Sheffield: JSOT Press.

———. 2011. "Against Historiography—In Defense of History." Pages 49–56 in *Enquire of the Former Age: Ancient Historiography and Writing the History of Israel*. Edited by Lester L. Grabbe. LHBOTS 554. ESHM 9. New York: Bloomsbury.

Knoppers, Gary N. 1994. *Two Nations under God: The Deuteronomistic History of Solomon and the Dual Monarchies*. Vol. 2. HSM 53. Atlanta: Scholars Press.

———. 2000. "Is There a Future for the Deuteronomistic History?" Pages 117–34 in *The Future of the Deuteronomistic History*. Edited by T. Römer. BETL 147. Leuven: Leuven University Press.

———. 2001. "Rethinking the Relationship between Deuteronomy and the Deuteronomistic History: The Case of Kings." *CBQ* 63:393–415.

Koch, Ido, and Oded Lipschits. 2013. "The Rosette Stamped Jar Handle System and the Kingdom of Judah at the End of the First Temple Period." *ZDPV* 129:55–78.

Kofoed, Jens Bruun. 2005. *Text and History: Historiography and the Study of the Biblical Text*. Winona Lake, IN: Eisenbrauns.

Kolk, Bessel A. van der. 2014. *The Body Keeps the Score: Brain, Mind, and Body in the Healing of Trauma*. New York: Viking.

Kolk, Bessel A. van der, and Onno van der Hart. 1995. "The Intrusive Past: The Flexibility of Memory and the Engraving of Trauma." Pages

158–82 in *Trauma: Explorations in Memory*. Edited by Cathy Caruth. Baltimore: Johns Hopkins University Press.

Koptak, Paul E. 2014. "Identity and Identification in the Book of Lamentations." *CovQ* 72:199–215.

Krašovec, Jože. 1992. "The Source of Hope in the Book of Lamentations." *VT* 42:223–33.

Kupelian, Diane, Anie Sanentz Kalayjian, and Alice Kassalian. 1998. "The Turkish Genocide of the Armenians: Continuing Effects on Survivors and Their Families Eight Decades after Massive Trauma." Pages 191–210 in *International Handbook of Multigenerational Legacies of Trauma*. Edited by Yael Danieli. New York: Plenum.

Laato, Antti. 2005. "Making History for Israel—Foundation, Blocking and Policy." *SEÅ* 70:145–76.

Labahn, Antje. 2002. "Trauern als Bewältigung der Vergangenheit zur Gestaltung der Zukunft: Bemerkungen zur anthropologischen Theologie der Klagelieder." *VT* 52:513–27.

LaCapra, Dominick. 1994. *Representing the Holocaust: History, Theory, Trauma*. Ithaca, NY: Cornell University Press.

———. 1998. "History, Language, and Reading: Waiting for Crillon." Pages 90–118 in *History and Theory: Contemporary Readings*. Edited by Brian Fay, Philip Pomper, and Richard T. Vann. Malden, MA: Blackwell.

———. 2001. *Writing History, Writing Trauma*. PRCS. Baltimore: Johns Hopkins University Press.

———. 2003. "Holocaust Testimonies: Attending to the Victim's Voice." Pages 209–31 in *Catastrophe and Meaning: The Holocaust and the Twentieth Century*. Edited by Moishe Postone and Eric Santner. Chicago: University of Chicago Press.

Lanahan, William F. 1974. "The Speaking Voice in the Book of Lamentations." *JBL* 93:41–49.

Lang, Berel. 2000. *Holocaust Representation: Art within the Limits of History and Ethics*. Baltimore: Johns Hopkins University Press.

Langer, Lawrence L. 1991. *Holocaust Testimonies: The Ruin of Memory*. New Haven: Yale University Press.

———. 1995. *Admitting the Holocaust: Collected Essays*. Oxford: Oxford University Press.

Lanzmann, Claude. 1995. *Shoah: The Complete Text of the Acclaimed Holocaust Film*. New York: Da Capo.

Laub, Dori. 1992a. "Bearing Witness, or the Vicissitudes of Listening." Pages 57–74 in *Testimony: Crises of Witnessing in Literature, Psychoanalysis, and History*. Edited by Shoshana Felman and Dori Laub. New York: Routledge.

———. 1992b. "An Event without a Witness: Truth, Testimony and Survival." Pages 75–92 in *Testimony: Crises of Witnessing in Literature, Psychoanalysis, and History*. Edited by Shoshana Felman and Dori Laub. New York: Routledge.

Law, David R. 2012. *The Historical-Critical Method: A Guide for the Perplexed*. London: T&T Clark.

Lee, Nancy C. 2002. *The Singers of Lamentations: Cities under Siege, from Ur to Jerusalem to Sarajevo....* BibInt 60. Leiden: Brill.

Lemche, Niels Peter. 1998. *The Israelites in History and Tradition*. London: SPCK.

———. 2005. "Conservative Scholarship on the Move." *SJOT* 19:203–52.

———. 2008. *The Old Testament between Theology and History: A Critical Survey*. Louisville: Westminster John Knox.

———. 2010. "The Deuteronomistic History: Historical Reconsiderations." Pages 41–50 in *Raising Up a Faithful Priest: Essays in Honor of Richard D. Nelson*. Edited by K. L. Noll and Brooks Schramm. Winona Lake, IN: Eisenbrauns.

———. 2011. "Evading the Facts: Notes on Jens Bruun Kofoed, *Text and History: Historiography and the Study of the Biblical Text* (2005)." Pages 139–63 in *Enquire of the Former Age: Ancient Historiography and Writing the History of Israel*. Edited by Lester L. Grabbe. LHBOTS 554. ESHM 9. New York: Bloomsbury.

Levi, Primo. 1996. *If This Is a Man/The Truce*. Translated by Stuart Woolf. London: Vintage.

Levinson, Bernard M. 2001. "The Reconceptualization of Kingship and the Deuteronomistic History's Transformation of Torah." *VT* 51:511–34.

Lifton, Robert Jay. 1991. *Death in Life: Survivors of Hiroshima*. Chapel Hill: University of North Carolina Press.

Linafelt, Tod. 2000. *Surviving Lamentations: Catastrophe, Lament, and Protest in the Afterlife of a Biblical Book*. Chicago: University of Chicago Press.

———. 2001. "The Refusal of a Conclusion in the Book of Lamentations." *JBL* 120:340–43.

Lipschits, Oded. 1998. "Nebuchadrezzar's Policy in 'Ḥattu-Land' and the Fate of the Kingdom of Judah." *UF* 30:467–87.

———. 2003. "Demographic Changes in Judah between the Seventh and Fifth Centuries B.C.E." Pages 323–76 in *Judah and the Judeans in the Neo-Babylonian Period*. Edited by Oded Lipschits and Joseph Blenkinsopp. Winona Lake, IN: Eisenbrauns.

———. 2004a. "From Geba to Beersheba: A Further Consideration." *RB* 111:345–61.

———. 2004b. "The Rural Settlement in Judah in the Sixth Century B.C.E.: A Rejoinder." *PEQ* 136:99–107.

———. 2005. *The Fall and Rise of Jerusalem: Judah under Babylonian Rule*. Winona Lake, IN: Eisenbrauns.

———. 2011a. "Persian-Period Judah: A New Perspective." Pages 187–211 in *Texts, Contexts and Readings in Postexilic Literature: Explorations into Historiography and Identity Negotiation in Hebrew Bible and Related Texts*. Edited by Louis Jonker. FAT 2/53. Tübingen: Mohr Siebeck.

———. 2011b. "Shedding New Light on the Dark Years of the 'Exilic Period': New Studies, Further Elucidation, and Some Questions Regarding the Archaeology of Judah as an 'Empty Land.'" Pages 57–90 in *Interpreting Exile: Displacement and Deportation in Biblical and Modern Contexts*. Edited by Brad E. Kelle, Frank Ritchel Ames, and Jacob L. Wright. AIL 10. Atlanta: Society of Biblical Literature.

Liverani, Mario. 2010. "The Book of Kings and Ancient Near Eastern Historiography." Pages 163–84 in *The Books of Kings: Sources, Composition, Historiography and Reception*. Edited by André Lemaire and Baruch Halpern. VTSup 129. Leiden: Brill.

Lohfink, Norbert F. 1993. "Distribution of the Functions of Power: The Laws Concerning Public Offices in Deuteronomy 16:18–18:22." Pages 336–52 in *A Song of Power and the Power of Song: Essays on the Book of Deuteronomy*. Edited by Duane L. Christensen. SBTS 3. Winona Lake, IN: Eisenbrauns.

———. 1999. "Was There a Deuteronomistic Movement?" Pages 36–66 in *Those Elusive Deuteronomists: The Phenomenon of Pan-Deuteronomism*. Edited by Linda S. Schearing and Steven L. McKenzie. JSOTSup 268. Sheffield: Sheffield Academic.

Long, V. Philips. 1994. *The Art of Biblical History*. FCI 5. Grand Rapids: Zondervan.

———. 2002a. "How Reliable Are Biblical Reports? Repeating Lester Grabbe's Comparative Experiment." *VT* 52:367–84.

———. 2002b. "Introduction." Pages 1–22 in *Windows into Old Testament History: Evidence, Argument, and the Crisis of "Biblical Israel."* Edited by V. Philips Long, David W. Baker, and Gordon J. Wenham. Grand Rapids: Eerdmans.

Luckhurst, Roger. 2008. *The Trauma Question.* London: Routledge.

Lyotard, Jean-François. 1988. *The Differend: Phrases in Dispute.* Translated by Georges Van Den Abbeele. THL 46. Minneapolis: University of Minnesota Press.

Machinist, Peter. 1976. "Literature as Politics: The Tukulti-Ninurta Epic and the Bible." *CBQ* 38:455–82.

———. 1997. "The Fall of Assyria in Comparative Ancient Perspective." Pages 179–95 in *Assyria 1995: Proceedings of the 10th Anniversary Symposium of the Neo-Assyrian Text Corpus Project.* Edited by S. Parpola and R. M. Whiting. Helsinki: Neo-Assyrian Text Corpus Project.

Maier, Christl L. 2008a. "Body Space as Public Space: Jerusalem's Wounded Body in Lamentations." Pages 119–38 in *Constructions of Space II: The Biblical City and Other Imagined Spaces.* Edited by Jon L. Berquist and Claudia V. Camp. LHBOTS 490. New York: T&T Clark.

———. 2008b. *Daughter Zion, Mother Zion: Gender, Space, and the Sacred in Ancient Israel.* Minneapolis: Fortress.

Mandolfo, Carleen R. 2007. *Daughter Zion Talks Back to the Prophets: A Dialogic Theology of the Book of Lamentations.* SemeiaSt 58. Atlanta: Society of Biblical Literature.

Marttila, Marko. 2012. "The Deuteronomistic Heritage in the Psalms." *JSOT* 37:67–91.

Mayes, Andrew D. H. 2000. "Deuteronomistic Ideology and the Theology of the Old Testament." Pages 456–80 in *Israel Constructs Its History: Deuteronomistic Historiography in Recent Research.* Edited by Albert de Pury et al. JSOTSup 306. Sheffield: Sheffield Academic.

McKenzie, Steven L. 1991. *The Trouble with Kings: The Composition of the Book of Kings in the Deuteronomistic History.* VTSup 42. Leiden: Brill.

———. 2000. "The Divided Kingdom in the Deuteronomistic History and in Scholarship on It." Pages 135–45 in *The Future of the Deuteronomistic History.* Edited by T. Römer. BETL 147. Leuven: Peeters.

———. 2006. "Saul in the Deuteronomistic History." Pages 59–70 in *Saul in Story and Tradition.* Edited by Carl S. Ehrlich. FAT 47. Tübingen: Mohr Siebeck.

———. 2010. "*Ledavid* (for David)! 'Except in the Matter of Uriah the Hittite.'" Pages 103–13 in *For and against David: Story and History in the*

Books of Samuel. Edited by A. Graeme Auld and Erik Eynikel. BETL 232. Leuven: Peeters.

Middlemas, Jill A. 2006a. "Did Second Isaiah Write Lamentations iii?" *VT* 56:505–25.

———. 2006b. *The Troubles of Templeless Judah*. OTM. Oxford: Oxford University Press.

———. 2009. "Going beyond the Myth of the Empty Land: A Reassessment of the Early Persian Period." Pages 174–94 in *Exile and Restoration Revisited: Essays on the Babylonian and Persian Periods in Memory of Peter R. Ackroyd*. Edited by Gary N. Knoppers and Lester L. Grabbe. LSTS 73. London: T&T Clark.

———. 2012. "Speaking of Speaking: The Form of Zion's Suffering in Lamentations." Pages 39–54 in *Daughter Zion: Her Portrait, Her Response*. Edited by Mark J. Boda, Carol J. Dempsey, and LeAnn Snow Flesher. AIL 13. Atlanta: Society of Biblical Literature.

Millard, Alan R. 2010. "The Book of Kings and Ancient Near Eastern Historiography." Pages 155–60 in *The Book of Kings: Sources, Composition, Historiography and Reception*. Edited by André Lemaire and Baruch Halpern. VTSup 129. Leiden: Brill.

Miller, Charles William. 2001. "Reading Voices: Personification, Dialogism, and the Reader of Lamentations 1." *BibInt* 9:393–408.

Mink, Louis. 1987. *Historical Understanding*. Edited by Brian Fay, Eugene O. Golob, and Richard T. Vann. Ithaca, NY: Cornell University Press.

Mintz, Alan. 1982. "The Rhetoric of Lamentations and the Representation of Catastrophe." *Proof* 2:1–17.

Mitchell, Mary Louise. 2008. "Reflecting on Catastrophe: Lamentations 4 as Historiography" Pages 78–90 in *The Function of Ancient Historiography in Biblical and Cognate Studies*. Edited by Patricia G. Kirkpatrick and Timothy D. Goltz. LHBOTS 489. New York: T&T Clark.

Morrison, Toni. 1987. *Beloved*. New York: Knopf.

Morrow, William. 2011. "Deuteronomy 7 in Postcolonial Perspective: Cultural Fragmentation and Renewal." Pages 275–93 in *Interpreting Exile: Displacement and Deportation in Biblical and Modern Contexts*. Edited by Brad E. Kelle, Frank Ritchel Ames, and Jacob L. Wright. AIL 9. Atlanta: Society of Biblical Literature.

Murray, Donald F. 2001. "Of All the Years the Hopes—or Fears? Jehoiachin in Babylon (2 Kings 25:27–30)." *JBL* 120:245–65.

Na'aman, Nadav. 2004. "Death Formulae and the Burial Place of the Kings of the House of David." *Bib* 85:245–54.

———. 2005. "Josiah and the Kingdom of Judah." Pages 189–247 in *Good Kings and Bad Kings*. Edited by Lester L. Grabbe. LHBOTS 393. ESHM 5. London: T&T Clark.

———. 2011. "The 'Discovered Book' and the Legitimation of Josiah's Reform." *JBL* 130:47–62.

Nelson, Richard D. 1981a. *The Double Redaction of the Deuteronomistic History*. JSOTSup 18. Sheffield: JSOT Press.

———. 1981b. "Josiah in the Book of Joshua." *JBL* 100:531–40.

———. 2005. "The Double Redaction of the Deuteronomistic History: The Case Is Still Compelling." *JSOT* 29:319–37.

———. 2013. "The Deuteronomistic Historian in Samuel: 'The Man behind the Green Curtain.'" Pages 17–37 in *Is Samuel among the Deuteronomists? Current Views on the Place of Samuel in a Deuteronomistic History*. Edited by Cynthia Edenburg and Juha Pakkala. AIL 16. Atlanta: Society of Biblical Literature.

Nicholson, Ernest. 2009. "*Traditum* and *traditio*: The Case of Deuteronomy 17:14–20." Pages 46–61 in *Scriptural Exegesis: The Shapes of Culture and the Religious Imagination. Essays in Honour of Michael Fishbane*. Edited by Deborah A. Green and Laura S. Lieber. Oxford: Oxford University Press.

———. 2014. *Deuteronomy and the Judaean Diaspora*. Oxford: Oxford University Press.

Nicholson, Sarah. 2002. *Three Faces of Saul: An Intertextual Approach to Biblical Tragedy*. JSOTSup 339. Sheffield: Sheffield Academic.

Nicol, George G. 1998. "David, Abigail and Bathsheba, Nabal and Uriah: Transformations within a Triangle." *SJOT* 12:130–45.

Niderland, William G. 1968. "Clinical Observations on the 'Survivor Syndrome.'" *IJPA* 49:313–15.

Nielsen, Kirsten. 2014. "Post-traumatic Stress Disorder and the Book of Job." Pages 62–70 in *Trauma and Traumatization in Individual and Collective Dimensions: Insights from Biblical Studies and Beyond*. Edited by Eve-Marie Becker, Jan Dochhorn, and Else Kragelund Holt. SANt 2. Göttingen: Vandenhoeck & Ruprecht.

Noll, K. L. 2001. *Canaan and Israel in Antiquity: An Introduction*. BibSem 83. London: Sheffield Academic.

———. 2007. "Deuteronomistic History or Deuteronomic Debate? (A Thought Experiment)." *JSOT* 31:311–45.

Noth, Martin. 1981. *The Deuteronomistic History*. Translated by Jane Douall et al. JSOTSup 15. Sheffield: JSOT Press.

O'Connor, Kathleen M. 1999. "'Speak Tenderly to Jerusalem': Second Isaiah's Reception and Use of Daughter Zion." *PSB* 20:281–94.

———. 2002. *Lamentations and the Tears of the World*. Maryknoll, NY: Orbis Books.

———. 2011. *Jeremiah: Pain and Promise*. Minneapolis: Fortress.

———. 2014. "How Trauma Studies Can Contribute to Osld Testament Studies." Pages 210–22 in *Trauma and Traumatization in Individual and Collective Dimensions: Insights from Biblical Studies and Beyond*. Edited by Eve-Marie Becker, Jan Dochhorn, and Else Kragelund Holt. SANt 2. Göttingen: Vandenhoeck & Ruprecht.

Oded, Bustenay. 1992. *War, Peace and Empire: Justifications for War in Assyrian Royal Inscriptions*. Wiesbaden: Reichert.

Odell, Margaret S. 2016. "Fragments of Traumatic Memory: Ṣalmê zākār and Child Sacrifice in Ezekiel 16:15–22." Pages 107–24 in *Bible through the Lens of Trauma*. Edited by Christopher G. Frechette and Elizabeth Boase. SemeiaSt 86. Atlanta: SBL Press.

Olyan, Saul M. 1996. "Honor, Shame, and Covenant Relations in Ancient Israel and Its Environment." *JBL* 115:201–18.

Oppenheimer, A. Leo. 1947. "Assyriological Gleanings IV: The Shadow of the King." *BASOR* 107:7–11.

Owens, Pamela Jean. 1990. "Personification and Suffering in Lamentations 3." *ASB* 105:75–90.

Page, Philip. 1992. "Circularity in Toni Morrison's *Beloved*." *African American Review* 26:31–39.

Pakkala, Juha. 2010. "Why the Cult Reforms in Judah Probably Did Not Happen." Pages 201–35 in *One God—One Cult—One Nation: Archaeological and Biblical Perspectives*. Edited by Reinhard G. Kratz and Hermann Spieckermann. BZAW 405. Berlin: de Gruyter.

Parker, K. I. 1992. "Solomon as Philosopher King? The Nexus of Wisdom in 1 Kings 1–11." *JSOT* 53:75–91.

Parry, Robin A. 2007. "The Ethics of Lament: Lamentations 1 as a Case Study." Pages 138–55 in *Reading the Law: Studies in Honour of Gordon J. Wenham*. Edited by J. G. McConville and Karl Möller. LHBOTS 461. New York: T&T Clark.

———. 2010. *Lamentations*. THOTC. Grand Rapids: Eerdmans.

———. 2011. "Lamentations and the Poetic Politics of Prayer." *TynBul* 62:65–88.

Partner, Nancy F. 1998. "Making up Lost Time: Writing on the Writing of History." Pages 69–89 in *History and Theory: Contemporary Readings*.

Edited by Brian Fay, Philip Pomper, and Richard T. Vann. Malden, MA: Blackwell.

Pearce, Laurie E. 2006. "New Evidence for Judeans in Babylonia." Pages 399–411 in *Judah and the Judeans in the Persian Period*. Edited by Oded Lipschits and Manfred Oeming. Winona Lake, IN: Eisenbrauns.

———. 2011. "'Judean': A Special Status in Neo-Babylonian and Achaemenid Babylonia?" Pages 267–77 in *Judah and the Judeans in the Achaemenid Period: Negotiating Identity in an International Context*. Winona Lake, IN: Eisenbrauns.

Perlitt, Lothar. 1994. "Der Staatsgedanke im Deuteronomium." Pages 182–98 in *Language, Theology and the Bible: Essays in Honour of James Barr*. Edited by Samuel E. Balentine and John Barton. Oxford: Clarendon.

Perry, Campbell, and Jean-Roch Lawrence. 1984. "Mental Processing outside of Awareness: The Contribution of Freud and Janet." Pages 9–48 in *The Unconscious Reconsidered*. Edited by Kenneth S. Bowers and Donald Meichenbaum. New York: Wiley & Sons.

Pham, Xuan Huong Thi. 1999. *Mourning in the Ancient Near East and the Hebrew Bible*. JSOTSup 302. Sheffield: Sheffield Academic.

Porteous, N. W. 1961. "Jerusalem—Zion: The Growth of a Symbol." Pages 235–52 in *Verbannung und Heimkehr: Beiträge zur Geschichte und Theologie Israels im 6. und 5. Jahrhundert v. Chr.* Edited by Arnulf Kuschke. Tübingen: Mohr.

Provan, Iain W. 1988. *Hezekiah and the Books of Kings: A Contribution to the Debate about the Composition of the Deuteronomistic History*. BZAW 172. Berlin: de Gruyter.

———. 1990a. "Feasts, Booths and Gardens (Thr 2,6a)." *ZAW* 102:254–55.

———. 1990b. "Reading Texts against an Historical Background: The Case of Lamentations 1." *SJOT* 4:130–43.

———. 1991a. *Lamentations*. NCBC. Grand Rapids: Eerdmans.

———. 1991b. "Past, Present and Future in Lamentations iii 52–66: The Case for a Precative Perfect Reexamined." *VT* 41:164–75.

———. 2000. "In the Stable with the Dwarves: Testimony, Interpretation, Faith and the History of Israel." Pages 281–319 in *Congress Volume Oslo 1998*. Edited by A. Lemaire and M. Sæbø. VTSup 80. Leiden: Brill.

Provan, Iain W., V. Philips Long, and Tremper Longman III. 2003. *A Biblical History of Israel*. Louisville: Westminster John Knox.

Pyper, Hugh S. 2001. "Reading Lamentations." *JSOT* 95:55–69.

Rad, Gerhard von. 1962. *Old Testament Theology*. Vol. 1. Translated by D. M. G. Stalker. New York: Harper & Row.

Ramadanovic, Petar. 2001. *Forgetting Futures: On Memory, Trauma, and Identity*. Lanham, MD: Lexington Books.

Reimer, David J. 2002. "Good Grief? A Psychological Reading of Lamentations." *ZAW* 114:542–59.

Renkema, Johan. 1998. *Lamentations*. Translated by Brian Doyle. HCOT. Leuven: Peeters.

Ricoeur, Paul. 1984. *Time and Narrative*. 3 vols. Translated by Kathleen McLaughlin and David Pellauer. Chicago: University of Chicago Press.

Römer, Thomas. 1994. "The Book of Deuteronomy." Pages 178–212 in *The History of Israel's Traditions: The Heritage of Martin Noth*. Edited by Steven L. McKenzie and M. Patrick Graham. JSOTSup 182. Sheffield: Sheffield Academic.

———. 2003. "The Form-Critical Problem of the So-Called Deuteronomistic History." Pages 240–52 in *The Changing Face of Form Criticism for the Twenty-First Century*. Edited by Marvin A. Sweeney and Ehud Ben Zvi. Grand Rapids: Eerdmans.

———. 2010. "Book-Endings in Joshua and the Question of the So-Called Deuteronomistic History." Pages 87–101 in *Raising Up a Faithful Priest: Essays in Honor of Richard D. Nelson*. Edited by K. L. Noll and Brooks Schramm. Winona Lake, IN: Eisenbrauns.

Rong, Lina. 2013. *Forgotten and Forsaken by God (Lam 5:19–20): The Community in Pain in Lamentations and Related Old Testament Texts*. Eugene, OR: Pickwick.

Rorty, Richard. 1982. *Consequences of Pragmatism (Essays 1972–1980)*. Minneapolis: University of Minnesota Press.

———. 1991. *Objectivity, Relativism, and Truth: Philosophical Papers Volume 1*. Cambridge: Cambridge University Press.

Rose, Martin. 2000. "Deuteronomistic Ideology and Theology of the Old Testament." Pages 424–55 in *Israel Constructs its History: Deuteronomistic Historiography in Recent Research*. Edited by Albert de Pury et al. JSOTSup 306. Sheffield: Sheffield Academic.

Rösel, Hartmut N. 2000. "Does a Comprehensive 'Leitmotiv' Exist in the Deuteronomistic History?" Pages 195–211 in *The Future of the Deuteronomistic History*. Edited by T. Römer. BETL 147. Leuven: Leuven University Press.

Rosenfeld, Alvin H. 1978. "The Problematics of Holocaust Literature." Pages 1–30 in *Confronting the Holocaust: The Impact of Elie Wiesel*.

Edited by Alvin H. Rosenfeld and Irving Greenberg. Bloomington: Indiana University Press.

Rumfelt, Janet L. 2011. "Reversing Fortune: War, Psychic Trauma, and the Promise of Narrative Repair." Pages 323–42 in *Interpreting Exile: Displacement and Deportation in Biblical and Modern Contexts*. Edited by Brad E. Kelle, Frank Ritchel Ames, and Jacob L. Wright. AIL 9. Atlanta: Society of Biblical Literature.

Saebø, M. 1993. "Who Is 'the Man' in Lamentations 3? A Fresh Approach to the Interpretation of the Book of Lamentations." Pages 294–306 in *Understanding Poets and Prophets: Essays in Honour of George Wishart Anderson*. Edited by A. Graeme Auld. JSOTSup 152. Sheffield: JSOT Press.

Salters, Robert B. 2000. "Structure and Implication in Lamentations 1?" *SJOT* 14:293–301.

———. 2007. "Text and Exegesis in Lamentations 4:21–22." Pages 327*–37* in *Shai le-Sara Japhet: Studies in the Bible, Its Exegesis, and Its Language*. Edited by Moshe Bar-Asher et al. Jerusalem: Bialik Institute.

———. 2011. "Acrostics and Lamentations." Pages 425–40 in *On Stone and Scroll: Essays in Honour of Graham Ivor Davies*. Edited by James K. Aitken, Katharine J. Dell, and Brian A. Mastin. BZAW 420. Berlin: de Gruyter.

Santner, Eric L. 1992. "History beyond the Pleasure Principle: Some Thoughts on the Representation of Trauma." Pages 143–54 in *Probing the Limits of Representation: Nazism and the "Final Solution."* Edited by Saul Friedlander. Cambridge: Harvard University Press.

Saussure, Ferdinand de. 1983. *Course in General Linguistics*. Translated by Roy Harris. La Salle, IL: Open Court.

Schäfer-Lichtenberger, Christa. 1995. "Die deuteronomische Verfassungsentwurf." Pages 105–18 in *Bundesdokument und Gesetz: Studien zum Deuteronomium*. Edited by Georg Braulik. HBS 4. Freiburg: Herder.

Schaudig, Hanspeter. 2001. *Die Inschriften Nabonids von Babylon und Kyros' des Grossen: Samt den in ihrem Umfeld entstandenen Tendenzschriften*. AOAT 256. Münster: Ugarit-Verlag.

Scheffler, Even. 2007. "Criticism of Government: Deuteronomy 17:14–20 between (and beyond) Synchrony and Diachrony." Pages 124–37 in *South African Perspectives on the Pentateuch between Synchrony and Diachrony*. Edited by Jurie le Roux and Eckart Otto. LHBOTS 463. New York: T&T Clark.

Schipper, Jeremy. 2005. "'Significant Resonances' with Mephibosheth in 2 Kings 25:27–30: A Response to Donald F. Murray." *JBL* 124:521–29.

Schmid, Konrad. 2010. *Genesis and the Moses Story: Israel's Dual Origins in the Hebrew Bible.* Translated by James D. Nogalski. Siphrut 3. Winona Lake, IN: Eisenbrauns.

Schwartz, Baruch. 2016. "The Pentateuchal Sources and the Former Prophets: A Neo-Documentarian's Perspective." Pages 783–93 in *The Formation of the Pentateuch: Bridging the Academic Cultures of Europe, Israel, and North America.* Edited by Jan C. Gertz et al. FAT 111. Tübingen: Mohr Siebeck.

Scurlock, JoAnn. 2006. "Josiah: The View from Mesopotamia." *BR* 51:9–24.

Seitz, Christopher. 1998. *Word without End: The Old Testament as Abiding Theological Witness.* Grand Rapids: Eerdmans.

Seow, C. L. 1985. "A Textual Note on Lamentations 1:20." *CBQ* 47:416–19.

Shea, William H. 1979. "The *qinah* Structure of the Book of Lamentations." *Bib* 60:103–7.

Smelser, Neil J. 2004. "Psychological Trauma and Cultural Trauma." Pages 31–59 in *Cultural Trauma and Collective Identity.* Edited by Jeffrey Alexander et al. Berkeley: University of California Press.

Smend, Rudolf. 2000. "The Law and the Nations: A Contribution to the Deuteronomistic Tradition History." Pages 95–110 in *Reconsidering Israel and Judah: Recent Studies on the Deuteronomistic History.* Edited by Gary N. Knoppers and J. Gordon McConville. SBTS 8. Winona Lake, IN: Eisenbrauns.

Speckhard, Anne. 1997. "Traumatic Death in Pregnancy: The Significance of Meaning and Attachment." Pages 67–100 in *Death and Trauma: The Traumatology of Grieving.* Edited by Charles R. Figley, Brian E. Bride, and Nicholas Mazza. Washington: Taylor & Francis.

Spieckermann, Hermann. 1982. *Juda unter Assur in der Sargonidenzeit.* FRLANT 129. Göttingen: Vandenhoeck & Ruprecht.

Stampfl, Barry. 2014. "Parsing the Unspeakable in the Context of Trauma." Pages 15–41 in *Contemporary Approaches in Literary Trauma Theory.* Edited by Michelle Balaev. London: Palgrave Macmillan.

Stern, Ephraim. 2001. *Archaeology of the Land of the Bible.* Vol. 2, *The Assyrian, Babylonian, and Persian Periods 732–332 BCE.* ABRL. New York: Doubleday.

———. 2004. "The Babylonian Gap: The Archaeological Reality." *JSOT* 28:273–77.

Sternberg, Meir. 1985. *The Poetics of Biblical Narrative: Ideological Literature and the Drama of Reading.* ISBL. Bloomington: Indiana University Press.

Steussy, Marti J. 1999. *David: Biblical Portraits of Power.* SPOT. Columbia: University of South Carolina Press.

Steymans, Hans Ulrich. 1995. *Deuteronomium 28 und die adê zur Thronfolgeregelung Asarhaddons: Segen und Fluch im Alten Orient und in Israel.* OBO 145. Göttingen: Vandenhoeck & Ruprecht.

Stiebert, Johanna. 2003. "Human Suffering and Divine Abuse of Power in Lamentations: Reflections on Forgiveness in the Context of South Africa's Truth and Reconciliation Process." *Pacifica* 16:195–215.

Stinespring, W. F. 1965. "No Daughter of Zion: A Study of the Appositional Genitive in Hebrew Grammar." *Enc* 26:133–41.

Strawn, Brent. 2016. "Trauma, Psalmic Disclosure, and Authentic Happiness." Pages 143–60 in *Bible through the Lens of Trauma.* Edited by Christopher G. Frechette and Elizabeth Boase. SemeiaSt 86. Atlanta: SBL Press.

Stulman, Louis. 2016. "Reflections on the Prose Sermons in the Book of Jeremiah: Duhm's and Mowinckel's Contributions to Contemporary Trauma." Pages 125–39 in *Bible through the Lens of Trauma.* Edited by Elizabeth Boase and Christopher G. Frechette. SemeiaSt 86. Atlanta: SBL Press.

Sutherland, Roy K. 1992. "Israelite Political Theories in Joshua 9." *JSOT* 53:65–74.

Sweeney, Marvin A. 1995. "The Critique of Solomon in the Josianic Edition of the Deuteronomistic History." *JBL* 114:607–22.

———. 2005. "King Manasseh of Judah and the Problem of Theodicy in the Deuteronomistic History." Pages 264–78 in *Good Kings and Bad Kings.* Edited by Lester L. Grabbe. LHBOTS 393. ESHM 5. London: T&T Clark.

Tadmor, Hayim, Benno Landsberger, and Simo Parpola. 1989. "The Sin of Sargon and Sennacherib's Last Will." *SAAB* 3:3–51.

Tal, Kalí. 1996. *Worlds of Hurt: Reading the Literatures of Trauma.* CSALC. Cambridge: Cambridge University Press.

Taylor, J. Glen. 1993. *Yahweh and the Sun: Biblical and Archaeological Evidence for Sun Worship in Ancient Israel.* JSOTSup 111. Sheffield: JSOT Press.

Thomas, Heath Aaron. 2008. "The Liturgical Function of the Book of Lamentations." Pages 137–47 in *Thinking towards New Horizons.* Edited by Matthias Augustin and Hermann Michael Niemann. BEATAJ 55. Frankfurt am Main: Lang.

———. 2011. "'I Will Hope in Him': Theology and Hope in Lamentations." Pages 203–21 in *A God of Faithfulness: Essays in Honour of J. Gordon McConville*. Edited by Jamie A. Grant, Alison Lo, and Gordon J. Wenham. LHBOTS 538. New York: T&T Clark.

Thompson, Thomas. 1992. "Historiography: Israelite Historiography." *ABD* 3:206–12.

———. 2000. *The Bible in History: How Writers Create a Past*. London: Pimlico.

Tiemeyer, Lena-Sofia. 2007. "Genealogy and Textual Allusions: Interpreting Isaiah xl–lv and Lamentations as Judahite Texts." *VT* 57:367–85.

Tigay, Jeffrey. 1996. *Deuteronomy: The JPS Torah Commentary*. Philadelphia: Jewish Publication Society.

Tollington, Janet E. 1998. "The Book of Judges: The Result of Post-Exilic Exegesis?" Pages 186–96 in *Intertextuality in Ugarit and Israel*. Edited by Johannes C. de Moor. OtSt 40. Leiden: Brill.

Trudinger, Peter. 2008. "How Lonely Sits the City: Reading Lamentations as City and Land." Pages 41–52 in *Exploring Ecological Hermeneutics*. Edited by Norman C. Habel and Peter Trudinger. Leiden: Brill.

Uehlinger, Christoph. 2005. "Was There a Cult Reform under King Josiah? The Case for a Well-Grounded Minimum." Pages 279–316 in *Good Kings and Bad Kings*. Edited by Lester L. Grabbe. LHBOTS 393. ESHM 5. London: T&T Clark.

Valkama, Kirsi. 2010. "What Do Archaeological Remains Reveal of the Settlements in Judah during the Mid-Sixth Century BCE?" Pages 39–59 in *The Concept of Exile in Ancient Israel and Its Historical Contexts*. Edited by Ehud Ben Zvi and Christoph Levin. BZAW 404. Berlin: de Gruyter.

Van Seters, John. 1983. *In Search of History: Historiography in the Ancient World and the Origins of Biblical History*. New Haven: Yale University Press.

———. 2009. *The Biblical Saga of King David*. Winona Lake, IN: Eisenbrauns.

Vonnegut, Kurt. 1969. *Slaughterhouse-Five or the Children's Crusade: A Duty-Dance with Death*. New York: Dell, 1969.

Webb, Barry G. 1987. *The Book of the Judges: An Integrated Reading*. JSOTSup 46. Sheffield: JSOT Press.

Weippert, Helga. 1972. "Die 'deuteronomistischen' Beurteilungen der Könige von Israel und Juda und das Problem der Redaktion der Königsbücher." *Bib* 53:301–39.

Westermann, Claus. 1994a. *Die Geschichtsbücher des Alten Testament: Gab es ein deuteronomistisches Geschichtswerk?* TBAT 87. Gütersloh: Kaiser.

———. 1994b. *Lamentations: Issues and Interpretation.* Translated by Charles Muenchow. Edinburgh: T&T Clark.

White, Hayden. 1973. *Metahistory: The Historical Imagination in Nineteenth-Century Europe.* Baltimore: Johns Hopkins University Press.

———. 1978. *Tropics of Discourse: Essays in Cultural Criticism.* Baltimore: Johns Hopkins University Press.

———. 1987. *The Content of the Form: Narrative Discourse and Historical Representation.* Baltimore: Johns Hopkins University Press.

———. 1998. "The Historical Text as Literary Artifact." Pages 15–33 in *History and Theory: Contemporary Readings.* Edited by Brian Fay, Philip Pomper, and Richard T. Vann. Malden, MA: Blackwell.

———. 2010. *The Fiction of Narrative: Essays on History, Literature, and Theory 1957–2007.* Edited by Robert Doran. Baltimore: Johns Hopkins University Press.

Whybray, R. N. 1999. "What Do We Know about Ancient Israel?" Pages 181–87 in *Israel's Past in Present Research: Essays on Ancient Israelite Historiography.* Edited by V. Philips Long. SBTS 7. Winona Lake, IN: Eisenbrauns.

Wiesel, Elie. 1978. "Why I Write." Pages 200–206 in *Confronting the Holocaust: The Impact of Elie Wiesel.* Edited by Alvin H. Rosenfeld and Irving Greenberg. Bloomington: Indiana University Press.

———. 1981. *Night.* Translated by Stella Rodway. Harmondsworth: Penguin Books.

Willey, Patricia Tull. 1997. *Remember the Former Things: The Recollection of Previous Texts in Second Isaiah.* SBLDS 161. Atlanta: Scholars Press.

Williamson, H. G. M. 2003. "The Family in Persian Period Judah: Some Textual Reflections." Pages 469–85 in *Symbiosis, Symbolism and the Power of the Past: Canaan, Israel and Their Neighbors from the Late Bronze Age through Roman Palaestina.* Edited by William G. Dever and Seymour Gittin. Winona Lake, IN: Eisenbrauns.

Williamson, Robert, Jr. 2008. "Lament and the Arts of Resistance: Public and Hidden Transcripts in Lamentations 5." Pages 67–80 in *Lamentations in Ancient and Contemporary Cultural Contexts.* Edited by Nancy

C. Lee and Carleen Mandolfo. SymS 43. Atlanta: Society of Biblical Literature.

Wilson, Robert R. 1999. "Who Was the Deuteronomist? (Who Was Not the Deuteronomist?)." Pages 67–82 in *Those Elusive Deuteronomists: The Phenomenon of Pan-Deuteronomism*. Edited by Linda S. Schearing and Steven L. McKenzie. JSOTSup 268. Sheffield: Sheffield Academic.

Wissmann, Felipe Blanco. 2008. *"Er tat das Rechte ...": Beurteilungskriterien und Deuteronomismus in 1Kön 12–2Kön 25*. ATANT 93. Zurich: TVZ.

Wong, Gregory T. K. 2005. "Is There a Direct Pro-Judah Polemic in Judges?" *SJOT* 19:84–110.

———. 2006. *Compositional Strategy of the Book of Judges: An Inductive, Rhetorical Study*. VTSup 111. Leiden: Brill.

Würthwein, Ernst. 1994. *Studien zum deuteronomistischen Geschichtswerk*. BZAW 227. Berlin: de Gruyter.

Yee, Gale. 2003. *Poor Banished Children of Eve: Women as Evil in the Hebrew Bible*. Minneapolis: Fortress.

Younger, K. Lawson, Jr. 1994. "Judges 1 in its Near Eastern Literary Context." Pages 207–27 in *Faith, Tradition, and History: Old Testament Historiography in Its Near Eastern Context*. Edited by A. R. Millard, James K. Hoffmeier, and David W. Baker. Winona Lake, IN: Eisenbrauns.

———. 1999. "The Underpinnings." Pages 304–45 in *Israel's Past in Present Research: Essays on Ancient Israelite Historiography*. Edited by V. Philips Long. SBTS 7. Winona Lake, IN: Eisenbrauns.

Ancient Sources Index

Inscriptions

Modern Authors Index

Subject Index

CPSIA information can be obtained
at www.ICGtesting.com
Printed in the USA
FSHW021130080819
60826FS